THE TRUCE
THE DAY
THE WAR STOPPED

THE TRUCE
THE DAY
THE WAR STOPPED

CHRIS BAKER

AMBERLEY

First published 2014

Amberley Publishing
The Hill, Stroud
Gloucestershire, GL5 4EP

www.amberley-books.com

British Library Cataloguing in Publication Data.
A catalogue record for this book is available from the British Library.

ISBN 978 1 4456 3490 6 (print)
ISBN 978 1 4456 3511 8 (ebook)

Typesetting and Origination by Amberley Publishing.
Printed in the UK.

Contents

Acknowledgements

Research for a book such as this relies heavily upon the assistance of the primary archives of contemporary material. I particularly thank the staff of the National Archives, Imperial War Museum, the British Library, the Special Collections at the Brotherton Library at the University of Leeds, the BBC Written Archives and the documentation centre at In Flanders Fields museum in Ypres.

Dr Jack Sheldon, ground-breaking author of so many titles on the German armies on the Western Front, was of great help in identifying units and pointing me in the direction of German sources. I thank Malcolm Brown and Shirley Seaton, whose masterly work *Christmas Truce* provides such a strong factual basis for anyone's education in that subject. Andrew Thornton, Jeremy Banning, Alan Hewer and Joseph Bogaert have all assisted too, with copies of rare material. Members and pals at the internet Great War Forum directly, and in some cases unwittingly, also provided valuable information and suggestions.

I also thank the owners of copyright material who have so willingly given their approval for use of their works. All efforts have been made to identify copyright holders where this was not immediately evident. I urge anyone who believes that a copyright work has been used without appropriate permission to contact me via the publisher.

Finally, thanks to my long-suffering wife Geraldine, who gives up so much to allow me to concentrate on my First World War work and, on this occasion, to my son Lawrence, who helped with war diaries and officers' service records at the National Archives.

PROLOGUE
Christmas Greetings

It was not unreasonable to think the British General Post Office would forecast that the usual 'Christmas rush' of mail would be somewhat reduced in 1914, in comparison with previous years. After all, normal trade was disrupted, people were not feeling quite so jolly and many were being rather more careful with their money. In peacetime, an additional 11,000 temporary workers had been engaged to handle the extra parcels, cards and packages at Christmas, but it was decided that 10,000 would be sufficient for this year. Even this was believed to be on the high side of what would be needed, but with so many postal workers having enlisted since August 1914, it would fill the gaps to cope with the expected volume.

The GPO was already handling the masses of post being sent to soldiers overseas. Comforts of all kinds had been going at an average rate of 20,000 parcels every day since the British Expeditionary Force had first moved to France in August 1914. The sorting offices and mail trains had grown accustomed to dealing with it. But the GPO had not counted on the extraordinary effect that Christmas would have on people's wish to send something to their men in France. Cards, cakes and puddings, smokes, woollens, socks and all manner of gifts, both useful and frivolous, were being bought, or lovingly made. In the six days up to the last posting date of 12 December, 250,000 parcels were sent. The GPO was stretched to the very limit, and things were not helped by the fact that many people did not how to address a package so that it reached the right soldier.[1]

The Royal Engineers Postal Section, which was responsible for receiving and distributing the post arriving in France, had no recent previous experience upon which to draw when it came to estimating how many men, vehicles and facilities it would need in order to handle the expected Christmas post. It was arranged that the 900 men of the Section should be temporarily increased to 1,500, but how to transport the mountains of mail proved more difficult. A special postal and gifts railway train was organised, which would run from the main postal base at Le Havre to the station at Boulogne, where the trucks would be separated and coupled to trains going to each railhead. The goods would then be taken on by lorry to the units at the front. On finding no spare lorries available in France, the director of postal services had to make a special appeal to the War Office. The depots were searched and forty-four additional vehicles were sent for postal work, plus two for each of the eight divisional supply columns, along with another six for work on the lines of communication in the rear.[2]

Somehow they just managed to handle the huge numbers of letters and parcels. The men in the front lines received their cards, puddings and cigarettes by the 'sandbag-full'. As an example, the 2nd Northamptonshire Regiment recorded in their daily war diary that, while in billets in La Gorgue on 21 December 1914, 'the number of presents received became almost embarrassing; mufflers, belts, scarves abounded while the number of cigarettes amounted, at one time, to a hundred and twenty a man.' Eighty tons of plum puddings were delivered to the railheads between 24 and 26 December.[3]

The British public would have been generous in sending their sons, fathers, brothers and cousins in uniform something for Christmas, without being told or persuaded to do so. They may have also been inspired by an idea that came direct from Buckingham Palace. *The Times* of 16 October 1914 published an appeal by Princess Mary for donations to raise £100,000, 'to send a Christmas present to every sailor afloat and every soldier at the front. Could there be anything more likely to hearten them in their struggle than a present received straight from home on Christmas Day?' Promised donations, amounting to almost £4,000, from benefactors including the Rothermeres, the Rothschilds, the Duke of Devonshire and others from the 'rich list' of the day, showed that the Princess had already drummed up some support. More donations rolled in over the next months and, at Christmas, the troops each received a small brass tin containing tobacco or sweets for the non-smokers among them. The 'Princess Mary box' is one of the most common personal artefacts in family and museum collections to this day.

The men at the front wrote home whenever possible. Field postcards that were uncensored, but which only gave brief details such as 'I am well', along with locally bought picture postcards and souvenir embroidered cards, all came from France in their thousands. Many a soldier had his photograph taken and sent home when he had his turn out of the front line. Letters home often went through censorship so sensitive military details were not mentioned, but they were often sent, even if only to ask after the family's health and to assure them that the soldier himself was 'in the pink'. As Christmas approached, men's thoughts turned increasingly to home and family.

I will wish you a very merry and happy Xmas. I should love to be home so as to be able to spend it with you, but I still pray and hope I shall be home soon after Xmas, when we shall make up for it. (11 December 1914)

We tried our hand at making a raisin pudding. It was not so bad, the only thing it was a bit heavy. We thought of using it against the Germans! I hope you had a merry Xmas. We shall spend ours in the trenches amongst mud and water, but I daresay we shall be fairly happy by making the best of things.[4]

(21 December 1914)

In the days immediately after Christmas 1914, many of the letters bore excited explanations of a most unexpected turn of events. Men described how the fighting had stopped and how barely a shot had been fired for some time. They wrote about how they had heard the Germans singing, and how they had themselves sung back; how a few brave fellows had actually gone out and met the Germans in no man's land; how some of the enemy spoke English and had lived or worked in Britain; and how they had exchanged cigarettes or other token gifts. The men simply could not believe it, even though they had witnessed it for themselves.

There was also a flow of post of a more sober and devastating kind. War Office letters brought terrible official news, such as: 'Deeply regret to inform you that Private 1234 James Smith was killed in action 19 December 1914. Lord Kitchener expresses his sympathy.' Personal hand-written letters from a soldier's commanding officer would typically say:

I very much regret to inform you that your son Private Smith died bravely on 19 December. He was shot by a German sniper. His death was instantaneous and he did not suffer. He was very popular with officers and men alike and the Company deeply sympathises with your loss.

Parcels and letters returned home, battered after a journey to France and back, were marked 'Missing' or 'Dead', on occasion arriving before the official notification. They came in their appalling numbers. In this period that is most remembered for the inspiring and hopeful truce in no man's land, no fewer than 3,356 British and Indian soldiers lost their lives in France and Flanders, seventy-seven of them on Christmas Day itself.[5]

Introduction

This book was researched and written in the centenary year of the events it describes. Starting long before the 100th anniversary of Britain's entry into the war, on 4 August 1914, there has been a deluge of media coverage, release of new and reprinted books, articles, exhibitions and the unveiling of new memorials to the conflict we still call the Great War. Interest in the period has possibly never been greater than during the terrible years of the war itself. To some extent, this has been fuelled by increasing accessibility of information and a boom in family history as a hobby; but there is more to it than that. The war is now firmly in the realms of history, yet close enough to our own times that many of us had parents or grandparents who took part. The sheer horror of the devastation, and the suffering behind the numbing casualty statistics, make the subject somehow compelling. We have difficulty in comprehending how and why men tolerated it all; we can only stand in awe at their endurance, bravery and stoicism. We find solace in their humour, knowing that for some men and women it was the making of their lives. The positive aspects of the human spirit occasionally shine though the gloom of one the blackest periods of our history.

No event or period of the First World War is richer in human spirit than the unofficial truces that took place in France and Flanders during Christmas 1914. The story that ordinary soldiers stopped the war, met their enemy in no man's land, exchanged conversation and mementos, shook hands and even played football together, is both heart-warming and rather odd. The truce period is well-documented, with several good, objective books already existing on the subject. Yet it also remains the source of persistent symbolism which obscures the truth of what happened and why. Football is central to this, and is increasingly being used as a totem for the international peace and understanding implicit in the truce. A mid-2014 visitor to Prowse Point Cemetery, near Ploegsteert, wrote that they were 'remembering the Football

Truce' by being there. A simple, wooden cross, planted in 1999, a private marker that a group (known as the Khaki Chums) had spent some time in a trench they had dug where the truce took place, is now always festooned with scarves, rosettes, shirts and other football memorabilia. The psychology of visitors leaving such keepsakes would make a good study in itself. This year, the football organisation UEFA is marking the centenary with high-profile football events in Flanders. Nowadays, there is rarely a mention of the truce without football being at the forefront, if not to the exclusion of all else. It masks a more difficult and complex truth.

In reality the truces – many of which started well before Christmas – emerged from battlefield squalor. There was a sudden freeze after weeks of lashing rain had made the trenches an unbearable and impractical quagmire. There were hundreds of unburied bodies of recently-dead men lying out in no man's land; the hopes of the armies had been exhausted; the burden of the loss of friends all combined into a despair that no end was in sight, yet, at the same time, a hope that victory was just around the corner. These aspects are now rarely included in tales of the truce, but they form its vital backbone. In this book, I attempt to examine the events leading up to Christmas to understand the prevailing atmosphere.

Despite its positive symbolism of hope, and that the 'little man' can have an effect on great events, in retrospect we can see that the truce made no difference to the war. It neither shortened nor lengthened it, and made no impact on the way the war was being conducted. In a gigantic struggle between the world's wealthiest nations with their global futures at stake, a day or two of cessation of fighting on small parts of the front would not change things, nor could it be allowed to. The truce was not universal or particularly large in its scope. Hostilities ceased completely in some areas, yet bitter fighting went on in others, with men dying nearby. After a while, units on both sides were ordered to resume action. In some cases, this was done in a gentlemanly manner, with warnings given to the other side before shots were fired.

' A great many of those who had been present at the truce did not live to see another Christmas, and knowledge of their individual contributions to these stirring events was lost forever. Our evidence for what had happened comes principally from contemporary official accounts, letters and diaries. They are unvarnished and written during, or soon after, the event. Further information comes from interviews and memoirs written at much later dates, but these accounts are not always completely trustworthy. Many of the memories of men who took part were not recorded until the 1960s or later. In searching for evidence, I have excluded some of these later accounts, as it is appears that the memory of the old soldier had been affected by repetition and absorption of things they have heard over the decades. Some had been asked leading questions that shaped the answers that were given. I have also excluded some narratives that had been featured in accounts of the truce before – like that of the author Henry Williamson, an officer who was present. In this book, readers will find many more letters, memoirs and interviews that mention the truce – in such profusion that some selection was inevitably necessary.

The book is about the experience of the men who were in France and Flanders during the month of December 1914, and how the truce came about as a hopeful aberration in an otherwise terrible period. I hope that in some small way, this exploration of their tale will play some part in their remembrance.

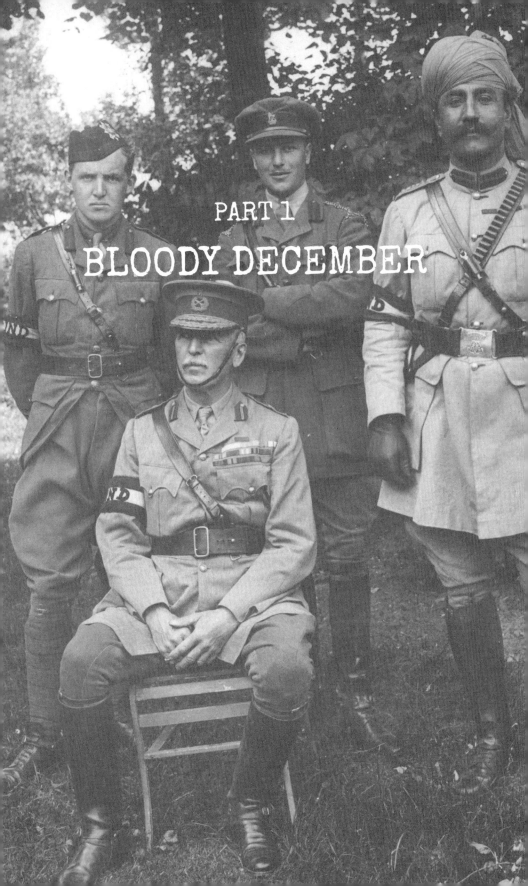

PART 1
BLOODY DECEMBER

1

Turning Point

A War of Movement Becomes a War of the Trenches

The last two months of 1914 marked a turning point in the progress of the war on the Western Front in France and Flanders, and the beginning of an awful period of entrenched warfare that would last until the spring of 1918. Up to now, it had been a war of movement – of huge armies marching and manoeuvring, and of some of the costliest fighting of the war for France and Germany. During November it had reached a stalemate, with the two sides dug in, glaring at each other across the no man's land in between. For the military planners and the staffs of the armies of both sides, the fighting since August had proved to be disappointing and perplexing. At first, the Germans, having attacked France with the objective of a rapid victory, had made great progress, but their hopes had been decisively crushed in the titanic Battle of the Marne in early September.

The French, believing their best form of defence was to advance across the border into Germany, sustained appalling casualties for no significant gain. Since the Marne, both sides had been forced to reappraise the situation, as their original plans were no longer relevant. Germans and French alike improvised the disposition of their forces, attempting to advance around the northern limit of their opponent's armies – a move known as outflanking the enemy. Every effort to do so was met with enemy doing the same thing, and led to severe fighting as the two sides clashed. The outflanking movement was blunted, and ended with the two sides digging in where they stood, unable to advance further. This was repeated in a series of steps towards the north that became known, inappropriately, as the race to the sea. Neither side was trying to reach the sea: they were trying to turn the enemy's flank. As each successive attempt was brought to a halt, it meant making attacks nearer and nearer to the North Sea coast.

These attacks finally came to an end at the coast itself. The small and embattled Belgian army, having lost the vast majority of its own territory under enormous German pressure, took the drastic step of flooding the hinterland. By the end of October, the two sides had dug a continuous entrenched front form in all over the Franco-Swiss border to Nieuport on the Belgian coast. Regardless of which side tried it, every effort to attack the enemy's line was met with a hail of fire and rapidly brought to an end. By mid-November, the armies were exhausted, had effectively used up their ammunition stocks and could move no further. They faced the enemy from the line that they had dug for protection, and now began to improve them, deepen them and make them impregnable. The two entrenched lines became the focus of fighting for the next three years. It became a world of its own, understood only by those who had the misfortune to be there. One twenty-five-year-old transport officer with the 5th Scottish Rifles memorably described the scene:

> In front of us, two hundred yards ahead, the trench line stretched to right and left – the usual little spots of light from fires, hurricane lamps and candles, that extraordinary sight. Supremely moving in terms of what it signified. War Cabinets, munition works, patriotic speeches, national efforts of every kind, all the gigantic machinery and paraphernalia of an Empire at war, patrol ships, bases, depots, railheads, hospitals, clearing stations, GHQ, Army, Corps, Divisional and Brigade HQ; it all fined down in the end to a thread of twinkling lights. This was in fact the war.[1]

Descent into static trench warfare was not an inevitable consequence of conditions. It resulted from a deliberate German decision to go onto the defensive in France. In his 1919 book *General Headquarters 1914–1916 and its Critical Decisions* General Erich von Falkenhayn, who took over as chief of the general staff after the crushing disappointment on the Marne, said that,

> At the beginning of November, GHQ could not conceal from itself that a further thorough-going success was no longer to be obtained here [in France], in the face of an opponent who was continually growing stronger.
>
> It was now debated whether by suddenly shifting the pressure a breakthrough should be attempted against a portion of the enemy's front on which he had weakened himself for the sake of the defence of Flanders. The district of Artois ... came under consideration for this purpose. The idea, however, soon had to be dropped.

Falkenhayn ordered his army to stand fast on the entrenched line, but adopting a defensive stance only, with no more costly attacking attempts. His decision allowed the Germans to remove a number of divisions from France and send them to reinforce the Eastern Front, where offensive operations were to be continued against the Russians.

After the East had been provided with the reserves at hand, both men and ammunition, the forces in the West were no longer sufficient for ... realisation [of a breakthrough].

Trench Warfare Comes to Flanders

Flanders is an ancient region, spanning either side of the Franco-Belgian national border. The definition of lands included in the region have fluctuated over time, but, by the early twentieth century, it covered the northern provinces of West and East Flanders, the Dutch province of Zeeuwse Vlaanderen, and the border area of France often called French Flanders.[2] It is, by and large, a rural area, although it contains the larger cities and towns of Antwerp, Ghent, Bruges, Ostend, Courtrai and Ypres (all Belgium), Armentières, Lille and Dunkirk (France).

Neither German nor French military planners would predict the northern region of Flanders might become the key battleground that it did in 1914, despite it having played an important part in wars in Europe since the days of knights in armour. Their plans for war, although on the German side based on an advance through Belgium, were focused onto areas further south, ensuring that Flanders remained unmolested for a number of weeks after the war began.

In September and October 1914, two developments brought war to the area. Sadly for the people of Flanders, it remained there for the next four years. After it had played such a gallant and important part in defending Liège in August, the Belgian army began a northerly withdrawal to its 'national redoubt' – the fortified city and port of Antwerp. A German corps was deployed to keep it pinned there, while the main body of the German forces continued the advance on France. The Belgians carried out several offensive 'sorties' against the corps, until the Germans eventually ordered a bombardment and capture of the city. Too late, a British formation known as the Royal Naval Division went to assist, followed by a more significant force in the shape of IV Corps. By the time they arrived, the Belgians had reluctantly decided to evacuate from the city and withdraw its force westwards along the coast, crossing into West Flanders and digging in along the River Yser. The Royal Naval Division suffered something of a disaster when large numbers of its men crossed the frontier from Antwerp into the neutral Netherlands, where they were then interned. The British IV Corps, having arrived in the Ghent area from Britain, withdraw alongside the Belgians, finally arriving at Ypres, where they too dug in.

At the same time, the French and German forces were engaged in the effort to outflank each other, which saw forces creeping up from the Aisne, across Picardy and Artois into the strategically critical high ground of the Vimy and Lorette ridges, and to the drab industrial and mining area of Lens and Béthune. The British Expeditionary Force (BEF), after much debate, was moved *en bloc* from the Aisne to the north of this extended line, to take its place on the left of the French forces – the north being in Flanders.

The period of October to November 1914 proved to be the final phase of the 'race to the sea', and the cause of the German decision to go onto the defensive in the West. It is not the intention of this book to cover this fighting, except to say that it was arguably the second decisive battle of the war, in that it ended Germany's hopes of a decision in France. In retrospect, one might also say that, from November 1914, Germany could not win the war at all.

For the purposes of providing a basis for the official histories and the awards of battle honours to regiments engaged, after the war the British resorted to a committee to decide definitions for the periods of fighting, the areas they covered and the units involved. This 'Battles Nomenclature Committee' reported in May 1921. It gave titles to the actions of October and November, all under the general heading of 'Operations in Flanders, 10 October–22 November 1914'.

From south to north, these battles were: the Battle of La Bassée (10 October–2 November, fought by the British II and Indian Corps); the Battle of Armentières (10 October–2 November, fought by III Corps); the Battle of Messines (12 October–2 November, fought by the Cavalry Corps and various units from II and Indian Corps) and the Battles of Ypres (19 October–22 November, and more often known as the First Battle of Ypres).[3] At the same time, to the north of the BEF, the Belgian army was engaged in the Battle of the Yser. In German, this fighting is known as *Schlacht bei Lille* and the *Erste Flandernschlacht*. Their Sixth Army held the line up to the Ploegsteert area and the Fourth Army north of that to the sea.

By mid-November 1914, the two sides had dug in, exhausted by these climactic battles. The continuous line now crossed the La Bassée canal at Givenchy-lez-la-Bassée, east of Béthune; ran up to skirt Armentières and Ploegsteert Wood on its eastern side; bulged westwards with the important ridge line of Messines and Wytschaete in German hands; ran around east of Ypres, in a shape that would be forever known as the Ypres Salient, and then followed the Yser canal and River Yser to the sea at Nieuport.

The Allies Go Onto the Offensive

As the Ypres fighting appeared to have died down, the British Commander-in-Chief, Sir John French, summed up the situation in a Special Order of the Day, issued to the army on 22 November 1914:

The value and significance of the splendid role fulfilled since the commencement of hostilities by the Allied forces in the West lies in the fact that at the moment when the Eastern Provinces of Germany are about to be over-run by the numerous and powerful armies of Russia, nearly the whole of the active army of Germany is tied down to a line of trenches extending from the fortress of Verdun on the Alsatian frontier round to the sea at Nieuport, east of Dunkirk (a distance of 260 miles), where they are held, much reduced in numbers and morale by the successful action of our troops in the west.

What the enemy will do now we cannot tell. Should they attempt to withdraw their troops to strengthen their weakened forces in the East, we must follow them up and harass their retreat to the utmost of our power.[4]

A Special Order was almost a public statement. In the more private communications, Sir John indicated to his corps commanders that the cessation of German attacks on Ypres may simply indicate a lull, while the enemy drew breath and regrouped to continue their offensive. He advised on the necessity for vigilance and the positioning of reserves for rapid reaction to anything that might develop.

Despite the impasse and uncertainty about German intentions, it was inconceivable that the French and British allies would adopt anything but an aggressive stance. There was no question that they must continue offensive operations against the German entrenched line. France had gone to war with the deep desire to wrest back her former provinces of Alsace and Lorraine, which she had lost to Germany in 1870. She not only failed to achieve that, but now had Germany controlling a significant part of her land, population and industrial base. France would stop at nothing to rid herself of the occupier. For Great Britain, it was not enemy occupation of the homeland that was the issue, but the fact that Germany now held the North Sea coast of Belgium. From the ports of Antwerp, Zeebrugge and Ostend, the German surface fleet and U-boats posed a major threat to British naval dominance and her ability to supply an army in France. The then First Lord of the Admiralty, Winston Churchill, had implored Sir John French in a letter dated 26 October 1914:

I do trust you will realise how damnable it will be if the enemy settles down for the winter on lines which comprise Calais, Dunkirk or Ostend. There will be continual alarms and added difficulties. We must have him off the Belgian coast even if we cannot recover Antwerp.[5]

By mid-November it was all too evident that the Germans now held the coast and were not going to be easily prised away from it. This was so clear a danger that, on 9 December 1914, Foreign Minister Sir Edward Grey advised the ambassador to France, Sir Francis Bertie, that the British public would 'regard any losses entailed by an offensive action taken by our troops against these coastal positions as fully justified'.[6] Removal of German forces from the Belgian coast remained a British objective throughout the war – an objective that remained unfulfilled until October 1918.

The French and, to some extent, the British, also felt an obligation to maintain pressure on Germany in the West in order to alleviate pressure on their ally Russia, in the East. Germany had a strategic advantage of 'interior lines' and had the capability to move forces from West to East as needed. This advantage could not be broken by Allied military action, but could be minimised by pinning down the enemy troops in the trenches of the West.

The entrenched position presented the French and British military staffs with a great dilemma, an almost insuperable problem that defeated every technological and tactical development until 1918 – how to break through the German defences. Since 1918, some contemporary commentators, and many observers since, have viewed the military's attempts to solve this problem as brainless, dull thinking that recklessly sent men to do the impossible, while meeting an inevitable death in trying. Modern academic historians see a 'learning curve', with lessons learned the hard way in the 1915–17 period, eventually catalysing into techniques that fundamentally changed the war in 1918. During the 'race to the sea' phase, the German and French armies first encountered the terrible difficulty of attacking an entrenched enemy that was equipped with the awesome firepower of modern weapons. The original BEF had its first taste of things to come during a few weeks on the heights above the River Aisne in late September, when facing German troops dug in on slopes above them. But, in the autumn of 1914, such a position was not the norm and had not yet settled; commanders would hope to break that line, or to outflank it. The Aisne was seen by the British command as an aberration in a war of movement. By late November 1914, it had become horribly evident that the Germans had gone onto the defensive, and the trenches were no longer something unusual or temporary, but the way the war was going to be. Sir John French and French Gen. Ferdinand Foch, who in late 1914 was Assistant Commander-in-Chief to General Joseph Joffre, both later wrote of their thoughts on the situation. In essence, they agreed that the Allies were facing siege warfare on a vast scale. Sir John believed that the Allies could affect nothing of importance unless there was either 'a considerable augmentation of our forces, including a vastly increased supply of heavy artillery, machine guns, trench artillery and ammunition, or the enemy's forces on the Western front must be so weakened by the necessity of sending troops to the East.'[7] Foch said much the same: 'It seems to me that the organisation of this war has got to be carefully studied. What are its requirements? A large number of siege guns, with plenty of ammunition, heavy enough to breakdown the obstacles opposed to them'.[8] He went on to call for grenades, mortars, mining and tunnelling to blow up the German positions from below.

There was some debate between the Allies, not with regard to *whether* to attack the Germans, but *where* and *when*. The decision that emerged was a French one, and not for the first nor last time, the BEF found itself agreeing to undertake operations for which it was neither ready, nor to which it could devote its whole-hearted backing. It was a consequence of coalition warfare, in which France was the dominant senior partner in land operations. For political reasons, the British were disinclined to take firm a stance against French proposals even when they meant ignoring or de-emphasising the North Sea coast problem. As early as 19 November – the critical fighting at Ypres had only begun to slow down a week before – Foch was proposing that when the Allies did go onto the offensive, it should begin with a blow between Antwerp and Namur, and be followed by another against the River Meuse between Namur and Liége. Expected resistance on the Meuse could be overcome by a further attack starting from Verdun. His thoughts set a basic pattern for every Allied offensive up to late 1917, in that they envisaged a huge converging pincer attack in the North and South against the salient that the Germans had pushed into France. It was never considered that the BEF would play a significant part in such an action, but their support would be needed. Quite apart from it being a relatively small force in comparison with the French and German Armies, Joffre and Foch both held reservations about the British, especially regarding their offensive capability. Sir John French was still nervous of the possibility that the Germans had not yet gone onto the defensive, merely resting and massing troops for a fresh blow. He instructed his various corps to be alert to this possibility on 22 November.[9]

On 6 December 1914, Foch went to meet with Joffre. There was some new intelligence that the Germans were removing forces from the West.[10] Despite his foresight in analysing the requirements for a successful breakthrough, Foch effectively ignored the fact that such resources and techniques were simply not yet available, forming an opinion that the moment for offensive action had arrived. In particular, he believed that an attack in the area of Wytschaete-Hollebeke would relieve the precarious situation south east of Ypres. It was enough to persuade Joffre. On 8 December, he issued general instructions to the French army that stated that main attacks would now be carried out.

One, starting from the region of Arras, in the direction of Cambrai and Douai, to be executed by the Tenth Army reinforced. The other in Champagne, in the direction of Attigny, by the Fourth Army. In addition, secondary operations will be carried out on various parts of the front, more particularly by the Eighth Army and the left of the British Army, attacking in a convergent direction on Wervicq [Wervik]; by the Second Army, attacking in the direction of Combles.[11]

Foch formally requested Sir John French's assistance in committing the BEF to join the offensive. Alternative British proposals for a North Sea coast operation, which would require the BEF to be moved from its position south of Ypres up to the Dunkirk-Furnes-Nieuport area, were put to the French just as these plans were being announced. Despite support from British Secretary of State for War Lord Kitchener, Churchill and Sir John French, they were not received well. The latter would later write, 'It was quite evident that they [the French] had no intention of leaving the British forces in sole charge of the Allied left, but they agreed to regard the question as a military one and to refer it to General Joffre. I had several conversations with him on the subject, but there appeared to be no disposition on his part to acquiesce in my plans.' Sir Edward Grey advised Bertie to adopt the line that 'co-operation with the contemplated French effort to drive the Germans back would be rendered far more effective', if the BEF was moved and the coastal operation undertaken, but it cut no ice with French high command. Such were the impossibilities of being the junior partner in a military coalition. 'Yielding thus to French representations, our government began to weaken. Churchill adhered to his views throughout, but was not supported.'[12] With such weak political support, Sir John was in no position to refuse the French. The die was cast. It was in December that, under Joffre's instructions formalised into British orders, the BEF would make its first attempts at storming the continuous, entrenched Western Front.

A Plan Emerges

Even before Joffre issued his formal instructions on 8 December, he had written to Foch and Sir John French saying that a thinning out of German forces was now so evident that they should proceed with partial attacks without waiting for final preparations. Time was of the essence.

It was the job of Sir John's Chief of the General Staff (CGS), Lt-Gen. Sir Archibald Murray, to turn the general instructions into a practical operational plan. He had been given the job as CGS at the beginning of the war, but it had proved an unhappy appointment. His performance during the first months had been decidedly shaky, and he was not well-liked by his peers or juniors. One staff officer summed Murray up as 'incompetent, cantankerous, timid and quite useless'.[13]

Intelligence from various sources gave Murray a reasonably accurate picture of the opposing forces within the area. From south to north, the British Indian, IV and III Corps from Cuinchy (on the Béthune to La Bassée road) stretching up to the River Douve north of Ploegsteert, were faced by the German 29th Division, VII Corps and XIX (Saxon) Corps. From the Douve to Wytschaete hospice, II Corps faced the 6th Bavarian Division and part of II Bavarian Corps. The British I Corps was in reserve. On the north of the British, and extending the line up to beyond Ypres, was the French Eighth army. On the immediate left of the British came that army's XVI Corps, who faced the rest of the II Bavarian Corps. Overall, this gave the Allies a theoretical manpower advantage. The British force, including I Corps, of ten infantry divisions (and cavalry in reserve) was confronted by fewer than seven German divisions.

A resumption of offensive operations had been the subject of speculation among the senior officers of the BEF for some time. Commander of II Corps, Lt-Gen. Sir Horace Smith-Dorrien, had written to his divisional commanders that it was 'unnecessary and unprofitable at this juncture to enter into a discussion of possible plans', saying that it was the Commander-in-Chief's business to agree this with the French, but it was fairly plain that his Corps would be called upon to capture the Wytschaete–Messines ridge. All they could do in the meantime was improve their trenches with a view to attacking from them.[14]

Information was coming through to Saint-Omer that the French were planning to attack on a fairly large scale, not only in Flanders but in the Vosges, the Champagne, on the Aisne and in Artois. Joffre met with Sir John French to request that, on 14 December 1914, the BEF should play a part in this offensive by attacking all along its front, but with particular weight on the Messines–Warneton sector. He assured the British commander that General Victor d'Urbal's Eighth army would attack alongside in the Hollebeke-Wytschaete area. The operation would be carried out by XVI Corps under General Paul-Francois Grossetti.[15]

British General Headquarters issued its own detailed instructions at 7 p.m. on 12 December 1914, under Murray's signature. It called for an offensive action beginning on 14 December, which would be carried out by the BEF with the French on their left, and with the intention of advancing to reach a line from Le Touquet (a hamlet 3 miles south of Warneton) to Warneton and Hollebeke. By doing so, the enemy would be driven from the left bank of the River Lys. The British element was responsible for capturing Messines and Warneton. On the left, II Corps would take high ground at Wytschaete (the French being responsible for the village itself), Hill 75 and Messines. On the right, III Corps would advance on Warneton once II Corps had also captured Messines. In other areas, IV Corps and the Indian Corps would not attack, but would 'carry out local operations with a view to containing the enemy'. The attack would be supported by 'powerful artillery bombardment' and the Cavalry Corps. I Corps and the 1st Indian Cavalry Division would remain in reserve, but the instructions remained silent on what they would actually do in the event of success.

The plan was clear enough, even if it was watered down somewhat from Joffre's request that the BEF attack all along its line. But it does not reveal the full story. Sir John French had been discussing matters with his corps commanders, and orders for preparations to be made had gone down to the divisions for several days before Murray's instruction emerged from Saint-Omer. He had told Smith-Dorrien that the French and II Corps attack on Wytschaete would precede any move by III Corps, by as much as several days.

A conference held at the town hall in Bailleul, on 12 December 1914, brought Sir John together with his corps commanders. What emerged, and what became the basis of operations regardless of Murray's instruction, was curious and half-hearted. Far from an 'attack all the way along the line', even in the Messines–Warneton sector the attack would not be made as one. Instead, each division of II and III Corps would attack independently in succession, in a sequence beginning on 14 December, with 3rd Division of II Corps on the extreme British left. After that, no division was to advance and get ahead of the one on its left. While waiting for Messines to fall to II Corps, the two divisions of III Corps would actively harass the enemy by sapping, sniping and use of artillery. By taking this approach, it was inevitable that relatively small forces would attack and be exposed to enemy fire from ahead, left and right, while the units on their right waited to see if the attack had succeeded before they too went forward.[16]

Rarely can there have been a plan so devoid of imagination and practicality, rarely have military planners so thoroughly abandoned all known military principles, and rarely can an army have taken so little account of the resources and operational capabilities of the forces at its disposal, to say nothing of the capabilities of the enemy it faced and the nature of the ground over which it was to advance. The Germans would later call the battle the *Dezemberschlacht in Französisch-Flandern.*

2

The British Army in December 1914

By December 1914, the BEF comprised ten infantry and four cavalry divisions, with all of the lines of communication and headquarters needed for effective control and supply of the force. In all, some 270,000 officers and men of the British and Indian Armies were now in France and Flanders, making the force considerably larger than the original BEF, which had crossed to France in the August.[1]

The army was now quite different to that which had landed with high hopes and expectations in those high days of summer. The original divisions of August had effectively been in continual combat ever since, and those that had arrived in September and October had endured the intense and critical fighting of the Aisne, the climactic battle at Ypres and in the less well-known but equally vital battles of La Bassée, Armentières and Messines. The BEF could certainly look back with pride at its recent achievements in stemming the German attack, but they had come at enormous cost – the army had, by 30 November 1914, suffered the horrifying total of more than 89,000 casualties that had been killed, wounded or missing. British official historian, Brig.-Gen. Sir James Edmonds, said in his second volume on the 1914 fighting that, by November, 'the old British army was gone past recall, leaving but a remnant to carry on with the training of the New Armies.'

From a purely numerical viewpoint, this is overstating things. On 1 August 1914, the entire regular army, including its reservists, was 456,000 strong, not including the Territorial Force, the vast resources of the Indian army or the forces of the Dominions. Even by December 1914, Britain could still call upon very significant numbers of men who could be considered to be its 'old army'. It was more from the viewpoint of quality and experience of its infantry, that the pre-war army could be said to have largely been lost. The cavalry, artillery, transport, engineering and medical arms had not sustained the same degree of loss.

Edmonds reported that of the British infantry battalions that had fought at the Marne and Ypres, an average of one officer and thirty men who had landed in France in August 1914 scarcely remained. An infantry battalion at full strength comprised 30 officers and 977 men. Those battalions had received drafts during the fighting, and many of those had already become casualties. During late November and December 1914, most of the battalions received more drafts to bring them up to at least three quarters of their planned establishment numbers. This was achieved for most units, although those of the 7th Division were still at low strength by mid-December. The training depots were being combed of any men who were fit enough to go to France. They were a mixture of men, of regulars who, for various reasons, had not yet been sent out; of reservists recalled in August and who had been in training ever since; of men who had already been wounded and patched up sufficiently for a return to duty; and even men of no previous experience, who had enlisted since the outbreak of war.[2] The losses to some units in the recent fighting had been such that the drafts they needed were very large.

On 1 December, the 2nd Border Regiment received a draft of four officers and 570 men, bringing the battalion up to a total of thirteen officers and 973 men. The 2nd Wiltshires received two officers and 300 men on 18 December, almost doubling the size of the battalion. A good deal of work would be needed to organise and assimilate these drafts before they could go into an offensive. Experienced survivors of recent fighting were quickly promoted in order to manage these affairs, and men who had gone to war as privates suddenly found themselves as section corporals or platoon sergeants. Such rapid promotion had been unheard of in peacetime. The Borders' and Wiltshires' diaries make no mention of the type and quality of men they received, but it is evident that at least some of the adjutants and regimental sergeant-majors of the battalions looked askance at the arrival of the drafts. The 1st Gordon Highlanders are a prime example. They happened to be one of the units that would be ordered into the first attack. In the ten days before their assault on Petit Bois on 14 December 1914, the Gordons received drafts of 405 men, and a number of officers from its 3rd (Reserve) Battalion at Aberdeen. This represents more than half of the men who would go 'over the top'. The battalion notes in its war diary that the drafts included some very old soldiers, one of whom had seen service at Tel-el-Kebir in 1882, and others physically unsuited for a winter campaign in the trenches. With them were younger men who appeared to have had practically no military training, with total service varying between three and ten weeks.[3] The official French history reported that it was suffering from similar problems, with barely trained drafts being sent to replace losses to units recently in action.

Most battalions had suffered significant losses to their regimental officers, and many of the regiments had effectively exhausted their pre-war stock of subalterns by mid-November.[4] Many of those now arriving to replace losses were wartime volunteers with no military experience. In many cases, they had been commissioned simply on the basis of good schooling, good manners and soldierly appearance. Some had been with a school or university Officer Training Corps, but they had not had time to be imbued with the regimental ethos, with precious little opportunity to learn from the veterans before they were pitched into the battles of December. It is hard to argue that they could have been anything but tactically naïve. The numbers of such novices, together with the few elderly regulars found from commands in the Special Reserve, from the Indian army or from exotic administrative postings around the Empire, constituted the weakest unit leadership of any period in the war. Many such officers arrived just days before the offensive began, and the time available for getting to know their peers, their men and the conditions they faced was short indeed. In the higher formations, a shortage of officers properly trained in staff methods would hamper British operations for a considerable time ahead.

The army's method of operation, right down to the smallest detail, was encapsulated in the 1909 version of *Field Service Regulations*. Every officer and man was expected to be trained in, and know, the aspects that affected his activities. The regulations included a devolved system of command, giving responsibility to the 'man on the spot' rather than a central and remote staff. It relied on experience and judgement, and gave commanders latitude to make rapid, localised decisions. This also tended to make for difficulties, as will be appreciated when we examine the fighting of December 1914. Lessons, probably wrong as it turned out, were learned from this period. As the army grew, command became more centralised and more standardisation was required. The balance swung back in the light of experience of the major battles of 1916 and 1917, and the army's command and control structure in 1918 was very much devolved, even down to platoon level.

By December, the regular units of the BEF were supplemented by the arrival of fourteen battalions of the Territorial Force. Despite reservations about them being 'Saturday night soldiers', part-timers before they were called for full time service soon after war was declared, the 'Terriers' soon proved their value, playing an important part in the story of the month. With the exception of the 5th and 6th Divisions, which had received one each, all of the British divisions now included two territorial units.[5]

The most important reinforcement of the BEF was the Indian Corps, which comprised the 3rd (Lahore) and 7th (Meerut) Divisions. They would play a central part in the fighting in December – less so in the truce. The army was also anticipating the imminent arrival of reinforcements in the shape of 27th Division, but this took place too late for the events described.

Sustained action was also beginning to have baleful effects on the army's physical and material resources. To some extent, this was true of all of the armies on the Western Front. Artillery pieces, already fired numerous times and in some cases transported over long distances, were increasingly breaking down due to jolting and wear while in use, and the barrels of many guns and howitzers were worn out. Although the science of artillery would rapidly develop throughout the war, it was already appreciated that barrel wear had a significant effect on the accuracy and reliability of the gun. With the trench lines close together, and especially when soldiers went into an attack, it was vital to be able to fire repeatedly and accurately. By December 1914, this was a severe problem for many British batteries.

The BEF was also finding that it faced an enemy equipped with hand grenades and trench mortars, weapons that were of immense value in entrenched siege warfare. The British had no such weapons, and although they would develop excellent capability in this regard over time, in December 1914 it was a question of improvisation. Men would continue to pay for this with their lives for many months. It was the result of a general failure to foresee and prepare for siege warfare. There was a doctrinaire belief that the way to victory was through closing in on the enemy with the bayonet, along with years of Treasury parsimony where tight budgets were spent on the Royal Navy rather than the army. Despite numerous pleas for something to be done, the War Office response was slow. The army in France found itself having to invent and manufacture its own weapons, or borrow them from the French. In many cases, the early designs proved to be more dangerous to the British troops than to the enemy. The war diary of 20th Infantry Brigade (7th Division) headquarters for 4 December 1914 described how all of the division's brigade and artillery commanders were summoned to a demonstration held at Bac St Maur near Estaires. It proved to be

quite one of the most dangerous mornings of the campaign. The mortar guns we tried experimenting with were two French guns marked '1848'. The first shot proved quite successful, being fired with a light charge, and the round shot was not charged with gun cotton. It went some 200 feet in the air and landed about 150 yards away. Encouraged by this, a heavier charge was used and the gun given more elevation. What happened to the shell we don't know, but the gun went off with a roar, there was a great crash amongst the boughs of an apple tree above the heads of the spectators standing behind, and the gun was seen to be pointing the reverse way to which it had been aimed.[6]

It would be funny if this had not been serious experimentation with a mortar that may have had to be used in the trenches in the absence of anything else. The war diary of 3rd Division headquarters similarly reported wearily, '6 December: a new trench mortar was tried and universally condemned as it weighed over half a ton and was most inaccurate.'[7] The lack of a reliable trench mortar, and the paucity of heavy and siege artillery, put the British at a grave disadvantage. In particular, there was a desperate need to counter the enemy's 'Black Maria' shells, which exploded with an enormous bang and gave off plumes of black smoke (they were also known as 'Jack Johnsons', after a black American boxer). In December 1914, there simply was no answer available. Manufacturing defects and poor handling practices also contributed to problems, with munitions coming from the factories at home. 7th Division headquarters reported that a large proportion of Hales rifle grenades were proving to be 'duds', that is, they could be fired but would not explode. 50 per cent of them were reported by one brigade and 30 per cent by another. By 26 December, the same division reported that it had cadged 500 hand grenades from the French; the 8th Division had none of these. 7th also had 320 'hairbrush' bombs and 100 'jam tins' made locally by the Royal Engineers. 8th Division had 950 'jam tins'. It seems that during the fighting before Christmas 1914, not one grenade was supplied by the Master-General of the Ordnance at the War Office to the troops who faced plentiful, excellent German grenades.

Despite the solid foundation of Field Service Regulations, the BEF had to learn 'on the job' in just about every aspect of its operations. With the trench lines settling down, and with British divisions remaining in place for periods of time, there was now an opportunity to rotate units holding the firing line. They would remain in the trenches only for a short while, then have a few days in close support and then a period further in the rear. Support positions would often be houses, barns or trenches within a few hundred yards of the firing line. Villages up to a mile or two behind the trenches would be used for rest (and all too often the men were called upon to carry out manual work or take supplies forward to their comrades in the trenches). From time to time, entire brigades would rotate.

The army also had to learn to deal with the many civilians still living and working within its area of operations. Some areas began to be forcibly evacuated. This was less for the safety of the civilians, and more to give the army unhindered space to operate and access places that might be used for billets, headquarters, communications and stores. The army was simply not used to the detailed logistical planning required to support very large forces, constantly on the move between the rear and the front. The 7th Division tested the response time for its units in reserve. One brigade, on receiving a message from headquarters, took almost 1.5 hours to put the unit on the march and actually depart. Many factors were noted, including the fact that there was no lighting in the barns in which men were billeted. With the army, in most places, only being able to move in hours of darkness, such things were of crucial importance. The lessons were being learned.

Early in December, there was a newsworthy and memorable event for many men – King George V came to visit the BEF. Detachments from most

3

A Curious Interlude

Once Falkenhayn had ordered his armies onto the defensive, things quietened down along the front lines. The diaries and intelligence summaries of units holding the trenches generally report little warlike activity, other than sporadic shellfire and sniping in both directions. Much work was done at night, when materials would be carried forward for strengthening the trenches and erecting barbed-wire defences. Many infantrymen were ordered to dig saps out into no man's land for use as listening posts.[1] The 2nd Essex Regiment reported that it was having difficulty with this work, as they found themselves digging into quantities of buried Germans – men who had been killed in earlier fighting. Patrols would probe into no man's land during the night in order to gain information about the enemy's defences and activities and, on occasion, localised firefights would develop if a patrol was spotted. On the whole, however, the period up to mid-December remained fairly calm.

The weather sharply deteriorated in late November, bringing heavy rain and sleet which lasted for most of December. The temperature also dropped, with nights frosty. For both sides, the rain brought misery, for it flooded the trenches (in many places to knee or waist height), causing unsupported trench sides and dugouts to collapse. Drummer 7322 Frederick Waring, of the 2nd Battalion of the Border Regiment, suffocated to death when a dugout collapsed, burying him.[2] There was little shelter from the weather, even in a well-constructed trench. In such conditions, extreme personal discomfort became the norm, bringing an increase in sickness, rheumatism, frostbite and that painful affliction known as 'trench foot' to the shivering men. By 3 December, the recently arrived 8th Division was already reporting that it had lost 1,580 men to conditions caused by frozen feet. For the most part, Flanders is an area easily flooded, with a high water table criss-crossed by drainage channels dug over centuries. Many of these channels and ditches had been used for cover during fighting, and had been developed into trenches.

When the rains came they became a natural conduit. The little rivers Douve, Warnave and Layes rose quickly, as did the larger Lys. The water table rose to some 2 feet below the surface, and the infantry found themselves in a morass. Behind the lines, the roads and tracks connecting the rear area with the trenches was little better. The artillery found their guns, stockpiled shells and limbers sinking into the mud. The substratum of practically all of the roads in northern France, except for those which were paved, was chalk. After rain and frost it reduced to a pulp with no resisting power. All but the most lightly loaded vehicles would sink, and transport units reported that the mud was three inches deep on the roads by 29 November (they got worse during December). Mud plastered the men, vehicles and horses alike; it clogged rifles and oozed into every haversack, pack and box taken into the front line. The Royal Engineers brought pumps forward, but to little avail, and front-line troops spent more time baling out their trench than worrying about their enemy – for he was engaged in the same struggle. In such circumstances, the number of men holding the firing line was reduced as far as possible, but enough had to be left in place to ensure that any enemy attack could be beaten off. Certainly, by 7 December, official thoughts were turning to building up breastworks from sandbags and any other materials to hand, rather than relying on trenches. From late November, improvised cold and wet-weather clothing was issued to British infantry in the form of leather jerkins, goatskins, and what the 4th Middlesex Regiment described as 'fur waistcoats'. The many knitted caps, balaclavas, scarves, mittens that were arriving from home were put to good use too. Thigh-length gumboots were issued but were in short supply, and men's leather boots simply could not cope with continual wear and soaking. Some units received an issue of straw for the men to bind around their legs.[3] Some of the Scottish regiments had a particularly difficult time, for they wore shoes rather than boots. The 6th Gordon Highlanders, a newly arrived territorial unit, had to physically drag three of their men from the mud during their first period in the trenches, reporting that fifteen of their soldiers lost their shoes. Within a week, their brigade was reporting that the battalion was beginning to feel the strain, and that discipline was becoming a problem as a result.

In the midst of this cocktail of hostile activity and war against the wet and cold, one section of the front line appears to have developed a unique atmosphere. The area in question was that held by the British 4th Division, the left-hand division of III Corps. Their front ran from the valley of the River Douve, north-west of St Yves, down past the eastern edge of Ploegsteert Wood and on past Le Gheer towards Frélinghien. For much of this stretch, the two opposing trench lines were only 100 yards, or fewer, apart. In the area between Le Gheer and Le Touquet, which the Germans referred to as the Pont Rouge sector, they were particularly close.

Life in the trenches, while being terribly uncomfortable, was beginning to develop into tedium. When men on both sides were not on sentry duty, or the seemingly never-ending work of carrying or digging, or making trenches more habitable, the hours passed slowly. With the enemy close by, so close that you could hear them – sometimes smell their cigarettes or breakfast, hear their conversation and occasionally glimpse a man – it is not surprising that soldiers became curious about their enemy. Most British soldiers had never met a German, and vice-versa – certainly not at war. Were they the monsters of the propaganda in the press? Germans always seem to have been portrayed as fat, bewhiskered and baby-eating, or alternatively diminutive and bespectacled weaklings. The soldiers had learned the hard way that their enemy was there to fight, and was not to tempt the unwary. It was a brave man who would think about getting closer to them, and yet there was a certain attraction in doing so.

On 17 November 1914 – only a week or so since the Germans closed down the Ypres offensive – the 1st King's Own (Royal Lancaster Regiment) reported to 12th Infantry Brigade that the Germans were singing and clapping their men, although if anyone raised their head above the trench parapet they would be fired upon. During that day, the two battalions holding the front lost twenty-three men.[4] This curious incident was repeated, although hostilities continued and no man ventured out of the trenches. The brigade noted that singing and cheering was heard on 25 November. Gradually, the two sides began to make contact. Five days later, after a certain amount of 'promiscuous shelling' by the enemy, which included a near miss to the 2nd Essex's headquarters and twenty shells falling just behind the King's Own, staff at 12th Infantry Brigade wrote that 'semaphore communication [had been] established with the enemy, but his signallers are so bad that their replies cannot be read … Germans report verbally that they are being relieved and are going back for a fortnight's rest.' It was certainly a novel and unexpected situation. Neither brigade nor divisional headquarters appears to have been unduly concerned, and no action was taken to halt or encourage this dialogue. The 2nd Essex perhaps took rather less interest in the Germans on that particular day (30 November), for they managed to pierce a sewer pipe that promptly began to flood their trenches.

The 2nd Lancashire Fusiliers came into the line on 29 November, relieving the King's Own. They immediately joined in the cross-trench banter. By 1 December, the brigade was reporting that the

Lancashire Fusiliers are offering Germans bully beef in exchange for helmet badges and [the] bargain is complete except for a slight disagreement as to who should come out of his trench first and fetch his share … the Germans in front of the [2nd] Essex have been relieved by a rather surly lot. They will not answer when spoken to.

There were continued reports of shouting across the trenches over the next few days.

Some senior British officers already recognised the possibility that a lengthy period of static warfare, especially in poor conditions, might encourage such contact with the enemy. On 4 December, George Forestier-Walker, Brig.-Gen. on the general staff of II Corps, wrote to 3rd and 5th Divisions:

> It is during [such a] period that the greatest danger to the morale of the troops exists. Experience of this, and every other war, proves undoubtedly that troops in trenches in close proximity to the enemy slide very easily, if permitted to do so, into a 'live and let live' theory of life. Understandings – amounting sometimes to almost unofficial armistices – grow up between our troops and the enemy, with a view to making life easier, until the sole object of war becomes obscured, and officers and men sink into a military lethargy from which it is difficult to arouse them ... this attitude of our troops can be readily understood and to a certain extent compels sympathy ... such an attitude is, however, most dangerous for it discourages initiative in commanders and destroys offensive spirit in all ranks ... Friendly intercourse with the enemy, unofficial armistices (e.g. 'we won't fire if you don't, etc') and the exchange of tobacco and other comforts, however tempting and occasionally amusing they may be, are absolutely prohibited.[5]

This insightful but firm attitude does not appear to have existed in III Corps, or at least in 4th Division. Contact escalated on 10–11 December. The 2nd Essex Regiment had been relieved and briefly housed in the *Brasserie de la Lys*, an old brewery on the northern outskirts of Armentières, when it was ordered to relieve the 2nd Monmouths in the trenches at the Estaminet du Bon Coin on 7 December.[6] They found the firing line and communication trenches still flooded. The Royal Engineers had brought up a pump, but the men still had to spend much time bailing out, without marked success. Things were so bad that during daylight the garrison was withdrawn from the trenches and placed in houses just in rear, and a new trench was begun nearby. When the battalion returned to the firing line, three men were wounded by snipers and heavy firing was heard from the Houplines direction on 9 December, but otherwise all was quiet. Next day, the Essex learned from shouted messages that the XIX Saxon Corps was facing them: 'they had half-masted the German flag and were fed up with the war.'

On a foggy and cold day on 11 December, the battalion diary noted that, at '10 a.m. officers and men of A and D Companies met Germans half way between the trenches. Germans say they were fed up. Regiment occupying trenches [is] 181st Regiment of 19th Saxon Corps. Trenches appeared to be held in about the same strength as ourselves and in same state.'[7] A report submitted to the brigade by the battalion's temporary commanding officer, Captain Lumley Jones, is more specific.[8]

> Second Lieutenant Spooner, commanding a trench of my right, Second Lieutenant Brabazon and Sergeant Flin have been out of the trenches and have met the Germans half way and have talked to them. They have 181 on their shoulder strap and a 12 on the button. Germans state that they are very 'fed up' and that they keep sniping so much in order to stay awake, and that it is only the youngsters that do it. He also reports that some men of D Company (the company on his left) have been in the German trenches and returned. The orderly who brought the message here states that the Germans are standing in water up to their waist and have sacks on, sewn up the middle between the legs.[9]

In this report are shades of the fraternisation that would take place along this front at Christmas, but as yet this was an isolated case. Brig.-Gen. Frederick Anley, previously of the 2nd Essex, but since October in command of 12th Infantry Brigade, thought that things were getting out of hand. Fraternisation was an act that could lead to the most severe punishments under British military law. If the soldier was found guilty of 'treacherously holding correspondence with or giving intelligence to the enemy', he was liable to a death or a lesser sentence. If 'without due authority [he] either holds correspondence with, or gives intelligence to, or sends a flag of truce to an enemy', he would suffer penal servitude.[10] Jones's report is marked 'shown to Corps Commander but not forwarded.' On 13 December, Anley ordered, 'There will be no further parleying with the enemy in any form. The Germans will be informed of this as soon as possible but no further communication of any sort will be made to them.' His orders continued, to specify that short but heavy fire would be opened against the enemy at 11 a.m. and 3 p.m. There is no further mention of fraternisation between the Saxons and 12th Infantry Brigade, and within a matter of days they were hard at battle.

4

The Attack at Wytschaete, 14 December

The British Part in the Offensive Whittles Down to Two Single-Battalion Attacks

Around 8 December 1914, Smith-Dorrien, at the British II Corps headquarters, learned that his formation would probably soon have to undertake an offensive operation against German positions in the Wytschaete area, alongside the French XVI Corps on his left. He soon became aware of the emerging idea of a sequential attack, and that as he was on the left of the British front, he would be called upon to undertake the first assault. He already had the 3rd Division holding the left of his Corps' front, next to the French. The division was commanded by Maj.-Gen. (James) Aylmer Haldane, and had been in almost continuous action since Mons in August 1914.[1] The plan was gradually confirmed over the next few days, amid a rush of meetings between GHQ, II Corps and the commanders of its constituent divisions and brigades. Early on 9 December, a motor car arrived to take Brig.-Gen. William Bowes to meet with Smith-Dorrien. Bowes commanded the 8th Infantry Brigade of Haldane's division. Although records do not confirm so, it appears that it was at this point that Bowes' brigade was selected to undertake the first attack once it was finally ordered. The brigade had been relieved from the trenches and was resting at Westoutre at this time, remaining so until just before the attack.[2]

The commanders of the Royal Artillery of the 3rd, 4th and 5th Divisions were summoned to a conference at II Corps' advanced report centre on the Scherpenberg hill in the morning of 11 December. Part of the artillery of 4th Division, a formation of III Corps was going to be used to supplement that 3rd and 5th Divisions of II Corps. The three officers were briefed with an outline of the plan, and told that,

> Orders for the attack will be sent, when drafted, for the information of the artillery
> commanders, but these cannot be issued until the commander of the French Eighth

Army has issued his orders to the commander of the XVI French Corps, and the final scope, and time of commencement of, the attack is finally settled.

The three went away to arrange appropriate dispositions of their brigades, organise ammunition stocks and begin the process of ranging the batteries onto the probable targets.[3] At the same time, the men of 3rd Divisional Signal Company of the Royal Engineers, notably Number 3 Section under Lieutenant Robert Dammers, laid telephone cable from the barn that would be used as an advanced brigade headquarters to the firing line and support trenches.

While these discussions and preparations were taking place, the general situation on the Flanders front remained relatively quiet, although punctuated by the arrival of disquieting news. A battalion of the Royal Scots Fusiliers reported that the Germans were strengthening their defences, employing 'poles on trestles with barbed wire'. The Royal West Kents of 10th Infantry Brigade (4th Division) found that the Germans had brought field guns forward, to within 300 yards of their front line. During this 'quiet period' of 6 to 13 December 1914, no fewer than 342 officers and men of the BEF lost their lives, such was the daily toll of trench warfare.[4] Among them were three officers and forty men of two companies of the 1st Lincolnshire Regiment (9th Infantry Brigade, 3rd Division), who had carried out a localised attack against Petit Bois at 10 p.m. on 8 December. Soaked and cold, to the extent that men had to help each other climb from their flooded trench, they had been cut down by enemy fire coming from the wood. Most of the casualties fell within yards of their own trench, hit as they plodded through deep mud. Only on the extreme right of the frontage attacked did the battalion manage to cut the barbed-wire defences and enter the edge of the wood. They found a firing line some yards into the trees full of water, and could see other lines of trenches further on. Two German machine guns appeared to be located centrally within the wood. The survivors fell back to their start point. Sketches of the German positions were delivered to brigade headquarters.[5]

Later, on 11 December, the commanders of the four battalions of 8th Infantry Brigade met with Bowes. The general plan of attack was disclosed to them, but not the date. Bowes ordered the 2nd Royal Scots and 1st Gordon Highlanders to begin preparations for an assault; they would be supported by his other battalions the 4th Middlesex Regiment and 2nd Suffolk Regiment. Officers of the attacking companies were to spend a day in the trenches on 12 December, with a view to making themselves familiar with the situation. Poor Second Lt Alexander Pirie, who was to lead a company of the 1st Gordons, was shot through the head while doing so. He died of his wounds next day.[6]

Smith-Dorrien finally issued written orders at 1.30 p.m. on 13 December, based on the instructions he had received from Murray. They called for the capture of Wytschaete and Hollebeke by a combined attack of the British II Corps and the

French Eighth army. The latter would employ its XVI Corps and XXXII Corps, and would advance in the direction of Oostaverne and Houthem. The 32nd Division of XVI Corps would be on the immediate left of the British, with the boundary on the line Vandenberghe Farm–Wytschaete Hospice–Wambeke. II Corps would deploy its 3rd Division for the attack, which 'will be made in force and will be pushed with the utmost determination'. It would advance to capture Point 73, Maedelstede Farm and the eastern edge of Petit Bois: the same position that had repelled the Lincolnshires attack on 8 December. The 5th Division lay on 3rd Division's right, with the operational boundary being the crest of a ridge running eastwards from Point 73, through Point 74 to Wytschaete. 5th Division would not make an infantry attack, but would 'arrange by activity in its trenches to convey the impression that an attack is going to be made', in the area south-west of Messines. The Cavalry Corps would be in reserve, ready to exploit any breakthrough (it moved a brigade to the Scherpenberg–Westoutre area for the purpose, and caused most artillery and field ambulances to move to accommodate them). It was placed under temporary command of II Corps for the operation, as was a portion of the artillery of III Corps' 4th Division, and a single 4.5-inch howitzer battery from I Corps. Spotting work for the artillery would be carried out by 6 Squadron of the Royal Flying Corps, two machines being allotted to each of the 3rd and 5th Divisional artillery.

The attack was ordered to begin at 7 a.m. on 14 December, with a preliminary bombardment lasting 45 minutes, at which moment the British and French infantry would begin their attack. The supply of artillery ammunition gave cause for anxiety. British GHQ had given sanction for a certain amount of expenditure of shells, with II Corps orders adding that if more was required for the tasks allotted, then it was to be used. The supply officers reported the numbers of shells that were in the forward area (between the divisional railheads and the gun positions), at the sanctioned rate of fire of 150 shells per day. For each 18-pounder, there was enough shrapnel shell for sustained action lasting 2.7 days, but for the 4.5-inch howitzers firing at sixty per day, there was less than a day of Lyddite high explosive shell although there was also 2.6 days of shrapnel. The paucity of ammunition, especially the threadbare stocks of high-explosives, was the critical factor. II Corps had to limit its attack to a single infantry brigade front, while the rest of the Corps in effect would stand by and watch to see what happened.

Shortly after II Corps issued their orders, so Haldane's headquarters issued at 3.30 p.m. more detailed orders to the units of 3rd Division. 8th Infantry Brigade would attack the German trenches fronting Petit Bois and at Maedelstede Farm. They would then go on to secure the rest of the wood and a location known as Point 73. The 2nd Royal Scots and 1st Gordon Highlanders had already been instructed to move to Kemmel during the evening, and to be in their assault positions by 5 a.m. the next day. The

4th Middlesex and 2nd Suffolks would also move to Kemmel, as would brigade headquarters, remaining there until called upon. The battalions of 9th Infantry Brigade would 'support the attack from their trenches and will take any opportunity of gaining ground'. 7th Infantry Brigade would remain in a reserve position near Locre. During the afternoon of 13 December, Captain the Hon. Henry Lyndhurst Bruce of the Royal Scots and Lt William Findlay Dobie of the Gordon Highlanders (both of whom had spent the day before in the trenches and who would lead a company into action) reported to the divisional Commander Royal Artillery (Brig.-Gen. Frederick Wing), to offer advice regarding their respective lines of advance and other details of the position. It is not clear whether Bruce was shown the sketch of the position his battalion would attack, for they were to advance over the same ground where the 2nd Lincolns had been cut down six days before. Neither officer would survive the next day.[7]

Shortly before dawn, on the fine morning of 14 December, Brig.-Gen. Bowes, his opposite number at 9th Infantry Brigade W. Douglas Smith, and their respective Brigade-Majors moved into the barn north of Kemmel, from where they had good observation of the attack front. They would be joined there by Lt-Col George Geddes of 42 Brigade RFA, the artillery unit in specific support to the assault units. Behind them on the Scherpenberg hill, staff of II Corps, 3rd Division and later Sir John French himself, would also study what was happening.

By the time the artillery bombardment opened, at 7 a.m. on 14 December, the French and British assault units had taken up their allotted positions. Plastered with mud and with the kilts of the Gordons heavy and sodden, they waited the 45 minutes while shells screamed above onto the enemy trenches a matter of 200 yards in front.

Somehow, the call for a British attack 'all along its front' had been whittled down to these two under-strength battalions. Many soldiers who had barely received training, and some of whom had not been in the trenches before, were wet and up to their ankles in mud, and about to attack a difficult set of defences. As the commander of I Corps, Gen. Sir Douglas Haig would note in his diary on 14 December, 'it is sad to see the offensive movement by the British army 280,000 strong resolve itself into an attack of two battalions!'[8] As if that was bad enough, the geography of the situation meant that they would have to attack in different directions, in effect as two single-battalion attacks.

The front line to be assaulted was not quite continuous. The Germans held the two woods that lay west of Wytschaete (the small, detached wood Petit Bois being nearest to the British trenches) and Maedelstede Farm which lay just north of the Wytschaete–Kemmel road. The German defences skirting the western edge of woods lay in a more or less north–south direction, and those skirting the northern side of the farm in a west–east direction. In other words, the 'line' formed a right-angle bend in between the woods and farm. The

2nd Royal Scots would attack Petit Bois advancing eastwards and downhill, and the 1st Gordons would attack the farm, advancing southwards and uphill. The further they advanced, the further apart they became. It proved to be a most difficult situation, in that German defenders holding the woods could not only fire into the Royal Scots coming towards them, but into the backs of the Gordon Highlanders advancing away from them and vice-versa.

Dead Men Can Advance no Further[9]

In early June 1917, the British Second Army carried out one of the most successful offensive operations of the war in finally capturing the Wytschaete–Messines ridge. Attacking on a front several miles wide and with enormous artillery resources, they advanced across the very same ground in which the fighting of 14 December 1914 had taken place. As a prelude to the attack, the British artillery fired a pulverising bombardment onto enemy positions that then gradually crept forward, allowing the infantry to advance in its wake and to a large extent unmolested. The German defences of Maedelstede Farm were obliterated by the explosion of an enormous underground mine. The shellfire and fall-out from the mine churned the ground and created a new landscape; countless numbers of German soldiers were killed, their bodies never found. The shells and debris also churned and fell on the old battleground of 1914, along and the weathered, broken skeletons and tatters of kilts of the 1st Gordon Highlanders who died there. They still lay where they fell because their advance had been brought to a shattering halt, the line barely moved over the next two and a half years, and it was simply too dangerous to attempt to recover the dead. After the 1917 advance, men of the 11th Royal Irish Rifles were ordered to clear this part of the battlefield, and in so doing they found the remains of the 1914 victims.[10] They identified the few they could, and buried the remainder with dignity. The burial place was named Irish House Cemetery, after a farm nearby. It had been just a few hundred yards behind 8th Infantry Brigade's line in December 1914. A single mass grave contains the unidentifiable remains of thirty men of the 1st Gordon Highlanders next to the graves of twenty-seven-year-old Lieutenant Dobie, who had co-ordinated with the artillery the day before he died, along with nineteen-year-old Lieutenant James MacWilliam and 9870 Company Quartermaster Sgt Archibald McKinlay.[11] Together with just four others named in other cemeteries, they are the only ones of 125 men of the battalion who were killed or died of wounds on the day to have a known grave. The poor 1st Gordon Highlanders lost three-quarters of their officers and over half of their men killed or wounded in the attack. And what of the 2nd Royal Scots? With the exception of two men buried in Locre churchyard, not one of their fifty-three officers and men who died in their attack on Petit Bois has a known grave today.[12] A further fifty-one officers and men were listed as wounded. On the left of the Royal Scots, the French 32nd Division also suffered significant numbers of casualties.[13] 453 Corporal George Cleghorn of A Company of the Gordons wrote home soon after the battle:

> I have just come from the trenches where I had my first baptism of fire. I will never forget it. The Gordons and Royal Scots had to take some trenches. This they did, but at some loss. In this my first ordeal under fire the noise did not trouble me, nor the shells, but when I saw my mates knocked over I felt a bit giddy. But this passes away, and it becomes part of the day's work. The ground was in an awful state. We were up to the knees in mud and water, shivering with cold.[14]

Seeds of Disaster

These terrible statistics tell a moving tale of disaster, which stemmed from what proved to be a wholly insufficient artillery bombardment and an unjustifiably optimistic view that it would clear the way for the infantry. Simple calculations reveal the terrible truth. II Corps arranged for a total of 143 field guns and howitzers from the artillery of 3rd, 4th and 5th Divisions to fire on targets on the front to be attacked by 3rd Division. Of these, ninety-six were 18-pounder field guns firing shrapnel, and the rest were 4.5- and 6-inch howitzers firing high explosive and shrapnel. This resource was spread to fire onto a number of different targets, with only seventy-two of the 18-pounders, eighteen of the 4.5-inch and thirteen 6-inch howitzers aiming at the trenches to be assaulted. There does not appear to have been a specific task for reduction and clearance of the enemy's barbed-wire defences. II Corps orders read,

> The attack will be preceded by an artillery bombardment of objectives, A, B, C and E. [The first three were the German trenches to be attacked; E was a feint against trenches near Messines]. When enemy's artillery opens, fire will be opened on them (objective G). The French propose to begin their preliminary bombardment about three quarters of an hour before the infantry attack commences. The bombardment will not be continuous, but will commence with a burst of intense fire for two minutes, then a cessation of fire for ten minutes, followed by a burst for, say, one and a half minutes, then a cessation of five minutes, and so on. A similar course will be adopted by the artillery under command of II Corps against objectives A, B, C and E. Bursts of fire need not be simultaneous against all four objectives.
>
> At the expiration of the period allotted to the initial bombardment [i.e. when the infantry should begin to advance] fire on objective C will switch sufficiently

to the East to allow the infantry attack on Petit Bois and Maedelstede Farm to proceed with danger from our own fire.

Brig.-Gen. Frederick Wing reported in the war diary that each 18-pounder had sixty rounds allotted to it for the preliminary bombardment; each 4.5-inch howitzer fifty rounds and each 6-inch howitzer just ten. They were to fire in four bursts that totalled 23 minutes of the 45-minute period. We can calculate from this that the bombardment of objectives A, B, C and E consisted of a total of 4380 18-pounder shells, 900 4.5-inch and 130 6-inch – some 235 shells per minute.[15]

The targets at A, B, C and E were defined in various orders, but not with great precision. At this stage of the war there were no trench maps, for the enemy's position had not been surveyed. The positions to be hit were only known by ground and air observation, and expressed in sketch maps. If we ignore E completely, it appears that the total trench frontage onto which the bombardment would fall was approximately 1250 yards, thus there were just over four shells to be fired for every yard of enemy trench. To the uninformed that sounds a lot. But with technical manuals showing that a new 18-pounder could expect to get only 50 per cent of its shells within a 42-yard range of target, and with most of the guns of the BEF being well worn by December 1914, it becomes evident that very few would actually hit the target. Add to this the shrapnel that was already known to have only minor effects on trenches and barbed wire, it can be appreciated just how the German defenders and defences were to all intents fully intact when the bombardment ended. Once the shells stopped falling, the British whistles blew and men began to advance with the bayonet – the German infantry simply had to man the parapet and open fire.

We should not leave the topic of artillery without mention of Second Lt Hew Kilner of the 35th Heavy Battery of the Royal Garrison Artillery.[16] He had landed in France on 1 December and had been given the unenviable task of assessing an experimental 5-inch 'trench howitzer', which fired a 50-pound Lyddite high-explosive shell. Ten men worked six hours per night for five nights to dig a suitable pit to house the beast. Fifty rounds of ammunition were brought forward, but had to be carried the last 3/4 of a mile by hand, as did the various sections of the howitzer that would be assembled in the pit. It took over thirteen hours to bring this material into place. By herculean effort, Kilner and his men had the new weapon ready by 6.45 a.m. on 14 December, and prepared to fire in the preliminary bombardment. Confidence in its potential effects was perhaps not high, as a few rounds had been fired before it was disassembled for the move into place and it had been found that the fall of shots varied by 200 yards. Frustration must have been intense when it was found that the howitzer and shells had become so muddy during the carry into the pit, that not a shot could be fired until they were completely cleaned. It finally came into action on 17 December.[17]

As soon as the Gordon Highlanders left their trenches and began to move up the gentle slope towards Maedelstede Farm, they came under heavy machine gun and rifle fire. Those men who somehow survived the hail of bullets found that the barbed-wire defences 50 yards in front of the German trenches were intact. The Gordons could advance no further. Losses mounted as men were picked off. Lieutenant James MacWilliam, described in a letter sent to his grieving father, was among them. He had led Nos 9 and 11 Platoons of C Company, encouraging his men forward. Having taken cover in front of the wire, he was shot when raising his head to try to find ways to make progress.[18]

The 2nd Royal Scots found their downhill advance a little easier at first, despite the D Company on the battalion's right front having to squeeze through a gap in a hedge that stood in front of their trench. The battalion also soon came under terrific fire, but quickly reached the German trench on the edge of Petit Bois, where they captured two machine guns and a number of men.[19]

Early reports reaching the II Corps were encouraging, although there was an absence of information from the Gordons, assigned to the fact that the telephone cables linking their front line to the brigade headquarters' barn were being continually broken by enemy shellfire. At 7.45 a.m., Smith-Dorrien received a message from the French XVI Corps that both of its divisions had reported at 7.30 a.m., and that everything had been carried out in accordance with orders. They also signalled at 8.30 a.m. that they had captured the first line of enemy trenches. Smith-Dorrien now informed GHQ that the two battalions of 8th Infantry Brigade had gone ahead with great dash, and troops were now well inside Petit Bois. A few minutes later, the news came that the Germans had evacuated buildings at Maedelstede Farm. This was all reasonably accurate.

The fog of war soon descended and thickened. No one seemed to be able to report what had happened to the Gordons, or exactly where the Royal Scots were, except that they were somewhere inside Petit Bois. In fact, the latter had sent patrols forward that had discovered an unoccupied but flooded trench line within the wood. One wonders whether the Scots had been given information that it existed, for it had been reported by the Lincolnshires after their attack. As early as 7.40 a.m., the 42 Brigade RFA was placed under direct orders of the 8th Infantry Brigade for close support, but did not open fire for some time, as the position of the infantry was so obscure. Although the British artillery had continued to fire in bursts ever since the infantry had advanced, they were now ordered to keep up a slow rate of 'fire on objective C' until the situation became clearer. In Petit Bois, the dwindling number of Royal Scots found British shells falling on their position and even behind them, especially around the south-west corner of the wood, adding to the heavy German fire still pouring from their front. Out of touch and unaware of what had happened to the Gordons on their right, and the French on their left, the battalion took cover as best it could. During this period, Pte 11340 Henry Robson carried out an act of exceptional bravery that eventually led to him being awarded the Victoria Cross. His citation reads,

> For most conspicuous bravery near Kemmel on the 14th December, 1914, during an attack on the German position, when he left his trench under a very heavy fire and rescued a wounded Non-Commissioned Officer, and subsequently for making an attempt to bring another wounded man into cover, whilst exposed to a severe fire. In this attempt he was at once wounded, but persevered in his efforts until rendered helpless by being shot a second time. [20]

Around two hours after the attack began, messages began to arrive from the French that their attack had not made the progress initially reported. They had not only suffered from machine gun and rifle fire from the trenches in the same way as the British battalions, but were also being troubled by German artillery east of Wytschaete. II Corps had employed only eleven heavy guns onto counter-battery work (that is, firing to destroy or neutralise the enemy's artillery) and it appears to have had little effect. The French attack was described in the history of the 18th Bavarian Infantry.[21]

> The French high command intended to unsettle the Germans by means of attack in mid-December all along the line. This was experienced by the 18th Regiment as well. On 14 December after a sharp artillery bombardment, the French launched forward against the German lines as it became light. We were not unprepared because the prisoners [this refers to French soldiers captured during a successful surprise German attack some days earlier which had led to the capture of 215 men] had stated that a major attack would take place in mid-December. But it was a much more modest affair than had been expected. All attacks were beaten off by the defensive fire of our machine guns, some of which could bring down enfilade fire on no man's land, together with that of our soldiers, who coolly manned the parapet and waited until the enemy closed right up to them. The courage of the French was absolutely remarkable. Led by officers with drawn swords, they launched forward repeatedly from their trenches, only to be shot down or driven back. A further attack was attempted the next day (15th), this time it was directed against Hill 58 which climbed away to the left of our position ... their dead littered the battlefield ... Our losses were only sixteen wounded.

By now, the attack had lost all cohesion, with elements of the Gordons and Royal Scots pinned down in the positions they had reached. The French units were in the much the same position, and were uncertain with regard to British progress. At 12.50 p.m., the 3rd Division finally signalled to II Corps that the Gordons were held up 50 yards short of the enemy front trench, and that the Germans had reinforced it. Corps passed this onto GHQ and the Cavalry Corps was stood down, for it was certain that no exploitable breakthrough was going to happen this day. Half an hour later, a message came from the French XVI Corps asking if the British were in possession of whole of Petit Bois, but all that could be said was that this was 'not clear but probable'. This was somewhat optimistic.

Sir John French had now arrived at the Scherpenberg to observe proceedings. He could have seen little forward movement, but he believed the German artillery fire to be less than the British, and on that basis authorised a renewal of the attack for mid-afternoon.

Half of the 4th Middlesex moved forward to give support to the 1st Gordon Highlanders, and the British artillery fired a bombardment described as 'stupendous' by the Royal Scots, but which the Gordon Highlanders reported as falling short. In essence, the proposed attack fizzled out and, by 5.30 p.m., the tired remnants of the two battalions had been relieved. A party of the Middlesex stretcher bearers, among others, helped the wounded Gordons to the dressing stations at Kemmel. As the Royal Irish Rifles would find in 1917, many dead men remained out in no man's land.

During the evening, orders were given that the offensive would continue the next day. GHQ was informed at 11.50 p.m. that Petit Bois had been captured. Over at I Corps, Haig had noted two days before that 'They [II and III Corps] seemed to me rather slovenly in their methods of carrying on war'. On 15 December 1914, he would write, 'Very little energy displayed by 8 Brigade (Bowes) of 3rd Division, II Corps in pressing their attack'.[22]

The Allied assault had not unduly worried the German high command or caused the Germans to make any significant changes to dispositions. In his diary, commander of Sixth Army General Rupprecht, Crown Prince of Bavaria simply noted, 'Various isolated attacks and attempts at attack occurred during the morning. I gained the impression that these were conducted reluctantly and only undertaken to demonstrate that at least something was happening.'[23] He was not far from the truth.

Sir John French would later write in his memoirs that the 'Gordons at dusk had captured the enemy's trenches surrounding Mendleston Farm [sic], but were again driven out of them by powerful machine-gun counter-attack'.[24] This was wishful thinking. French was attempting to deflect blame from rushed preparation, highly optimistic views with regard to the effect of artillery and the reduction of a potentially large-scale attack down to two pinprick assaults. The two battalions had been cruelly exposed to frontal and enfilading fire from positions that had already defeated a similar effort just days before. As one highly respected young British staff officer would call it, the brigade's attack had been 'little short of murder'.[25]

French Thinks Again

The failure of the 8th Infantry Brigade's attack led to a period of near-paralysis as far as British offensive operations in the Wytschaete and Messines areas were concerned. The grand plan for a sequential succession of attacks starting on the left had fallen at the first hurdle. The rushed nature of the arrangements made before 14 December now proved a hindrance, for with 5th Division and the III Corps beyond them not having been properly organised for immediate commencement of an attack, or given specific orders from GHQ other than to harass or 'demonstrate', no major effort could be made for some time. French met with commander of III Corps, Lt-Gen. Sir William Pulteney, on 15 December. From verbatim notes, it can be deduced that the Commander-in-Chief was both disappointed with an apparent lack of vigour shown by the 8th Infantry Brigade and ready to blame the French XVI Corps for uncertainty and lack of progress.[26] The 3rd Division made no serious attempt to renew the attack, despite the three French Corps continuing operations in the area of Bois Quarante and Piccadilly Farm (without marked success) over the next two days. Foch reported to Joffre that without the British engaging on his right, he was stuck.[27] Both sides kept up occasional artillery fire along much of the line. The Germans quietly reoccupied the trenches in the middle of Petit Bois during the night of 15/16 December. When replying to a French request for clarification of the position, the II Corps replied that 7th Infantry Brigade (which had by now relieved the 8th) held the western edge, although reports suggests that this was only a covering force 30 yards outside the wood, with the main body being back in the trench from which the 2nd Royal Scots had attached on 14 December.

Smith-Dorrien had no real intention of carrying on what he perceived to be quite useless, narrow-front attacks. Pulteney wrote to French, with a few rough ideas about how best to proceed. The Commander-in-Chief admonished him for sharing ideas regarding potential actions and developments on paper, due to the security risks he ran, and insisted that in future he did so verbally and in secret. Considering that news and tittle-tattle from headquarters was the subject of frequent whispering in London and Paris, this was correct, but somewhat harsh. Instead of taking heed of practicalities and waiting for the time when he did have proper forces and munitions for a serious offensive, French still found himself greatly under the influence of Foch and Joffre. He mulled over the possibilities and talked to his subordinates of considering an offensive with general view to recapturing the Belgian coast, but until that could be properly undertaken it was necessary to attack elsewhere, preferably north of the Lys, rather than to the south of it. The objective would only be to 'hold the enemy to his ground and occupy at least an equal German force, while a more extensive French force is attacking elsewhere'. Intelligence suggested that only two and a half German corps faced the entire BEF of five corps: French's view was that a locally vigorous offensive was required to compel the Germans to move force from elsewhere to face the aggressive British. Any attack to be made by the BEF was not aimed at any form of breakthrough, but was simply to attract and kill Germans while the French got on with winning the war. It was an admission of a limited offensive, a very far cry from Lord Grey saying that British public would be happy with losses if an important prize was won. When the orders finally emerged from British headquarters, they were an admission of the failure of the previous plan. There would be 'no attacks in succession from a flank, but a main effort continuously sustained till it is achieved'. Objectives should be allotted to one commander, unlike the rather shared approach previously adopted – the 'French and ourselves should not share the attack on an objective such as Wytschaete. The II and III Corps should not both attack Messines.' French considered various options but settled once more on the Wytschaete–Messines ridge, and that meant a main attack against Wytschaete; a holding attack from the Douve down to the Rue du Bois; standing on the defensive south of there. It was a confused and fragmented set of instructions. How would junior commanders explain to their men exactly what they were trying to achieve and when they would know they had achieved it? Even French's Generals needed to have a 'holding attack' explained before it made much sense. French did, however, encourage his army to use night attack, surprise and sapping as methods in the attacks and to aim at feasible tactical gains.

At 9 a.m. on 17 December, Murray's latest order emerged from GHQ saying that in addition to II Corps and Grossetti's Corps resuming the attack north of River Douve, 'It is in the intention of the C-in-C to attack vigorously all along the front tomorrow with the II, II, IV and Indian Corps. A powerful French attack is being made in the neighbourhood of Arras, and to assist that attack the III, IV and Indian Corps will demonstrate and seize any favourable opportunity which may offer to capture the enemy's trenches in their front. Operations will commence at 10 a.m.'[28] This was indeed as vague as an order could possibly be. A year hence these operations would have been viewed as mere raids, and orders arranged on that basis. This was sweeping and utterly without clarity. The main lessons of 14 December had not been learned. There was no time for preparation, or to bring fresh troops into the line, no massing of artillery to provide enough firepower to make a genuine difference, and ominously, allocation of ammunition was even less for than earlier attack. The 18-pounder field guns would now have only forty shells each, the 4.5-inch and 6-inch howitzers twenty and thirty respectively. GHQ left the decisions about what to attack, when, and with what force to the local corps and divisional commands, as long as it was all done within the next few days. In retrospect, it was possibly the lowest point of the entire war as far as committing British forces to a clear and reasonably well-thought-out operation was concerned.

5

Battles in the Lee of Aubers Ridge

Rawlinson's IV Corps

Henry Rawlinson's IV Corps did not carry out any significant operations in the period between 14 and 17 December, although units adjacent to the Indian Corps were ordered to open fire to support their attack on the 16th. In addition to this, the units occupying the front line trenches all along the Corps front kept up small-arms fire and, from time to time, the artillery fired salvoes at identified troublesome spots. This included their part in the 'demonstrations' while the 3rd Division attacked at Wytschaete. The Corps now commanded the 7th and 8th Divisions, both of which largely comprised units of the regular army that had been based at distant garrisons of Empire when war was declared. Those units had been recalled home, but in some cases had to wait until their place could be taken by an outgoing territorial unit.

The Corps, which at the time had included 7th Division and a rather under-strength 3rd Cavalry Division, had been despatched to Belgium in the first week of October 1914, with orders to assist the Belgian army that had been besieged at Antwerp. By the time it arrived, the Belgians were already withdrawing westwards from Antwerp, and 7th Division complied. In doing so, they became the first British formation to enter Ypres. They played a central role in the First Battle there, earning the title of the 'Immortal Seventh'. Both the Corps and Division had inevitably been improvised formations, for they did not exist before the war. The staffs were new, the units were unfamiliar with each other and for some men it was their first time in Europe for many years. Despite this, the division acquitted itself well, but holding the German attack was achieved at appalling cost. The 7th Division lost 364 officers and 9,302 men in little over a month since arriving in Belgium. All twelve of its infantry battalions had 500 men or more killed, wounded or taken prisoner; most lost more than 750, and in the case of the 1st Royal Welsh Fusiliers, a staggering total of 1,024. When at full strength, a complete battalion numbered 30 officers and 977 men. For all practical purposes, the division had to be rebuilt in late November and early December, and most of its units were still under-strength when Sir John French's orders for the offensive were received. The 7th Division was under command of Maj.-Gen. Sir Thompson Capper. Aged fifty-one, he was a well-regarded regimental and staff officer who had seen service in the Second Boer War.[1]

The 8th Division began to land in France in early November 1914, and was still completing assembly just as the First Battle of Ypres was dying down. On 14 November, it took over a stretch of the front line in the Rue du Bois–Fauquissart–Neuve Chapelle sector. For men so recently recalled from Malta, Egypt, South Africa and India, the change in climate and conditions came as a distinctly unpleasant development. The division was in a similar state of training to that of the 7th Division before the fighting at Ypres, in that its units were at reasonably high strength and well-trained, but the formation was new, the staff was new and of course the situation in which the division found itself was of a type no man had yet experienced. Maj.-Gen. Sir Francis Davies was in command. He too was a Second Boer War veteran, and had held regimental and staff posts in the intervening years. Davies was in the post of director of staff duties at the War Office when war was declared.

By early December, the two divisions were holding over 4 miles of front line from La Boutillerie down to Neuve Chapelle. This is a uniformly flat area, intersected by many drainage ditches. Behind the German front line lay the small River Layes (it crossed to behind British trenches near Pétillon), and a gentle incline to a ridge that peaks at a distance of about a mile from the trenches.[2] The ridge is only some 15–30 feet higher than the area to the west, but this gave it the advantage of being less liable to flooding. For the Germans, it provided useful observation points and ensured that some of its artillery was out of direct sight from the British-held area. Not far behind the German line lay the villages of Fromelles, Aubers and Neuve Chapelle, and behind the British lay Fleurbaix and Laventie, with the River Lys some 4 miles away. The whole area was farmland and was dotted with houses and barns. There was no particular tactical or other logic to the siting of the two opposing trench lines, in that they just happened to be where the fighting of October had settled down.

Facing Rawlinson's men was the German VII Armee-Korps under *General der Infanterie* Eberhard von Claer. Under his command came the 13th Division (*Generalleutnant* Kurt von den Borne) and 14th Division (*Generalleutnant* Paul Fleck). The Korps had seen much action since the start of the war, including battles at Liege, Namur, St-Quentin, on the Marne, at Arras and on the Lorette Ridge. It was a formation of the Prussian army, with its units drawn from the Westphalia region, and had moved into this sector in November. The boundaries differed slightly, but essentially the 13th Division faced the entire British IV Corps, while the 14th Division faced the Indian Corps south of Neuve Chapelle.

Throughout the period up to 18 December, this part of the front remained generally quiet but with occasional flare-ups. The artillery of both sides was active, firing on roads and sensitive points behind the lines. The trenches could sometimes be deceptively quiet while the troops strengthened defences or tried to make their lot more comfortable. Sniper fire picked off the unwary at vulnerable points, and localised firefights or small-scale infantry attacks often developed in an effort to eliminate the troublesome snipers. Casualties were small in number, but all too often included experienced officers and NCOs. Both sides sent patrols out into no man's land at night to probe the enemy's defences, and to identify units if possible by the capture of prisoners. The British were also keen to detect any sign that the Germans were sapping towards them.

In December 1914, a young officer of the Royal Engineers (whom we shall meet later) was involved in a perfect local raid during the night of 26/27 November. Units of the 8th Division's 23rd Infantry Brigade had reported problems from snipers located in a house near the German trenches. This was the large farmhouse north of Neuve Chapelle known to the British as the moated grange. Typical of many farms in northern France, the buildings surrounded a courtyard and midden on four sides, making a site 40 yards square.[3] Lt Philip Neame RE was ordered to take a party of twenty-four men to demolish the house, covered by eight men of the 2nd West Yorkshire Regiment under Second Lieutenant Loraine Macgregor Kerr. Waiting until after midnight due to the moon being so bright earlier on, Neame's men ran cables out to the house, which was found to be unoccupied, and despite occasional German rifle fire in their direction laid fourteen guncotton charges. Within an hour the two parties were back in the safety of their own trenches, undetected. Exploders were then connected up to the three cable circuits that had been laid, and the house was demolished on three sides. There were no casualties.[4]

On 16 December, patrols reported that the German barbed-wire defences in front of 7th Division were now 5 feet high in places, but with gaps and areas much less well covered. The enemy trenches appeared to be lightly manned, but the German infantry was 'making a big show' to suggest that there was a greater presence. A German prisoner interrogated on 19 December confirmed these findings, saying that the trenches were certainly no more strongly held than usual and had one man about every four to five paces.[5]

At 10.30 p.m. on 17 December, Capper and Davies were summoned for a meeting with Rawlinson at his headquarters in Merville. Their brigades, artillery and engineers were warned that fresh orders might be expected during the night. Orders from Murray at GHQ did not arrive until midnight.

After discussion, it was decided that the most effective way of ensuring that the Germans dare not remove any reserves from the front facing IV Corps, was for both 7th and 8th Divisions to make an attack. Rawlinson advised that this should take place at dusk, which was around 4 p.m. The two divisional commanders returned to their headquarters respectively, at Sailly-sur-la-Lys and Estaires respectively. Their subordinates were called and plans worked out.

Rawlinson issued an order from IV Corps headquarters at 9.20 a.m., stating the general objective but also giving divisional commanders latitude to select their own points of assault. With only some seven hours to go before the attack was launched, there was no time for any change in dispositions, or to bring rested men into the trenches; no time for any special reconnaissance, no time to think about surprise or deception, arrangements of supply or special arrangements for casualties.

For the attack by 7th Division, Capper decided upon an assault by 22nd Infantry Brigade, on a front 400 yards wide in the direction of Bas-Maisnil, against the three lines of German trenches in front of the brigade. The divisional artillery would open fire at 4 p.m., paying particular attention on to the enemy's front trench and those on its flank and on an area known as the 'Cabbage Patch'. The infantry would go 'over the top', at 4.30 p.m., and ten minutes later the guns would lengthen range onto the German support trenches and approach tracks. The artillery would also devote a certain amount of ammunition on breaking up the barbed-wire defences in front of 20th Infantry Brigade. This formation would attack at 6 p.m., but only with two half-battalions.

While this plan was being briefed to the units involved, the division's chief gunner, Brig.-Gen. Herbert Kendall Jackson, worked out that he only had ammunition for a 15-minute bombardment, and virtually all of that was shrapnel. It might keep German heads down for a while, but even the most optimistic soldier would now guess that the division's infantry was going to face uncut wire and trenches that had barely been damaged.

The 22nd Brigade: The Warwicks and Queen's

At 10 a.m. on 18 December, the commanding officers of the brigade's battalions met at brigade headquarters at Fleurbaix. They received instructions from Brig.-Gen. Sydney Lawford, an experienced officer who would later go on to lead the 41st Division and become the longest-serving British divisional commander of the war.[6] It was decided that the brigade was to attack on a 500-yard frontage east of La Boutillerie, with the left-hand end of the front at Well Farm. With no significant changes to dispositions being possible in time, the brigade would have to use the units that were already in the trenches. The 2nd Royal Warwickshire Regiment would lead, followed by two companies of the 2nd Queen's (Royal West Surrey Regiment). The rest of the Queen's would man the front line east of Well Farm. The general idea was to advance across the 250 yards of no man's land, penetrate the enemy's barbed-wire defences and capture their front-line trench. Work would then be undertaken to reverse the trench parapet and secure the flanks. Once this was achieved, a second advance would be made if the enemy was believed to be weak. Divisional instructions came, entreating the brigade to make sure that they had arranged for special wire cutting, hand grenade and machine gun detachments, to provide working parties with all the tools, equipment and materials they would need for isolating the captured area and revetting the trench as needed. They would also make preparations for bringing ammunition and all manner of trench stores forward, but should not dismantle anything from their old trench until the German line had been definitely secured. This was to prove somewhat optimistic.

The 2nd Royal Warwicks had been holding a sector of the brigade's front line for the past three days. In order to take their place as ordered for the attack, they had squeeze up into a shorter line by vacating the left-hand part of the trenches they were holding. A and B companies of the 2nd Queen's moved up from reserve into the vacated trench, and their C and D companies moved into a close support position ready to follow the Warwicks once they had advanced. All of this took place within a short distance of the enemy in driving rain, with men moving through already half-flooded trenches and deep mud. The Queen's were still moving into place when the divisional artillery opened up at 4.15 p.m., and had no time to pass details of the attack scheme to each soldier.

Although the Warwicks described the artillery as 'heavy' and the Queen's said it was 'terrific', simple mathematics and the admission by the divisional artillery commander suggests this cannot have been the case. The bombardment apparently did little damage to either the barbed-wire defences, the German trench or its garrison, but it did manage to wound several of the British troops awaiting the whistle at 4.30 p.m. and gave away any opportunity for surprise. The German artillery, according to the Warwicks, was so little troubled that it made hardly any reply. The infantry of the German 55th Infantry Regiment, manning the trenches of the La Boutillerie sector, were ready and waiting. The story of 22nd Infantry Brigade's part on 18 December is movingly told by the 2nd Royal Warwickshire's war diary:[7]

Attack was started by B Company on the right led by Captain Haddon, advancing in two lines; A Company advanced on the left in two lines with D Company in the centre. C Company formed the third line, with entrenching tools. A machine gun was on each flank. Immediately the attack was opened, the enemy opened a very heavy rifle and machine gun fire. The battalion advanced under this with steadiness, suffering very heavy casualties.[8]

The Queen's had managed to get into the trench from which the Warwicks attacked by about 4.45 p.m., but could only guess at the carnage ahead of them as it was now dark and the air full of smoke. About fifteen minutes later, an NCO from the Warwicks returned to ask for support from the Queen's, but there was no reliable information about exactly what had happened. Leaving half a company behind to defend the trench in case of a German counter-attack, the Queen's now also advanced into the continuous hail of fire. A message went to the 1st Royal Welsh Fusiliers, the brigade's reserve company, to prepare to move forward to reinforce the attack. The Queen's found that the Warwicks had apparently crossed the first half of no man's land without too much trouble, but the piled corpses and wounded near the German wire told their own story. Reports suggested that a party of the Warwicks had entered the German trench. As they crossed the fire-swept no man's land, the Queen's also took severe casualties – captains Lee and Fearon, who commanded the two companies, were both wounded. The Warwicks' commanding officer Lt-Col. Robert Brewis, and three of his officers, had been killed at the head of their men. Haddon was taken prisoner, and battlefield command inevitably broke down. The survivors of both battalions were scattered in groups, taking cover as best they could. Runners sent to take information back to battalion and brigade headquarters failed to arrive and, even by 6 p.m., Lawford had no clear idea of the progress made by his men, or their position. The British artillery fire, having stepped forward as instructed, continued to fall on the German support trenches, and had no effect on the fight for the front line. At 7.15 p.m., Capper instructed Lawford to call off the attack, but it appears to have been at about 7.52 p.m. when Capt. Francis Montague-Bates, who was in command of the 2nd Queen's and back in the original trench, ordered the men to withdraw from no man's land and sent out parties to attempt to bring in the wounded. These tired remnants arrived in their old front line, finding them now full of the recently arrived 1st Royal Welsh Fusiliers.

When roll call was taken, it was found that the Warwicks had lost twelve officers, with 383 men killed, wounded or missing. The Queen's had lost six officers and eighty-nine men: a terrible toll for no gain whatever.

At daybreak next day (19 December), the survivors of the two battalions that were still in their front line saw the Germans beckoning at them, indicating that they could come out to bury the dead. It must have been with some trepidation that several officers and some thirty men went out, meeting with a slightly larger enemy in no man's land. An informal ceasefire was arranged and men of both sides set to the grim task of identifying and burying the bodies. One report states that of the Warwicks, 'between 200 and 300 were buried on the ground'. The records of the Commonwealth War Graves Commission in fact list 116 dead.[9]

The majority of the men killed were more than halfway across no man's land and close to the wire defences, which meant that search and burial parties were working near the German trenches. It was as a result of this proximity that two officers of the Queen's were taken prisoner. This was not noticed until the ceasefire was ended by British shellfire. One of those who went into captivity was Second Lt Charles Gardner Rought of C Company.

I was working until well into the night, with rescue parties. Many of our wounded were lying close up to the enemy lines and we had been unable to get to them. The men in our trenches stood to arms the whole night as we were expecting a counter-attack and just as it was growing light I heard some of them say the enemy were leaving their trenches. I looked over our parapet and saw some Germans bending over our wounded, but almost simultaneously some of our men fired and the Germans disappeared. About an hour later the Germans showed themselves again and our men were told not to fire. Seeing our doctor standing on the parapet and going out, and thinking I should be of help in getting some of the wounded in, (and also that by being in no man's land I might show our men that the Germans intended letting us bring in our wounded and that they must not fire) I followed the doctor out and, after looking at a few men I found to be dead, heard the Germans calling 'we are peaceful, we are peaceful, take your comrades'. I [went off] to the right to a point in the German advanced trench where I thought I might find Lieut. Ramsay, who we thought had been wounded the previous evening.

As I got up to the first line which was partly a firing trench and partly a natural ditch cross-wired, I saw a number of our wounded and was just starting to lift a man when a German soldier called 'Officer?' I said 'yes' and he replied 'our officer wishes to speak to you'. [The officer said] that our men might take back the wounded but the rifles must be left where they were. This demand I thought quite reasonable and shouted to the men within earshot accordingly. The German officer made one or two further remarks, amongst other things he said, pointing to our dead and wounded, 'the Englishmen are very brave'. I was now standing close to a sap, running from the advanced trench to the main firing line, and started to move off to lift one of our fellows who was lying close by. Several of our NCOs and men were by this time hard at work amongst Germans, who were also helping to rescue the wounded – but the German officer caught my arm and said I was not to go. For a moment I remonstrated and after saying something in German, the officer said 'war is war'. I made some remark in which I used the word 'treachery', whereupon I was pulled by some soldiers, evidently by command of their officer, into their sap and drawn into their main trench. The officer, holding a revolver to my chest, said that if I repeated my remarks he would shoot me. He cooled somewhat and stated that I must see his commandant and with his permission might return to my own lines, but as I had seen their position he must keep me.

It was now I noticed Lieut. Walmisley and saw the Germans taking his equipment from him. He was about 20 yards distant and they brought him and one or two men and sent us down their trench under escort. As we passed, away to our left we could still see Germans mixed up with our men attending to the wounded in no man's land. We were harangued by an officer with a red cross band round his arm. Speaking fluent English he said we had fired on the white flag and were to be shot.[10]

According to the 2nd Queen's diary, it was during the ceasefire that a German sniper picked off Lt Henry Bower of the 1st South Staffords, killing him instantly. Half of his battalion had now moved up into the trenches from which the 2nd Royal Warwickshires had attacked, and Bower – who had himself been wounded during the First Battle of Ypres – was shot while helping bring in the Warwicks' wounded. The Staffords' diary times his death at about 8.30 a.m., about the time that Rought and Walmisley were being taken prisoner.[11] The somewhat nervous truce ended not long afterwards.

20th Brigade: The Scots Guards and Border Regiment

Once Brig.-Gen. Frederick Heyworth, in command of 20th Infantry Brigade, had received his instructions from division, he had little time to conclude on how best to use his force to make an attack. It had already been decided that he would use two half-battalions (that is, two companies from each battalion) and would attack at 6 p.m., a full ninety minutes after 22nd Brigade had advanced on his left. Heyworth gave orders to move his brigade headquarters to a forward position at La Cordonnerie Farm, which was just behind the extreme left-hand portion of the attack frontage.[12]

The battalions holding the trenches, the 2nd Border Regiment and 2nd Scots Guards, were strung out over a longer line than usual, as the 7th Division's other brigade (21st) had been temporarily released to support the II Corps. Despite having little time, Heyworth decided that both battalions had to squeeze up in order to have enough men on the 400-yard front to be attacked. The space they vacated would be filled by other units that would have to move into place before the attack. While this appears to have been achieved, it meant a day of moving men and material, with precious little time for briefing or preparation for going 'over the top'. By the time that A and C Companies of the 2nd Borders were in their position, it was dark and no man knew exactly his correct front or the point of attack.

At 3.45 p.m., the two officers who would lead the attack met to co-ordinate orders. Capt. Giles Loder of the Scots Guards and Capt. Henry Askew of the Borders agreed that just before 6 p.m. their men would climb over their parapet, crawl under the British barbed wire and lie down.[13] Once they were in place, Loder would blow his whistle and all four companies would advance at the walk until the enemy opened fire, at which point they would rush the German trench. They had to cross a no man's land that varied between 80 and 150 yards in depth, along with the barbed-wire defences in front of the German trenches. As it happened, these defences were patchy, with some gaps between areas that were less easily penetrated. No man's land was flat and criss-crossed with small drainage ditches. Behind the German front lay a few farm houses and, away on the left, some small woods in front of the village of Fromelles, which sits on the gentle Aubers ridge. By 6 p.m., it was pitch black.

Across no man's land lay the *7. Lothringisches Infanterie-Regiment* No. 158 of 25th Brigade of the German 13th Division, supported by that division's guns of the *13. Feldartillerie-Brigade*.

About half an hour before the attack, rumours came through that the 22nd Brigade, about half a mile away on the left, had failed in theirs. There was no special preliminary artillery bombardment on the front to be attacked, although shelling was going on to some extent. Those units on the flanks maintained rifle and machine gun fire to make sure the enemy kept their heads down.

As his watch ticked round to 6 p.m., Giles Loder blew his whistle as hard as he could. 200 yards off to his left, Henry Askew and the two companies of the 2nd Border Regiment did not hear it amid the noise of gunfire. The Scots Guards got up as ordered, and quietly crossed no man's land, finding the gaps in the wire. Within minutes, those men who had been lucky enough to walk towards these gaps were jumping down into the enemy trenches and bayonetting every German they could find. Despite the evident tension in the air from the 4 p.m. attack, and that there had been much activity behind British lines during the day, the absence of a preliminary bombardment had helped the Guards achieve complete surprise. In Loder's section, they were in possession of the enemy trench and set about making it defensible – no easy task as it proved to be very deep. Pte 7792 Harold Bryan recalled his job:

> It was my duty to cut the wire with cutters. This I had to do lying down and it was to this that I owe my life, for hundreds of bullets passed over my head. When we were within 80 yards of them the signal was given and what a charge: we caught them getting out of their trenches, but few of them were left to escape. On these occasions no prisoners were taken. They either have to run, or stand and be killed. We held that trench for three days and then, owing to weight of

numbers, had to retire again to our own line. We weren't exactly sorry because our trenches are far better than theirs.[14]

Elsewhere the attack was breaking down. The Germans, alerted only at the last minute as the Guards were almost upon them, poured fire into those elements on whose front the wire defences had been present and intact. In other words, the German trench was only entered in patches, isolated from each other, while the survivors in the fire-swept areas also became isolated into small groups that took shelter as best they could. On the extreme right of the Scots Guards' front, F Company's progress was halted by an enemy machine gun firing from the vicinity of Delaporte Farm to Rouges Bancs, which scythed the guardsmen down as they attempted to breach the wire.[15] A detachment under-eighteen-year-old Lt Geoffrey Ottley was ordered to reinforce them, but they too suffered heavily from this fire.[16]

The 2nd Borders, having not heard Loder's whistle, did not advance until some time later. Their own war diary suggests this took place at 6.15 p.m. although the brigade diary says it was fifteen minutes later. Quite why it took so long for the two companies to begin to move is not clear – and many of those who might have reported why it was so did not live to tell the tale. With the Germans now fully alerted, the Borders met with heavy fire as they attempted to cross no man's land. It appears that some casualties were caused by the British artillery firing short, and those men who did manage to approach the German trenches were halted for an hour until messages could get back to the guns to cease firing, or lift onto the enemy's reserve trenches.

The *Sunderland Daily Echo* of 9 January 1915 included a letter written home by the 2nd Border's 9050 Sgt Charles Dobson. He had only arrived in France on 25 November and this was his draft's first time in action.

> I had my baptism of fire soon after I arrived here. Two days after my arrival my company went into the trenches for four days' duty. On the fourth night we made an attack on the enemy's trenches, which are only about 100 yards from ours, but our attack was unsuccessful, although we got to the enemy's barbed wire and some even got into the trenches. I had about 50 men in my platoon when we started but at the finish I only had 29; the others were mostly wounded. I thought I would never get back. Three times we went forward from our trench under a perfect hail of lead.

Eventually, the battalion's temporary commanding officer Maj. George Warren made his way to Brigade HQ at La Cordonnerie Farm. By this time it was apparent that the attack had failed and, other than the parties of Scots Guards, the brigade had nowhere penetrated into the German lines. Heyworth issued orders to call off the attack unless it could be carried on without heavy casualties. As Warren returned to his trench, he found that those company and platoon officers who had survived, had already withdrawn their men back to the cover of their own front line. 'Further operations ceased and the collecting of dead and wounded went on,' according to the battalion diary. Five officers and 123 men of the 2nd Border Regiment had been killed or wounded, including Henry Askew, the officer who had led the advance.[17]

The work of bringing in the wounded continued for the next two days. There was no ceasefire arranged in this area. Two soldiers of the battalion were awarded the Victoria Cross for their extreme bravery in bringing in wounded men during daylight. Privates 6423 James Alexander Smith and 10694 Abraham Acton share a common citation, which was published in the *London Gazette* of 18 February 1915:

> For conspicuous bravery on 21st December, at Rouges Bancs, in voluntarily going from their trench and rescuing a wounded man who had been lying exposed against the enemy's trenches for 75 hours, and on the same day again leaving their trench voluntarily, under heavy fire, to bring into cover another wounded man. They were under fire for 60 minutes, whilst conveying the wounded men into safety.[18]

It was not safe enough to bring in the dead who were lying near to the enemy wire and trenches. The brigade's war diary reported that there were many cases of wounded men being shot by the Germans as soon as they moved, and of one poor fellow who, despite being wounded in both thighs managed to drag himself back to the British parapet, only to be shot dead just as he reached it. But while this may be generally true, at least one officer saw things differently. Capt. Sir Edward Hulse of the 2nd Scots Guards wrote to his mother on 22 December:

> The morning after our attack, there was almost a tacit understanding as to no firing, and about 6.15 a.m. I saw eight or nine German heads and shoulders appear, and then three of them crawled out a few feet in front of their parapet and began dragging in some of our fellows who were either dead or unconscious close to their parapet. I do not know what they intended to do with them, but I passed down the order that none of my men were to fire, and this seems to have been done all own the line. I helped one of our men in myself, and was not fired at, at all. I sincerely hope that their intentions were all that could be desired with regard to our wounded whom they fetched in. I also saw some of them, two cases, where the two Germans evidently were not quite sure about showing themselves, and pushed their rifles out to two of our wounded and got them to catch hold, and pulled them on to their parapet, and so into their trenches. Far the most ghastly part of this business is that the wounded have so little chance of being brought in, and if heavy fire is kept up, cannot even be sent for. There were

many conspicuous acts of gallantry that night, in getting in the wounded under fire, but many had to be left out.[19]

With the attack of the 2nd Border Regiment having failed, those detachments of the 2nd Scots Guards that had reached the enemy line, and were now holding parts of the trenches, found themselves in a most dangerous situation. Their battalion's G Company under Hulse had been ordered to support the assault. He wrote in a letter home on 20 December that 'Directly the attack was launched, we began digging communication trenches under fire, (a dirty task) towards the line of German trenches which our other two companies had taken.' Capt Loder returned across the fire-swept no man's land around an hour after getting into the enemy trenches, in order to gather information and obtain reinforcement, but learned that brigade had now called the attack off. He was also ordered to organise a digging party for the same purpose – of sapping out towards the captured enemy position. It proved an impossibility to dig 180 yards across no man's land. A party of one officer and around ten men went across to reinforce the dwindling garrison, which had been in Loder's absence under Lt James Saumarez. This young officer, Harrow educated and son of a Baronet, had sustained nasty wounds as described in Hulse's letter:

Saumarez is severely wounded, and may lose his hand. He was pluckier than anything I have yet seen, as he also had a bullet in his side, apart from half his hand (right) blown off, and persisted in saying that it was so damnable that he would not be able to play polo again!

A stretcher was sent across and Saumarez was brought back to British lines with great difficulty. Of the six officers who had gone into the attack, only Loder survived unharmed. Around 180 men – about half of those who went into action – were killed or wounded, but their fates were in many cases not definitely known for a considerable time. Among those killed was Pte James Mackenzie, who was awarded a posthumous Victoria Cross. His citation, published in the same *London Gazette* as the two from the 2nd Border Regiment reads:

For conspicuous bravery at Rouges Bancs on the 19th December, in rescuing a severely wounded man from in front of the German trenches, under a very heavy fire and after a stretcher-bearer party had been compelled to abandon the attempt. Private Mackenzie was subsequently killed on that day whilst in the performance of a similar act of gallant conduct.

Twenty-five-year-old Mackenzie from Dumfries, has no known grave, and is commemorated alongside so many of his comrades at the Ploegsteert Memorial.

As the British attack petered out, shellfire on their reserve and communication trenches having little effect, the German 13th Division took the opportunity to reinforce. Close fighting with the detachments of Scots Guards took place and, by about 11.30 p.m., the Germans had recaptured some of their trenches. The rest of them were given up as the Guards withdrew to their own lines before dawn. They later reported that the Germans had allowed them to gather in the dozens of wounded men.

23rd Brigade: The Devons and West Yorkshires

Across the Sailly–Fromelles road, on the right of the 2nd Scots Guards, lay the operational boundary between the British 7th and 8th Divisions. The latter held the 3.5 mile stretch of line down to beyond the Port Arthur crossroads, south of Neuve Chapelle. On the left, the front line was occupied by 25th Infantry Brigade under Brig.-Gen. Sir Arthur Lowry Cole, on his right came the 23rd Infantry Brigade, the command of Brig.-Gen. Reginald Pinney. For much of the division's sector, the British front line lay south of and parallel to the Armentières–Neuve Chapelle road, which is named Rue du Bois (except for a section between the hamlets of Picantin and Fauquissart where it is known as Rue Tilleloy). The ground is flat and, other than the farmhouses and barns along the road, and the little River Layes that ran behind German lines, there were few features between the trenches and the Aubers Ridge a mile distant. In Pinney's area, the village of Neuve Chapelle lay directly ahead and behind German lines. Facing his sector on the left of the village lay the ruins of the moated grange. On the right, the trenches turned almost ninety degrees at the Port Arthur crossroads and followed the line of the Estaires–La Bassée road. Behind Neuve Chapelle, the sizeable wood – the Bois de Biez – sheltered German reserves.

Facing the 8th Division was the southern element of the German 13th Division, which by coincidence was also a 25th Brigade. On the German right, facing the left of the British 25th Infantry Brigade, were elements of the same 158th Infantry Regiment that had caused so much trouble to the 2nd Scots Guards, but most of the line opposite 8th Division was held by the 13th Infantry Regiment.[20]

The 8th Division received its instructions from Rawlinson around midnight on 17/18 December and, like the 7th Division, it had little time in which to plan what to do, although it had received some intimation that it was about to be ordered into offensive action. Shortly before midnight, divisional headquarters signalled to Lowry Cole for his brigade to cancel any work, keep as quiet as possible and generally avoid disturbing the enemy. At 9 a.m., the brigadier went to Estaires to meet with his superior (Davies). He was told to pin the enemy down while 23rd Infantry Brigade on his right made an attack near Neuve Chapelle. Lowry Cole returned to brief his battalion commanders at Fort d'Esquin, to which he moved brigade headquarters for the attack. It was now 1 p.m., just over three hours before the action was to begin. Although the brigade was not going to make a major assault, it was to engage the enemy with fire from all along its front, and its 2nd Rifle Brigade would advance on an 800-yard-wide front to capture the German front line, thus threatening the main enemy line south-west of the Fauquissart–Trivelet road. In order to carry it out, some adjustments of the disposition of the battalions of the brigade would be needed. At the time, all five battalions (the brigade had been joined in November by the territorials of the 13th London Regiment, also known as the Kensington Battalion) were in the front line, with only some companies in reserve, so it meant much shuffling along the trenches. The company commanders of the Rifle Brigade were briefed at 2.30 p.m., and the movement to get the right troops into place appears to have been completed by the time the artillery opened fire at 4.15 p.m. This was the same time as the attack of 22nd Infantry Brigade, but a full hour and a half earlier than that of 20th Infantry Brigade in between them. This fragmented approach can be assigned in large part to the army's doctrine of devolved command, leaving decisions to the 'man on the spot'. It inevitably led to differing decisions, and nowhere was this fragmentation more likely to occur than across a divisional boundary. One can only wonder whether the poor Scots Guards would have suffered so heavily from machine gunfire if they had attacked at the same time as the 20th Infantry Brigade, and had that brigade made a full attack instead of half-heartedly deploying only the 2nd Rifle Brigade.

While the bombardment was underway and battalions on either side added to the maelstrom with rifle and machine gun fire, at 4.20 p.m., four platoons of the Rifle Brigade slipped quietly out of their trenches and passed through the British wire defences. They managed to enter some German saps and advanced trenches, drawing German fire as they went. Behind enemy lines, two or three haystacks were set on fire, throwing a smoky illumination over the battlefield. An officer and four men were hit before the detachment was ordered to withdraw – which it did without further loss in the early hours of 20 December. The British artillery continued sporadic fire throughout the night.[21]

Capt. Ralph Verney, commanding B Company of the 2nd Rifle Brigade, which had been in reserve during the operation, wrote home that, 'the artillery fairly bombarded the enemy's trenches on our right front, and an attack was delivered successfully as far as we know, but we have not had any definite news yet of what happened.' He was referring to the efforts of the 2nd Devonshire and 2nd West Yorkshire Regiments near Neuve Chapelle.

At 4 a.m. on 18 December, Brig.-Gen. Pinney returned from divisional headquarters with orders to make at attack at Neuve Chapelle. Specifically, he would attack from that narrow portion of the front known as 'C Lines' (the 8th Division had subdivided its front into lettered sections). This was east of Neuve Chappelle itself, and faced the recently destroyed buildings of the moated grange. The brigade's front line skirted the ruins on the northern-western side and the German frontline trench lay along its south-eastern edge. The limited expectation of the operation was explained: the enemy front line would be captured, with a view to possibly outflank Neuve Chapelle. Pinney made arrangements to move brigade headquarters to the 'Red Barn' on the Estaires–La Bassée road near Rouge Croix, and called his battalion commanders there for a briefing. The orders were sketched out but not fully confirmed until a second briefing at noon.

The pattern of the day was similar to that experienced by the other brigades which had been ordered to attack. There was very little time to do anything, other than to order the 2nd Devonshire Regiment, which had moved into the front line the previous day, to lead the assault. They would be supported by the 2nd West Yorkshire Regiment, of which a grenade detachment under Lt Frederick Harington would be ready to go into the initial attack. The Devons would advance using their D and C Companies only, with B in support. Their A Company would come up from reserve on the right only if called upon. The four company commanders did not have a complete view of what was to take place and had to get back to their units until just fifteen minutes before zero hour.

At 4.15 p.m., the same time as for the attacks further north, the British artillery commenced its bombardment. This letter, written the next day by Lt-Col George Brenton Laurie, commanding officer of the 1st Royal Irish Rifles, which was in the F Lines trenches not far from assault battalions, paints a vivid picture of the start of the attack. He was situated in a farm house on the Rue Tilleloy.

> This morning your kind present of ginger cake, plum pudding, and mittens, also soap, arrived, for all of which many thanks. You will be interested to hear what was going on last night, which I did not like to tell you at the time I was writing. We had been summoned in the morning to receive the General's order for an attack on a trench by the Rifle Brigade. The real attack, however, was to be made by someone else on quite another part of the line. We were to demonstrate. Well, if you ever heard Hell let loose, it was whilst I was writing that letter. Probably over fifty guns took part in it, and the firing was quite close overhead. It may have been 100 guns really some very heavy ones. Then about 10 miles of trenches were blazing away at the Germans, and they were blazing back at us. Bullets were racing through our roof, and there I sat in a little room, shivering with cold for we could light no fire. I was not allowed to go into my firing line, but sat near the two telephones connecting me with the artillery and with my own regiment.[22]

There is inconsistency between the reports of the action as stated in the various war diaries, but there is a common theme in that the left-hand C Company of the Devons, under Maj. Walter Meridith Goodwyn, ran into problems which soon brought their advance to a standstill. Goodwyn was wounded crossing no man's land and, having had no time to have the attack properly explained to the platoon commanders and sergeants, the company began to drift too far towards its left.[23] The men encountered thick barbed-wire entanglements and were cut down by German fire as they attempted to negotiate them. Only a few men under Lt Thomas Joy reached the enemy front line, where they linked up with D Company, who had had a much more successful advance.[24]

The diary of the 2nd West Yorkshires suggests that the Devons did not even begin their advance on the right, blocking the trenches as the two companies of the battalion moved forward into the line the Devons should have vacated. This may be a misinterpretation for A Company on the Devons standing-by for orders to advance, and is perhaps an illustration of the lack of meaningful briefing of the assault units, and the confusion that inevitably arose. Despite the disaster befalling the left company and the confused picture on the right, Capt. Claude Lafone led the central D Company through the rubble of the moated grange, capturing the enemy trench beyond as ordered, assisted by wire cutters from 15 Field Company of the Royal Engineers.[25] Around 5.10 p.m., the two support companies of the West Yorkshires moved forward to relieve Lafone's company, taking tools and materials with them for the purpose of consolidating the position that had been won. Some soldiers escorted twenty-four German prisoners back to British lines. Work also began to sap out from the British trenches in an effort to link up with the captured German trench, effectively providing a communication trench that could shelter men moving between the two. It was undertaken by the West Yorkshires and No. 3 Section of the Field Company. The sappers had been forced by heavy enemy fire to take cover for an hour, even before they reached the British front line. When his officer, Lt McAllister RE, was then wounded whilst reconnoitring the German trench with Claude Lafone, the work was led by Sgt Cooper RE, and continued until around 4 a.m. No. 2 Section RE also joined in this work, digging out to link up with the right-hand of the captured trench.

At 5 a.m., the Field Company's No. 1 Section under Lt Philip Neame RE (the man who had blown up the moated grange in November) was ordered forward to relieve the tired No. 3. This proved to be most fortuitous. At around 7.30 a.m., troops of the German 13th Infantry Regiment, armed with sackfuls of grenades, stole up to the captured trench at the north-east corner of the moated grange. Although the mixture of West Yorkshires and Royal Engineers in the area also had grenades at their disposal, it proved to be a largely one-sided fight – the British had no really effective weapon with which to reply. Their home-made grenades proved to be most difficult to light, fiddly and slow to use and not lighting in the wet conditions. Most men simply did not know how to use them. Within the confines of a trench, the German grenades proved to be devastating. They appeared to have no fuze to light and could be thrown up to 40 yards. In the desperate close-in fighting of the West Yorkshires, 'nearly a platoon was knocked out'. To make matters worse, their trench and the recently-dug saps were rapidly filling with floodwater. Step forward Philip Neame:

> When I got there I saw the officer in command who said the Germans were counter-attacking with bombs, that his own bombers had all been wounded and that the bombs that were left would not go off. So I went up to talk to one of the remaining bombers ... and discovered that he could not light our own bombs because there were no fuzes left.[26]

Neame knew to light a grenade you had to hold a match-head on the end of the fuze and then strike a matchbox across it. He clambered up onto the parapet (really the parados of the German trench) and began to calmly fight off the enemy with the stock of grenades. This extraordinarily brave young man held the enemy at bay for 45 minutes, causing them a good many casualties too, while the West Yorkshires evacuated the captured trench and carried their wounded back to original front line. He was awarded the Victoria Cross for his part in this action, but of course he had also played an important part in previous ventures.

In this enterprise, the Devons had lost nine officers and 131 men killed, wounded or missing, including thee company commanders; the West Yorkshires' five officers and ninety-five men. There had been no opportunity to remove the dead. The Germans are likely to have dealt with those in the trenches, but the remains lay out in no man's land until Christmas. No one could be really sure, but the general report was that at least a hundred Germans had died in this fight for the trench behind the Moated Grange.

Serious lessons were learned from the grenade fighting, and part of it was that the army was just not yet effective in their manufacture or use. Within a day of the fight, the staff of IV Corps issued a stern instruction to 7th and 8th Divisions:

> The experience of the operations of the night of December 18th and 19th show clearly that more effective steps must be taken to make use of hand grenades and bombs. Men must be trained to throw them accurately and instructed carefully in the mechanism and construction of the weapons. Divisional commanders will arrange for at least 30 selected men per battalion to be trained as bomb throwers and the question of carrying the necessary numbers of hand grenades to ensure the supply of these weapons at the right point and at the right time should be

gone into carefully. It is evident that if cunningly handled and accurately thrown, a trench may be easily captured by following it along from traverse to traverse and throwing bombs well into each successive section of trench. This was done successfully by the Indian Corps and can be repeated with advantage.[27]

Whether trenches could be 'easily captured' remained to be seen, but there is no doubt that the army took this lesson seriously – so seriously, that by 1916, when the army had a plentiful supply of reliable grenades, many commanders were bemoaning the fact that rifle and bayonet skills had been abandoned, and that the units were becoming overly reliant on the grenade in trench warfare.

The simple fact of the matter was that men were not likely to be efficient grenade fighters if their grenades were poor and there were not enough of them. Rawlinson immediately wrote to Murray at GHQ to say it was imperative a better grenade with a larger explosive charge was produced in quantity, and quickly. 'I am very disgusted at losing the trenches after having captured them so successfully and owe these German bomb throwers a grudge which must be paid 'ere long.' He said that German prisoners thought nothing of the effect of the British grenades in use. His temper was not improved when Brig.-Gen. George Fowke of the Royal Engineers, senior munitions engineering advisor at GHQ, was reported to have said that the failure to hold the trenches had been 'too much attributed to the grenades from what he had heard of the matter', refusing the idea of a larger charge. Rawlinson retorted that he 'had better visit the hospitals and see the wounds they made. They are a horrible sight as the Medical Officers will tell you.' With numerous appeals from GHQ having already gone to the War Office to no apparent effect, a request was made for a supply of French hand grenades that the IV Corps had already tested and found acceptable. British unpreparedness for the siege fighting that they were now engaged in could hardly be more stark.

At 6 p.m. on 19 December 1914, GHQ orders talked of the 'marked success' of the previous day. Little wonder that these bulletins generally became known as the 'Comic Cuts'.

6

The Battle for the 'German Birdcage'

The failure of II Corps to make progress in the Wytschaete area had left Sir William Pulteney's III Corps in a quandary. The original GHQ instructions for each corps and division to attack in succession from the left, and that his corps should not proceed with an attack until II Corps had succeeded, rendered Pulteney immobile and wondering what to do. His Corps consisted of the 4th and 6th Divisions, both of which had arrived in France prior to the BEF move to Flanders, gaining experience on the Aisne and in the recent fighting. The 4th Division, commanded by Maj.-Gen. Henry Wilson, held the front from the River Douve, skirting to the east of the large Ploegsteert Wood and going on down to the Lys near Frélinghien.[1] From there, Maj.-Gen. John Keir's 6th Division carried on the line around the eastern side of Houplines and Armentières to the link-up with 7th Division south of Bois-Grenier.[2] From an offensive viewpoint, the area held by the corps was not ideal. As everywhere else, the trenches had settled where the fighting had died down in November 1914, and the III Corps were left hemmed in by two rivers. The larger of the two, the Lys, was a commercial waterway that ran in a low-lying area that was now flooding. It lay behind the 6th Division's trenches, but crossed where the two divisions met and was in front of the 4th Division. Any serious advance that the latter would make would have to negotiate the crossing of the swollen Lys. On the division's left flank was the much smaller tributary, the River Douve, streaming down from the Flemish hills about Kemmel to meet the Lys at Warneton. By December, this too had risen considerably and would prove a nuisance to any advance going in the direction of Gapaard between Warneton and Messines.

Behind Pulteney's lines, the 4th Division had the advantage of Ploegsteert Wood, which was large and thick enough to conceal breastworks, dugouts and many thousands of men. Just behind it was the height of Hill 63, which gave good observation across the wood into enemy-held ground. 6th Division had the mixed blessing of Armentières very close behind its trenches – initially very useful for finding billets and facilities for men in its factories, breweries and larger houses (with shops and entertainments too, for much of the civilian population chose to remain).[3] It was also, however, a magnet for German shellfire and problematic for withdrawal in the event of an enemy attack in the area.

Occupying the trenches opposite the III Corps was the German army's XIX *Armee-Korps* under *General der Kavallerie* Maximilian von Laffert. It was a corps from Saxony, as given by its fuller title as the 2nd Royal Saxon (*II. Königlich Sächsisches*). The Korps comprised the 24th (2nd Saxon) Division (*Generalleutnant* Hans Krug von Nidda) and 40th (4th Saxon) Division (*Generalleutnant* Leo Götz von Olenhusen). The divisions were raised in the Leipzig and Chemnitz regions respectively.

Pulteney would not have been particularly innovative or proactive once II Corps had failed to make progress. Throughout his time as a corps commander, he demonstrated a certain inflexibility of purpose and formality in approach. Sir John French had already recently rebuked him for submitting observations and questions on paper, concerning subtle matters of strategy that would have been better and more securely dealt with face to face. When, on 30 November, his peer Henry Rawlinson wrote to suggest that, due to the flooding, he may have to pull his left flank back a little to drier ground, he asked whether III Corps was in a position to comply by pulling their line back at the point where the two met. Pulteney wrote 'The tenor of my instructions from GHQ prevent my considering the question of altering my present line unless I am compelled to by the action of the enemy.' Such a high-handed response was hardly likely to endear him to the quick-witted and sociable Rawlinson. One wonders what the men who were up to their knees in cold muddy trenches would have made of it.

Sir John French met with Pulteney on 15 December to explain the changed circumstances, and the need to support the French assault near Arras. There would now be no successive attack and, in the light of the experience at Wytschaete, any major objectives would not be shared between any two adjacent commanders. The Commander-in-Chief ran through various possibilities in terms of a 'holding attack' that III Corps might be called upon to make, but concluded that best of all would be a move against the strongly held Messines ridge. It was not encouraging, especially when he went on to outline that 'The present object cannot be obtained without losses, and probably heavy losses.' His guidance to Pulteney was perplexing for a man of inflexible thought: 'at some points it might be desirable to prepare the attack by bombardment. At others it might be preferable to attempt a night surprise. At others it might suffice to advance our trenches by sap and to destroy the enemy's obstacles by explosives before attempting an assault.' As long as the enemy was 'fully occupied and made to fight', French left it all up to Pulteney.

At 12.45 a.m. in the morning of 18 December, the capable staff officer Maj. Charles Harington issued orders from III Corps headquarters at the town hall in Bailleul down to the two divisions. They were only to 'demonstrate and seize any favourable opportunity which may offer to capture the enemy trenches on their front'. Operations were to commence at 10 a.m. that day.

As early as 10 December, the staff at the 4th Divisional headquarters had been mulling over possible offensive operations. They proposed attacking Messines from the south should II Corps manage to capture Wytschaete. Pulteney authorised the division's proposal of using the 10th Infantry Brigade (and 21st Infantry Brigade, which was briefly used as a Corps reserve) to seize Avenue and La Douve Farms and the nearby St Yves bridge over the Douve. This would give a good starting position for such an attack and detailed plans were to be worked out.[4]

The 4th Division also considered undertaking local operations to eliminate a troublesome tactical position in front of Ploegstreet Wood and straighten their line there. The fighting had created an awkward series of bends in the trenches. In the centre, where a lane from La Basse-Ville runs directly towards the eastern edge of the wood, the Germans held a forward line that poked a snout out towards the British. This was called the 'German Birdcage' by the British; the front line of this feature had, until recently, been a British trench but was now in enemy hands. The main German trench ran more or less parallel to the edge of the wood, behind the forward line.

In between the two lines on the German right lay a number of houses, which were already proving to be problematic in that they housed snipers and, from the top floors, the British trenches on the edge of the wood could be observed. The Germans had recently built a small strong point south of this feature that they called the *Entenschnabel* (Ducks' Bill). The British line bulged out towards the German, forming two small salients. Armies do not like occupying salients, for the enemy can shoot at them from left, front and right, and the curved line is inevitably longer than a straight one and needs more men to hold it, for no real advantage. Division thought it would be good to eliminate the two salients and grab the 'Birdcage'. It was known that a much deeper advance would take them into even wetter trenches than those they already held and from previous experience they knew that the 'Birdcage' could be enfiladed by German guns north of Messines. If an attack was to be made here, it had only to be for distinctly limited objectives.

The battalions of 11th Infantry Brigade were asked to consider the matter on 10 December, at which point it was proposed that the attack would be made by the 1st Somerset Light Infantry and 1st Rifle Brigade. These battalions, and the others of the division, also had other urgent matters to deal with: their trenches were flooding and the parapets collapsing to the point where there was no bullet-proof head cover. For several days, the units in the front line spent their time pumping out, revetting the trench sides with timber, and laying bricks to improve tracks and communication trenches. The conditions of the front line were now so bad that men even had difficulty simply getting into it. L/Cpl 9090 Arthur Cook of the 1st Somerset Light Infantry recalled that, on Friday 18 December, his company moved up to relieve another. It was so dark he described it as pitch black. The hapless Cook, loaded with his rifle, ammunition, rations and a sandbag full of other supplies and equipment, fell into a number of shell holes on the way up and finally slipped into a trench 3 feet deep with cold water. It was too close to the enemy to be able to shout for help, and it was only after much splashing, slithering and no doubt a few calls to the Almighty that he managed to emerge, soaked, filthy and tired, to carry out his front-line duties. Cook was one of the men ordered into the attack, and was surely not the only one in this condition. Four lucky men of each battalion were spared the task, for they were sent to work with the division's transport to help with handling the arrival of Christmas gifts.

Holding the 'Birdcage' and a stretch of line on either side was the 8th Infantry Brigade of the Saxon 40th Division. Raised in the Zwickau area, it comprised the 133rd and 134th Infantry Regiments. Formally, these were the *Königlich Sächsisches 9. Infanterie-Regiment No. 133* and *10. Infanterie-Regiment Nr. 134,* under the command of *Oberst* Franz von Kotch and *Oberst* Schultz respectively.

Even before the blood that had been spilt in the 3rd and 7th Divisions' attacks of 14 and 18 December, it was all too evident that the German barbed-wire defences presented a considerable difficulty for any infantry attack. In front of the 'Birdcage', the wire was observed as being 6 feet high and 6 feet thick. Early lessons were being learned and new ideas tried for tackling such a barrier. Pulteney instructed the 4th Division to determine the best methods available, and to make a number of 'rabbit wire' mats stuffed with straw that could be thrown across the barbed-wire to form a bridge over which a man could run or lie down. Wooden planks were to be found that were long and strong enough for a heavily-laden infantryman to use to bridge a stream or trench. The men of 11th Infantry Brigade set about constructing these things, making bridges 15 inches wide and 8 feet long. They also carried out practice assaults to be made using these methods, cutting some lanes in their own barbed-wire defences in order to facilitate an advance from the edge of the wood into the 'Birdcage'. A test carried out by the Somersets showed that, by using the mats, four men could cross a German-style wire defence 5 feet 6 inches high in just over a minute. Patrols went out from the battalion and reported that while the enemy front line appeared to be lightly held, the ground of no man's land was broken up and was difficult to advance across – and that was without Germans firing at you. Nonetheless, the regimental history records that morale was high, and 'all ranks were in a state of feverish excitement' at the prospect of going into offensive action.

By 8.30 a.m. on 18 December, Pulteney had made up his mind. There was no real value in continuing preparations for an attack up towards Messines as it was evident that II Corps were not making progress. He now wanted 4th Division to attack the 'Birdcage' at 3 p.m. the same day and said so at a meeting he held at the division's headquarters at Nieppe. The 6th Division was also represented at the meeting, but was told it was only to 'demonstrate' and use as little artillery ammunition as possible. The question arose as to how many large siege howitzers were available to fire in support of the attack. The reply was hardly reassuring – it was one.[5] With only some six hours before zero, 4th Division commander, Wilson, flatly stated that the operation was not possible but he could plan for it to take place tomorrow (and gave orders to that effect). A gunner officer, Lt-Col. Francis Lyon, who was acting as a liaison officer for general headquarters, said that Wilson's proposal was not in line with Murray's order, and the attack must be made today. A message was sent for the commander of 11th Infantry Brigade to join the meeting, as his brigade would have to make the attack.[6] This was none other than Brig.-Gen. Aylmer Hunter-Weston. Another man who had war experience, he has not been well regarded by military historians, a response that mainly hinges on his later performance in higher commands at Gallipoli and the Somme. During the first months of the campaign in France, he appears to have been an energetic front-line commander, in so far as a brigadier can ever be. Arriving at Nieppe at 10.15 a.m., he heard the plan and simply said that it could not be done. The infantry could not be properly disposed and instructed, and sufficient artillery was not available to carry out the bombardment. Wilson's idea that the attack could be held on 19 December was approved instead. Despite the fact that this meant that the attack would be independent of all others being made by the British Expeditionary Force, and late to support the Arras attack, no one seemed to suggest that it should not go ahead at all. It poured with rain during the afternoon of the 18th. The trenches, already part-flooded, rapidly filled up and the dugouts were unusable – no man's land became a morass. The weather improved overnight and the early morning was fine, but it soon clouded over and began to rain again during the attack.

The final orders made no pretence at an advance of any significance, but simply the capture of the enemy salient of the 'Birdcage'. The orders called it a 'bight'. The 1st Rifle Brigade would attack astride the La Basse-Ville lane and reach the enemy trenches some 300 yards along past 'German House', which lay immediately in front of the British line. On their left, the 1st Somerset Light Infantry would reach the enemy breastworks. The 1st Hampshires and 1st East Lancashire Regiment of the same brigade would hold the front and do their best to occupy the enemy with fire, while the two battalions made their attack. Behind Ploegsteert Wood, the territorials of the London Rifle Brigade would act as a reserve, ready to move forward if called upon.[7] Small squads of the 7th Field Company of Royal Engineers were attached to each, equipped with crowbars and grenades for dealing with few houses in the enemy lines, and also with means of marking for aerial observation the ground that had been gained. The British artillery would fire on the area to be attacked, and, at the zero hour of exactly 2.30 p.m., would lengthen range. To the north, the 10th Infantry Brigade would also provide fire support, as would the 12th Infantry Brigade to the south.

During the morning of 19 December, the two assault battalions made their final dispositions, with platoons lining up in waves ready to go 'over the top'. British shellfire commenced as early as 9 a.m., with the divisional artillery (recently having fired from its positions west of Ploegsteert Wood in support of 3rd Division's attack at Wytschaete) firing in 2-minute bursts every 15 to 30 minutes throughout the morning, but constrained by the same shortages of ammunition as elsewhere.[8] No. 29 Brigade RFA, which was specifically allocated to support the attack, reported that it fired 1,100 shells in total during the day. It appears that not all of the rounds fell on the intended targets, for both 10th and 11th Infantry Brigades reported British shells falling in and around their trenches – the former were advised that the shells exploding around them 'could only be German'. The adjutant of the 1st Somerset Light Infantry was called to an artillery observation post near St Yves to advise the gunners whether a trench they were about to bombard with heavy shells was British or German. He had to tell them that, despite the British shrapnel raining down on it, the trench was in fact held by the 1st Hampshire Regiment.[9]

Through prodigious effort, No. 2 Mountain Battery of the Royal Garrison Artillery moved three of its light guns into the front line. One shelled German House for 18 minutes to give the Rifle Brigade's I Company cover while it moved into its assault position. It was ordered to be prepared to move forward to destroy the houses at close range.

During the morning, the brigade's machine gunners opened up in what proved to be a vain attempt to help clear the barbed wire. It was also seen that the enemy had erected poles holding up anti-grenade nets.

At 2.30 p.m., the whistles blew and men of the two battalions began to move. On the right, the advance was led by two platoons from the I Company of the 1st Rifle Brigade, and a party of an NCO and ten men under Captain the Honourable Richard Morgan-Grenville. It was laden with sandbags, picks and shovels, for it was assigned to work with the demolition party of the Royal Engineers. With the bombardment lifted, the German troops holding the trenches and strongpoints of the 'Birdcage' were free to man their defences. Morgan-Grenville was almost immediately killed by a shot coming from the third house, while the men of the lead platoons rushed forward and managed to capture the first two houses.[10] Captain the Honourable Francis Prittie, who went forward and was to have directed the operation from the front, was also killed.[11]

A machine gun detachment did manage to get forward and took up position in the second house. Behind them, in the reserve trenches and breastworks in the wood, other pairs of platoons moved in their wake, ready to join the attack when ordered. On the right front of the battalion, the advance could progress no further than a fence which was just beyond the second house, for it was brought to a standstill by the men desperately trying to negotiate the deep mud in the face of withering enemy fire. It had advanced no more than 300 yards. On the left front, nineteen-year-old Second Lt Archibald Daniell rushed his platoon forward, but they too found the mud, water, shell holes and British shellfire that fell short combined to make their task impossible. Daniell decided to try to work his way left to link up with the Somersets, but every man who followed him was hit, and no survivors could accurately report what had happened to him.

The deaths of Morgan-Grenville and Prittie, not to mention the fire-swept ground across which runners had to go in order to report back, meant that information was slow in getting to the battalion. The next platoon was ordered to advance, to reinforce those that had led before, and D Company of the 1st Hampshire was also sent forward. They could make no progress, halted by their own side's shellfire. After about an hour, the fragmented reports coming in from wounded men and message runners began to make sense. The enemy's main earthwork defences appeared to have been little affected by the shelling, but elements of the battalion had penetrated into the defences and were now held up. Some men were working along a German communication trench along the right of the La Basse-Ville road, and something of a firing line was being established there; others were east of the St Yves road but pinned down by fire. The machine guns were still working in the second house. Casualties were heavy and no further progress could be made due to insufficient covering fire and the sheer practicalities of the mud. Most of the men who had advanced, and who had so far survived, were sheltering behind the parapets of old German trenches and were mostly under water. Capt. William Seymour, temporarily commanding the 1st Rifle Brigade, could see that continued action was futile and halted further operations. He signalled to brigade at 4.40 p.m. that unless some serious support could come up on the right, he proposed to demolish the houses that had been occupied and then withdraw. Hunter-Weston told him to make sure his men linked up with the Somersets and to hold on in a continuous line, while the sappers blew up the houses and German defences behind them. They could then withdraw through the British front line. During the evening all were back where they had started. Any notion of continuing the attack was abandoned on 20 December after orders were at first issued to continue. It was wisely judged that no further gain was possible.

The experience of the 1st Somerset Light Infantry on the left of the Rifle Brigade was not dissimilar. Their B Company was to form the first line of the attack with C in support and H Company in reserve behind it. In position by

1 p.m., they watched helplessly as the deafening British artillery fire intensified at about 1.30 p.m. and continued for the next hour – with much of it falling short and shrapnel flying about the British trenches and breastworks. Arthur Cook ruefully recalled that one British shell killed about a dozen of his comrades. Barely one of the heavy howitzer shells fell on the eastern side of the Le Gheer–St Yves road, most exploding in no man's land and cratering the ground over which the Somersets were to advance.

With every other man carrying a set of wire cutters, and others encumbered by the mats they were to throw over the German barbed wire, the battalion's advance began exactly on time along with the Rifle Brigade. It soon came to a terrible standstill. Only some 40 yards from the edge of the wood, the platoons on the right were hit by a heavy British howitzer shell that caused many casualties. On the left, and only some 10 yards further ahead, heavy German crossfire from machine guns and rifles caused the British advance to melt away. C Company was ordered forward to bring fresh impetus to the attack, but it too suffered severely. As darkness fell, part of the company reached trenches along the Le Gheer–St Yves road, but found them full of water and untenable. They held on to an 80-yard stretch of the road as best they could. Brigade orders for a continuation of the advance next day were questioned, given the sheer impossibility of digging in to create a 'jumping off' line, and eventually the orders were cancelled. For all of the effort, 11th Infantry Brigade had succeeded only in clearing the enemy from the edge of the wood and pushing the line a few tens of yards forward. The Somersets had lost six officers during the attack, and twenty-four-year-old Lt Roger Moore was hit next morning, while reconnoitring the ground near German House.

The fighting settled down to an uneasy quiet over the next few days, while the dead lay out on the battlefield. The records of the Commonwealth War Graves Commission list thirty-four officers and men of the 1st Rifle Brigade who were killed in the attack, or who died of wounds or in the trenches shortly afterwards. Only two of them have no known grave. Twenty-four of them lie in Rifle House Cemetery, deep within the wood and which was in effect a battalion plot from November onwards. Two more lie in London Rifle Brigade Cemetery, which is on the south side of Ploegsteert village, and others in locations adjacent to casualty clearing stations and base hospitals. Of the Somersets, the records list forty-seven officers and men dead. The pattern is similar to that of the Rifle Brigade, in that the majority were buried in a battalion plot which now forms part of Ploegsteert Wood Military Cemetery. It is quite clear that they were buried at Christmas. We will shortly be returning to the wood.

III Corps planned to send its 6th Division into an attack opposite Frélinghien on 21 December, supported by its own and artillery of the 4th Division, but this enterprise was abandoned due to shortage of artillery ammunition.

7

Willcocks' Indian Corps

To the south of the IV Corps, the line was continued by the Indian Corps under Lt-Gen. Sir James Willcocks, comprising the 3rd (Lahore) and 7th (Meerut) Divisions. The divisions were commanded by Lt-Gen. Henry Watkis and Lt-Gen. Charles Anderson respectively. All three men had spent many years in India, and had experience of command there, but in circumstances of 'small wars' very different to that which now faced their Corps. At sixty-four, Watkis was among the oldest of British generals to command a division in France; both Watkis and Anderson were really at a corps command rank despite only having a division. It was the first time in which Indian troops had been called upon to fight, in what was still, in late 1914, essentially a European struggle. The divisions of the corps comprised a mixture of British and native Indian units. The latter generally had a mixture of British and Indian officers. As their name suggests, the divisions had been based in the Lahore and Meerut areas of northern (and of course pre-partition) India, and the native units were principally manned by men of the northern provinces. They included soldiers from a bewildering array of traditions and tribes. Sikh, Hindu, Muslim and other religions were all represented in the force; there were men who would describe themselves as Punjabis, Jats, Mahsuds, Pathans, Ghurkas, Dogras, Garhwalis, Mahrattas and Afridis.[12] Since the 1857 mutiny, the British army in India had learned to provide these men with suitable rations, uniform, equipment and an atmosphere in which their traditional requirements could be met, yet still remain within a structure and with regulations not unlike the British army itself.

The Corps, which otherwise went by the name of 'Indian Expeditionary Force A', for the government of India also despatched other forces to Mesopotamia and Africa during 1914, was largely supplied and funded from India. While the British regular army was relatively small and now fully deployed, the ability to obtain the manpower and material benefits of Empire gave Britain a significant strategic advantage, and the relatively rapidly-accessible and professional army from India was central to it. This was tempered by the Indian army having a perhaps undeserved reputation at the War Office, and among the British high command, as being poor, and the British officers with the Indians as being second-rate. Despite looking like two full divisions on paper, the corps was, in manpower terms, not much more than a single division. It was stripped of the Sirhind Brigade, which remained for a while in Egypt. Most of its units were Indian, operating at a smaller war establishment than their British counterparts. It was also deficient in artillery, using a heavy and obsolescent machine gun – both products of the fact that it had hitherto been mainly used as a frontier defence force in the mountains of the north of India.[13] Few had ever envisaged a deployment in a continental war in Europe.

The Lahore Division arrived in Flanders in time to play a part in the fighting on the Wytschaete–Messines front from late October 1914. On arriving in Europe, the troops had received a message from King George V:

> You are the descendants of men who have been great rulers and warriors ... you will recall the glories of your race ... Hindus and Muslims will be fighting side-by-side with British soldiers and our gallant French allies ... you will be the first Indian soldiers of the King-Emperor who will have the honour of showing in Europe that the sons of India have lost none of their martial instincts. In battle you will remember that your religious duty is your highest reward ... you will fight for your King-Emperor and your faith, so that history will record the doings of India's sons and your children will proudly tell the deeds of their fathers.

The call to men's martial instincts and religious duty soon withered on the Western Front. The Indians were no more impervious to bullets and high-explosives than Britons, Frenchmen or Germans. During the period up to December, which was also marked by the arrival of the Meerut Division and belatedly the Sirhind Brigade, the corps found themselves heavily engaged and playing an important part in the fighting in Flanders. It was soon honoured by its first Victoria Cross of the Great War, which was awarded to twenty-six-year-old Sepoy [Pte] Khudadad Khan, a machine gunner of the 129th (Duke of Connaught's Own) Baluchis. On 31 October, in action near Hollebeke, Khan's team was hotly engaged, preventing the Germans from making a breakthrough towards Ypres. The battalion's other gun was knocked out by a shell explosion, and eventually all the men of the machine gun team were killed except for Khudadad Khan, who, despite being badly wounded, continued to operate his gun. He was left for dead by the enemy as they advanced; despite his wounds, he managed to crawl back to his regiment during the night. Despite this, and many other cases of individual bravery and skill, the corps was regarded as not performing that well. There is no doubt that this stemmed from an understandable initial unfamiliarity with the harsh facts of life in France, but also that the British high command had not taken sufficient steps to ensure that the corps was briefed and prepared. It was also due to a failure of the officers of the corps to adapt their organisation and methods to the new warfare, or at least to do so quickly enough. Tactical lessons had still not been fully understood and corrective actions taken before the corps was pitched into the battles of December, and men's lives depended upon it. There were also reports that the men's sword-bayonets did not fit properly onto the rifles they had been issued just before leaving India. By the time the fighting in Flanders quietened down in mid-November, the corps had suffered significant numbers of casualties and now found Indian replacements hard to come by, for no reserve and reinforcement system yet existed. The loss of British officers – 187 of them by 1 December – and their replacement with new and unfamiliar men appears to have had a serious effect on the fighting ability of the units of the corps.

During the night of 29 October 1914, the Indian Corps took over a long stretch of front line from the II Corps. It now occupied the whole run from the La Bassée Canal, up past Festubert and Neuve Chapelle, to Rouges Bancs near Fromelles. By mid-December, the IV Corps had relieved the Indians from Neuve Chapelle northwards, and the 8th (Jullundur) Brigade of the Lahore Division had extended the line down across the La Bassée Canal past Cuinchy to the Béthune road, taking this sector over from the French. The published history of the corps describes the corps' line as,

> one of the least attractive sections, either from the picturesque point of view or from that of comfort. The only prominent objects, to some extent relieving the eternal monotony of the scene, was the Bois de Biez, so long a stronghold of the enemy, and in the distance the Aubers ridge, so near and yet so far.

South of the canal, the units of the Jullundur Brigade found themselves on the edge of a vast coal mining area, black with dust that was studded with slag heaps and pit winding heads, criss-crossed by railways and with the civilian population still present in lowly miners' villages. In the dark, the cold and the mud of late 1914, it could scarcely have been more different to the lands from which the men of the corps came.

The Indian Corps received Sir John French's order to carry out 'local operations with a view to containing the enemy now on their front', and stood by for the successive attack to be mounted from 14 December to come their way. Earlier in the month, Willcocks had made some changes to his dispositions, and the Lahore Division had extended its front and taken over some of the trenches from the Meerut, giving the latter a chance to move some of its units into the rear. According to his headquarters diary, although he was supportive of his front line, firing and making small 'demonstrations'. On

14 December, Willcocks 'considered it inadvisable, in view of the lack of a definite objective, to attempt any attack across the open'. Nonetheless, he decided to do just that, using the 7th (Ferozepore) Brigade of the Lahore Division on 16 December.

The Ferozepore Brigade Attack on 16 December

The enemy facing the Lahore Division in front of the village of Givenchy caused concern by sapping out towards the Indian front line. Two enemy saps on the front north-east of Givenchy, which was being held by the 15th Ludhiana Sikhs of the Jullundur Brigade, were judged as being particularly concerning. The purpose of the attack was to eliminate these saps and seize as much of the German front line as possible. The attack was timed to coincide with larger French operations across the canal, undertaken by their 58th Division. It was decided that the experienced 129th Baluchis would lead the attack, followed by the 57th Wilde's Rifles, 1st Connaught Rangers, and detachments of the Sappers and Miners, who would assist in demolition and building trench blocks and barricades as needed. A battalion of the French Territorial 142nd Regiment of Infantry was also attached to the brigade for this operation. The assault units were in billets in Béthune and, starting with the Baluchis at 2 a.m., moved forwards to cross from the south side of the canal by Pont Fixe, about an hour before zero at 6.30 a.m. Every man was issued with 200 rounds of rifle ammunition. On reaching the 15th Sikhs' headquarters somewhere on the road around 'Windy Corner' (it is not clear if this name was yet in use), the Baluchis moved into Givenchy under cover of the network of communication trenches. The other battalions remained in reserve in this position, ordered not to proceed further until the Baluchis attack began, and took shelter in the buildings along the road up from the bridge. With two battalions now in the trenches, there simply was no room to accommodate a third or fourth. Orders given verbally the previous evening are somewhat chilling. The second battalion was not to go into action until the first one was 'used up', and the third would follow when the second was similarly disabled. The Baluchis were to enter the German front line and then fan out to left and right, and by bayonet, bomb and fire were to capture as much of the trenches as possible. There was to be no preliminary artillery bombardment.

At 6.30 a.m., two detachments emerged from the British front line and, although under fire, quickly crossed just 25 and 50 yards of no man's land respectively, jumping into the two narrow enemy saps and driving forwards towards the German main fire trench. The defenders soon woke up to the attack. Fire across no man's land suddenly became so intense that it proved simply impossible for support to be moved forward, or for wounded men or messengers to attempt to return from the saps. The two detachments were on their own. In the left-hand sap, Maj. Henry Potter received a message from his own trenches by the simple expedient of someone tying the paper to a weight and throwing it from the front trench. It was at this point that the British weakness in grenades and portable mortars began to be ruthlessly exposed, for the Germans of 56th Infantry Regiment (79th Brigade of 14th Division) responded quickly and began bombing the Baluchis detachments back down the sap towards no man's land.[14] Both detachments were greatly reduced by casualties, in part because in places they were overlooked and the parapets of their saps were far from bulletproof. Several men were seen to attempt to climb out of the right-hand sap in an effort to return to their own trenches, but all were killed or wounded in the attempt. A barricade was somehow constructed which kept the enemy at bay to some extent, but the party in this sap was in a most dire siege situation for some hours.

The 15th Sikhs, supported by the Sappers and Miners, now worked feverishly under fire to drive saps out from their front-line trench to link up with the two isolated detachments in the German saps. Havildar 4072 Mastan Singh acted as a runner, taking messages to and fro over fire-swept ground to keep the diggers and the men in the sap informed of progress: this brave soldier was killed at about 1 p.m., on his third attempt.[15]

Around 2 p.m., the Germans made a concerted effort to destroy the remaining Indian garrison in the right-hand sap. A heavy fire was opened on the main British trench in order to keep men's heads down and minimise fire being able to stop the counter-attack. Curious as to why the volume of fire had suddenly increased, Lt Bairstow and Jemadar Bir Singh peered through a loophole (a metal plate with a small hole, built into the parapet of the British trench) and found that they could see the heads and shoulders of German soldiers firing down into the right-hand sap. Bairstow (who was the Adjutant of the 15th Sikhs) and Bir Singh opened fire on them, and are said to have accounted for a minimum of ten Germans; Lieutenant John Smyth is said to have hit four more.[16]

It became increasingly evident during the afternoon that the situation was untenable and orders were given to the sap parties to withdraw under cover of darkness. Of the right-hand sap, just twenty-one men emerged, in every single case having been wounded by grenades. A party of the 15th Sikhs managed to cross to the left-hand sap at about 6 p.m., whereupon Potter withdrew his party. For no gain whatever, and no effect on the French attack to the south, the 129th Baluchis lost two officers, fifty-three men killed, four officers and sixty-seven men wounded. The 15th Sikhs lost six killed and fourteen wounded.

The Gharwal Brigade Attack on 19 December

Despite the Ferozepore Brigade's costly and futile effort, pressure coming down from Sir John French caused the Indian Corps to undertake further offensive operations. This was to support the French attack to the south, and was therefore at the same time that the British pinprick and bloody attacks at the 'Birdcage', Rouges-Bancs and Neuve Chapelle were also being carried out. Corps headquarters at Hinges received orders from British GHQ, simply stating that it must attack but that it should concentrate 'only on such objectives as are reasonably feasible'. This was a considerable reduction in scope from the 'attack all along the line' that Sir John had called for only hours before. Other than easing local tactical problems caused by specific hotspots in the trench lines (such as eliminating a point where the British trench was overlooked, or where troublesome German mortars or machine guns were positioned), the Indian Corps had no clear geographic objective they could use to formulate a plan. There was no 'Aubers ridge' to go for, no river line whose capture might ease the problems of flooding of the trenches. The villages of Violaines and Chapelle St-Roch lay ahead, but other than that it faced miles of flat farmland, dotted with trees and cut by many drainage channels. There was little tactical gain to be had by advancing the line from where it already stood. The town of La Bassée lay beyond, but the Corps clearly did not have the resources to carry the offensive that far, and made no dispositions of its reserves that may have hinted that it was even considered. The Corps was in the invidious position of making attacks with no specific purpose other than to capture some trenches and kill Germans.

From the early hours of 18 December, Corps headquarters held a series of meetings with the two divisions in order to decide a plan of action. An initial operational order emerged at 10 a.m., but it called for an attack to begin as soon as 4.45 p.m. The Gharwal Brigade of the Meerut Division, which would have to carry out this attack, protested that it could not be ready at that time and at 11.30 a.m. requested a delay. More discussion followed, from which it was decided that zero hour should be postponed by eleven hours, and that the operation should commence at 3.45 a.m. on 19 December. During the day and a very stormy, cold and wet night, the brigade shuffled its units to bring those selected for the assault into the correct locations. It also moved headquarters from Lacouture to a more advanced position at Rue des Berceaux.

The plan was quite simple: the 2nd Leicestershire Regiment and half of the 2/3rd Ghurka Rifles would attack and capture a portion of the enemy line that was on the extreme left front of the next brigade to the south – the Dehra Dun. They would be supported by a company of the 107th Pioneers and detachments of Sappers and Miners. Should it succeed, that brigade would then mount a further attack. The Leicesters, led by Lt-Col Charles Blackader, began to move from the rear at 12.30 a.m. on 19 December, going into the front-line trench which at the time was held by the 6th Jat Light Infantry. They were to attack from a small feature in the British line known as 'Jat salient' or C Company salient. It is not far from the junction on the Rue du Bois known as 'Chocolat Menier Corner', after a large advertisement on the side of a house there. Without a long preliminary bombardment to give the game away, but a short and sharp burst fired by the 9th Brigade of the Royal Field Artillery, the Leicesters surprised the enemy and quickly crossed no man's land, capturing about 300 yards of the German line from the 57th Infantry Regiment (of the same brigade and division that had been attacked by the Ferozepore Brigade on 16 December). The G Company of the 2/3rd Ghurkas, under Maj. Walter Dundas, also advanced, his detachment going to the right where a gap had been noticed in the Leicesters' line. Casualties were minor and the capture of the trench remarkably easy, but it appeared that the enemy had simply retired to a reserve trench. A prisoner of the 11th Jaeger was taken and sent back to British lines.[17] Dundas's men managed to reach the German front trench and link up with the men of the Leicesters that were on the right, but all efforts to move along the trench to reach the main body of the Leicesters was brought to a halt by enemy fire. They found themselves in a difficult position, for the trench they had captured led directly into the main German fire trench and, on attempting to move further along it, ran into determined resistance. A barricade was built in an effort to seal off the trench and provide some protection against grenades and bullets. The men also began to work to create a parapet facing the right way.

By 10.10 a.m., it was becoming clear that no further progress could be made, with signs that the enemy was about to counter-attack. Airmen reported a build-up of German infantry in trenches around La Quinque Rue. By 11.20 a.m., the brigade was receiving reports that the enemy was intensively bombing the captured trenches, and it was now also understood that, in daylight, the position could be overlooked from some German trenches. Inevitably, without reserves and suffering from the same shortage of a reliable bomb that all other British units had experienced, the Leicesters and Ghurkas were gradually reduced and pushed into a smaller and smaller space. The Germans cut away the barricade separating them from the isolated detachment on the right by the expedient of firing at it with a machine gun from close range. Of course, the barricade exploded into matchwood, and German bombers began to advance onto the Leicesters and Ghurkas ahead. Dundas took the only sensible decision and withdrew his men back to the British front line. The main body of the Leicesters held on.

On the right of this activity, the Dehra Dun Brigade had made preparations for its attack, which, if the Leicesters succeeded, would take place from the line now held by the 6th Jat Light Infantry and the 2/2nd King Edward's Own

Ghurka Rifles.[18] Any chance of carrying this out was eliminated during the afternoon, as heavy German shell and mortar fire was directed onto their position and casualties mounted. Enormous trench mortar rounds exploded with a fearsome roar, blasting men and trenches to fragments. The Ghurkas' Lt-Col., Charles Norie, in his report to brigade, would call them 'wreaker bombs' – a vivid title. The Ghurkas were forced to withdraw from a small orchard they were holding, to a position some 40 to 60 yards in the rear. Two companies of the 1/9th Ghurka Rifles came up to assist in the digging of this new line, which proved most difficult with the ground being so wet that the sides would constantly fall in, and with German shrapnel bursting over the men during the rainy night. At dawn, detachments were sent to quietly retrieve whatever they could from the abandoned orchard: bombs, flare pistols, rifle grenades and telephone equipment were all saved. The orchard is shown in sketch maps as being in the north-east angle of the junction where the road from Chocolat Menier Corner meets the Rue des Cailloux, also known as Brewery Road. All hope of reinforcing the beleaguered Leicesters still holding the enemy trench evaporated and, during the late afternoon and evening, Blackader withdrew his force to where they had begun the day. The effort had cost the Gharwal brigade four dead, 17 missing and 77 wounded.

The Sirhind and Ferozepore Brigades Attack on 19 December

The story of this attack was not dissimilar to that of the Garhwal, but ultimately with much heavier casualties and, and as things turned out, producing much greater risk to the security of the British position at Givenchy. The plan was concocted during the meetings on 18 December and was launched at 5.30 a.m. next day – almost two hours after the Leicesters had commenced their attack, and by which time the German defences were fully alerted and projecting enormous volumes of fire onto the British lines.

Described in orders as a 'simultaneous and conjoint' operation between the Sirhind and Ferozepore Brigades, the action took place east and north-east of Givenchy. Their objective was the capture of enemy trenches on a front about 150 yards in breadth. On the left, four waves of men of the Sirhind Brigade, comprising the 1st Highland Light Infantry and 1/4th Ghurka Rifles, would advance. It was their first significant operation since arriving in France from Egypt. On the right, the 59th Scinde Rifles was lent for this operation by the Jullundur to the Ferozepore Brigade. It received orders late, and from 2 a.m. moved through the night from billets at Beuvry. Not a man had had a wink of sleep since the previous night. The battalion reported to the headquarters of the 129th Baluchis, still in the line after their attack three days before, and after some hasty discussion was led into the communication and support trenches. The Baluchis cleared 200 yards of the front to allow the Scinde Rifles to take up their attack position. It was dark, and not a man had ever been near this position before. They arrived a matter of minutes before the signal for the launch of the attack, which was a 4 minute bombardment of the enemy trenches by 18 Brigade and one section of 57 Howitzer Battery of the Royal Field Artillery. Before they had any opportunity to get into contact with the Sirhind Brigade units on their left, they were off into action.

During this brief bombardment, the first wave of the left-hand group (the Sirhind Brigade) left their trench and moved out into no man's land. The moment it stopped, they rushed the last 180 yards or so and entered the enemy fire trench with very few losses. They had achieved an element of surprise, regardless of the generally alerted enemy, and sent some eighty prisoners back to British lines. In accordance with orders, the Pioneers, Sappers and Miners moved in to consolidate the trench and make it defensible. The second and successive waves also began to move forward. So far, so good. The Scots of the Highland Light Infantry and the Ghurkas now moved on to the reserve trench, finding that stage relatively straightforward, with the second wave arriving soon afterwards. The advance was halted there. The two captured trenches, so narrow in extent, were now so crammed with men that a message was sent back to the third and fourth waves to halt their advance and return. The position that had been captured also included a sap, running out from the German lines, towards the trenches from which the brigade had attacked: the 104th Pioneers began work to dig to connect it up, effectively to form a new communication trench. In the event, this effort failed. One report assigns it to the early death of a British officer ('they ceased work' stated the 1st Highland Light Infantry) but more likely is that it was the result of a serious problem had developed on the right.

The 59th Scinde Rifles were not only tired, and not sure of where they were or where they were supposed to be attacking, they found it terribly difficult to climb out of the flooding and muddy trenches. There had been no time or orders to create prepared exits, and the men had to slither up the trench sides as best they could. In so doing, the battalion practically lost all sense of direction. First out was a platoon on the battalion's right under Jemadar Mangal Singh; they advanced well and captured a trench. Although it ran in parallel with the main German fire trench, it was in fact an offshoot of a sap and was some tens of yards short of the main line. Mangal Singh and his men held this sap all day, until relieved early on 20 December.

A position was also reached on the extreme left. No one could report quite how, but a party under Lt William Bruce veered so far to their left that they ended up entering the German main trench across into the Sirhind Brigade's area of operations. Bruce was wounded and later died in the trench that day. He was awarded a posthumous Victoria Cross, with his citation reading,

> For most conspicuous bravery and devotion to duty. On the 19th December, 1914, near Givenchy, during a night attack, Lt. Bruce was in command of a small party which captured one of the enemy's trenches. In spite of being severely wounded in the neck, he walked up and down the trench, encouraging his men to hold on against several counter-attacks for some hours until killed. The fire from rifles and bombs was very heavy all day, and it was due to the skilful disposition made, and the example and encouragement shown by Lt. Bruce that his men were able to hold out until dusk, when the trench was finally captured by the enemy.

The citation tells us the outline of what happened, but for greater detail we have a report from Havildar Dost Mohammed of 'H' Company,

> I and my platoon reached the German trenches. Lieutenant Bruce was the first man in the trenches. The enemy said they would surrender and handed up rifles but men who put their heads over the trenches were killed. The writer Mohammed Hussein was killed in this way; eventually we got into the trench. Lieutenant Bruce told me to fortify and hold the left. [He] was wounded in the neck and later killed. Our men held on all day and killed many Germans, [but] our [rifle] bolts jammed and we could not fire much. Lots of Germans were piled up in the trenches on both sides and they seemed to be all round us. The Germans soon brought up a bomb gun into action. I told our men to go but they refused for they said the Sahib had told them to stay. Finally I when I went all others were dead – killed by bombs. I and another wounded man stated off up a sap. There was a British officer there who told us the Germans held this sap. We went into the opening and taking a wrong turning found ourselves in front of a hostile trench. We waited until the bursting of shells showed us our line and we crawled up to our firing line, which fired on us. I shouted out that I was a man from India and a Sergeant said 'come on'. I went in and then went back to bring in the other wounded man. The Sergeant said I ought not to go back.

Dost Mohammed's terrifying account is supported by others that talk of close-in fighting in the enemy trenches and bayonets, with the Scinde Rifles using bayonets in the dark. The trenches were crammed with men: German, British and Indian, and an awful confused fight took place with severe casualties to both sides.

On the left of the Ferozepore Brigade's area, a German detachment in a sap, and with cover of an embankment, had simply been missed as the British units on their left and right advanced towards the German lines. They had the advantage of observation across no man's land, and into the backs of those men of the Sirhind Brigade now in the saps and trenches of their enemy. Fire from this detachment, as well as from the German lines and artillery not only caused casualties to those men, swept the space between the two front lines. Once again, it became almost impossible to bring reserves or messages forward, or to evacuate wounded or bring messages back. Many a man was killed or wounded in the attempt.

At 10 a.m., one of the tragedies of the day took place. A platoon of the 1/1st Ghurka Rifles of the Sirhind Brigade, originally meant to attack at 5.30 a.m., but unable to do so as it was not ready, began to advance. It did not need to do this, as its order had been cancelled. Capt. Thomas Burke, Lt Lionel Rundall and one man were immediately killed, and twenty-three others wounded. Their brave attempt was over in moments and only a remnant returned unwounded to their trench.[19]

As it was evident that progress was improbable for some hours, that casualties were great and that the efforts to link up the sap on the right of the Sirhind Brigade's front had foundered, the 1/4th Ghurkas' Maj. Bernard Nicolay took the decision to withdraw. By around 5 p.m., the captured position was given up. The losses to the attacking units had been heavy, but for the two brigades the battle had barely yet begun.

The Defence of Givenchy, 20–21 December 1914

German retaliation to the Indian Corps' attacks was swift and heavy. From dawn on 20 December, in the cold and torrential rain, the German artillery subjected the whole Corps' front line trenches to a deluge of high-explosive shells, which was also supplemented by the fearsome trench mortars. Behind the German front, men of the 57th Infantry Regiment (of 79th Brigade, 14th Division) took up an assault position, facing the front between La Quinque Rue and Givenchy.[20] The epicentre of the bombardment was the front held by the Sirhind Brigade, against which on this occasion the Germans had an extra ace to play. Of course, the brigade was still in the process of recovering and reorganising after the fighting of the previous day, and its front line was being held by a very mixed set of units. On the brigade's right, a company of the 1st Highland Light Infantry, two double companies of the 1/4th Ghurkas and two machine gun teams from the 125th Rifles held the line. On their left came another company of the 1st Highland Light Infantry and two double companies of the 1/1st Ghurkas. Parts of the 1st Highland Light Infantry, 1/1st Ghurkas and 125th Rifles were not far behind, in local reserve on the Festubert road.

While shells were still raining down and the men of the brigade were doing as best they could to take shelter in the flooded trenches, the area north of

Givenchy (east of Le Plantin) was shaken at 9 a.m. by the sudden, deep and violent explosion of underground mines. Givenchy would acquire a terrible reputation as being a place for that most feared of trench fighting techniques, and the explosion under the brigade's trenches was the harbinger of many horrors yet to come. In comparison with later mine warfare, this was small beer., but it was enough to cause much consternation A captured report suggested that ten mines each of 50kg of explosive were used, with a 300kg charge under Picquet House failing to explode, causing carnage and confusion. The timing of the explosions had been set in order to give the German engineers daylight in which to test the electrical circuits, and to make any improvements needed before the switches were thrown. The Sirhind Brigade had been caught out by the very thing that all British units had been warned to look out for – the Germans digging saps out from their front line towards the British. From the sapheads closest to the brigade's parapets, just 3 metres away, German engineers had tunnelled below and quietly laid the charges. To some extent, this explains the strong resistance shown during the previous day's fighting, when men of the Indian Corps had stormed into some of the saps. For the infantry, the underground explosions were a terrible and new development. The technique was one of classical siege warfare from previous centuries and could not have been entirely unexpected, although it is apparent there was no intelligence that the Germans had yet commenced any operations to actually undermine the British trenches. It was not unexpected, because the British Royal Engineers had been having similar thoughts. Some days previously, a tunnel 70 feet deep had been dug to within 13 feet of the German lines on the front held by the Dehra Dun Brigade. Activity was detected, however, and the mine shaft near the orchard and nearby trenches were destroyed by mortars.

It was not until later that an assessment could be made of the exact effect of the German mines, but it was immediately evident that it had been very grave. On the brigade's right front, one of the double companies of the 1/4th Ghurkas were simply erased, apparently without survivors. The greater part of half a company of the 1st Highland Light Infantry suffered the same fate. A report from German VII Corps, captured later, stated that 'In dugouts of the trenches which were destroyed by the mines, a large number of Indian corpses were found still sitting; they had apparently been suffocated.'[21]

Within moments of the mine explosions, storming parties of German infantry and pioneers issued from each of the ten saps and very quickly entered the devastated British trench. They were followed by other parties who crossed the open between the saps, commencing the 'mopping up' the survivors by the use of hand grenades, and what the captured report described as 'incendiary torches'. Once cleared, a working party with timber, sandbags and other materials came across to the captured line and attempted to make it defensible.

The remainder of the 1/4th Ghurkas were ordered to retire from their trenches, a Ghurka officer and some forty to fifty men of the Ferozepore Brigade joined them in doing so. The machine gun detachments of the 1/4th Ghurkas, and those from the 125th Rifles, remained to cover this retirement, but another violent explosion was heard and it is believed that they perished or were captured, to a man. Of the units holding the left of the brigade's front, only a small number of the Highland Light Infantry on the extreme left appear to have survived the mines and initial enemy assault. In touch with the 1st Seaforth Highlanders of the Dehra Dun Brigade on their left, they fell back to a support the trench and barricaded it against further attack. This detachment held on for the next 24 hours. The German infantry poured through the gap, pushing on in the centre towards Le Plantin. On the British left, Picquet House, the Orchard and the brewery fell into enemy hands as the Germans advanced on Festubert itself. The 1st Seaforth Highlanders and the 2/2nd Ghurkas of the Dehra Dun Brigade found themselves under heavy attack. The 58th Rifles were ordered to assist and the 6th Jats were also engaged on the left. Desperate fighting took place, but the brigade more or less held its line. On the right, the Germans moved quickly through the increasingly ruined Givenchy, gaining advantage of the marginally higher and drier ground of the 'Mound' near the village church. East and south east of Givenchy, parts of the 9th Bhopal Light Infantry and 57th Rifles held their ground. No doubt some of this number came later in the day, but the captured German report said that nineteen British officers and 815 other ranks were taken prisoner on 20 December – the majority would have been in this first rapid assault.

At 11.15 a.m., the 1st Manchester Regiment of the Jullundur Brigade received orders to move from reserve and go to Gorre, where it would come under command of the Sirhind Brigade. The men were fed up, for they had spent the best part of two days at Béthune being ordered to be ready to move and then being stood down again. Marching off at noon, things changed again and the battalion was now instructed to move along the towpath of the La Bassée canal to Pont Fixe. On arrival, the battalion was ordered to make a counter-attack against German-held trenches east of Givenchy: this was misleading and disastrous for the battalion. The 2nd and 3rd battalions of the French 142nd Régiment of Territorial Infantry under Lt-Col. Cantau also moved in support, and took up a position near Pont Fixe.

Moving off at 3.15 p.m., the lead elements of the Manchesters soon found that Givenchy was strongly held by the enemy. The 3/142nd Battalion now moved up on the Manchesters left, passing north of the church. It took some time to clear the village, during which time twelve prisoners were taken (a small number given the close-in nature of fighting in a built-up area, hinting that men fought to the last) and, by the time the Manchesters entered the old communication trenches on the east side, it was too dark to see where the enemy was. The battalion was also now in unfamiliar, cratered ground. Companies of the 1/4th Suffolk Regiment, also ordered up from reserve, joined the Manchesters in and around Givenchy at this time. The French 3/142nd, commanded by Captain Salle, reached a similar position in the communication trenches, some 200 yards short of the German main firing line. They were out of touch with the Manchesters on their right and had nothing at all on the left. Salle, although badly wounded, remained in command until the morning, when Captain Ribes took over.

Patrols sent out during the night to reconnoitre the area met with heavy fire and sustained serious losses. At 6.30 a.m. on 21 December, the Manchesters and B Company of the Suffolks attempted to advance. They met with heavy and sustained machine gun fire, resulting in a heavy toll of casualties. Things had not been helped by the men being seen clear silhouette, illuminated by two haystacks burning behind them.

At 11 a.m., heavy German artillery fire fell onto Givenchy and the three units now in the communication trenches east and north of the village. A strong infantry attack, again by 57th Regiment, followed 45 minutes later. At this point, it becomes difficult to know exactly what happened, not least as the war diary of the Manchester Regiment suggests that the French unit gave way on its left, and the 142nd Régiment says that it stood firm. It does appear that Capt. Ribes was wounded, a patrol sent to get into contact with the Manchesters was wiped out, and the French were isolated north of the village church. The fighting remained intense for much of the day, ebbing and flowing. The British were pushed out of Givenchy again, only for the Manchesters to counter-attack at about 2 p.m., and the Germans to regroup and push again at about 3.20 p.m. The trenches and dugouts of Givenchy became a charnel house, with men of both sides dying and bleeding in large numbers as the fight boiled on.

During the fight, the British 1st Division, part of Haig's I Corps and headquartered at Hazebrouck, was welcoming a new commanding officer, Brig.-Gen. Richard Haking.[22] At 2.30 p.m., Haking received an urgent order to send one of his brigades to assist the Indian Corps. Less than an hour later, he was instructed to send another. The 1st and 3rd Infantry Brigades, resting at Borre-Pradelles and at Strazeele respectively, set off for Béthune. During the evening, the 2nd Infantry Brigade also began to move, for a decision had been taken to relieve the Indian Corps completely.

While Haking's men began their journey from rest to the hell of the Givenchy–Festubert front, the fighting continued. Reinforcements had been ordered into the area, in the shape of dismounted men of the Secunderabad Cavalry Brigade, to which had now been added the 47th Sikhs from the reserve of the Jullundur Brigade and the 2/8th Ghurkas from the Bareilly Brigade. The 780 cavalrymen, who came from the 7th Dragoon Guards, 34th Poona Horse,

20th Deccan Horse and Jodhpur Lancers (what images of Empire!) moved to Essars via Annezin on 19 December. They were commanded at first by forty-seven-year-old Boer War veteran Lt-Col. Henry Lemprière. He was killed in their intervention in the battle, becoming one of 174 British and Indian officers and men of the detachment to die, be wounded or taken prisoner. On arriving in the forward area, Lemprière was ordered to use 200 men of the 7th Dragoon Guards and the 47th Sikhs to mount a counter-attack in the area south of Festubert, attacking in a north-easterly direction up towards the area of Picquet House and the Orchard. Delays were encountered as contact was made with the French battalion (which was on the right of where the detachment would attack) and the Jullundur Brigade beyond. It was necessary to file the detachment forward across a narrow bridge at one point. Having left Gorre for Festubert at 6.15 p.m. on 20 December, it was not until 11.30 p.m. that the force was in place. Their counter-attack commenced in pitch darkness at 1 a.m. on 21 December. Their attempt was forlorn. Men reached the former British support trenches, but came under heavy enemy fire from their left front. Col Lemprière, who had gone forward with another officer to try to determine where they were and to locate the enemy's line, was shot in the head as he made his way back.

Soon after 2 a.m., the detachment was ordered to retire to Festubert. This was not the end of the brave effort by the cavalrymen, for, having regrouped in Festubert they were ordered at 3.50 a.m. to try again. This time an advance would be made by a first line consisting of the 47th Sikhs and half of the 2/8th Ghurkas and second line of the rest of the Ghurkas and the 7th Dragoon Guards. It proved as unhappy as the first. Moving off at 5 a.m., units got mixed up, did not know where they were, were out of touch with units on either idea and found themselves under heavy and sustained machine gun fire from both left and right. On nearing the enemy's fire trench, a party – believed to be Ghurkas – gave a cheer before they rushed forward. Few were ever heard of again. Some of the 7th Dragoon Guards got into the enemy trench and began to move along it to their right, but ran into such intense fire they could advance no further. The 2/8th Ghurkas reported that two of their men had drowned in a flooded trench on the left. The situation was simply untenable, and the wise decision was made to withdraw the force.

The units of 1st Infantry Brigade moved up through Beuvry in the morning of 21 December and took part in an attack, with 3rd Infantry Brigade on its left during the afternoon. After heavy, confusing fighting through the trenches, dugouts and ruins of Givenchy, the brigade succeeded in ejecting the enemy. The units of 3rd Brigade made some progress, but found flooded trenches and dykes made an advance far from straightforward, to say nothing of continued determined enemy resistance. At the same time, the 2nd Infantry Brigade began to relieve the Dehra Dun in the Le Touret sector. During the night of

21–22 December, the units of this brigade also began to attack, but found the original trenches that they were meant to capture so obliterated they were hard to identify. Fighting continued throughout 22 and 23 December, as the relatively fresh units of 1st Division deployed and continued press. By now, the German attack had lost its initial impetus through sheer exhaustion, but the 57th Regiment fought on doggedly and no ground was given up easily.

Losses on both sides had been severe. The Manchesters lost 5 officers and 280 men, the Highland Light Infantry 10 officers and 390 men; several Indian battalions lost more than 200 men. The German VII Corps reported approximately 1,250 casualties. By 24 December, things began to settle down to an uneasy quiet. After all, it was Christmas.

PART 2

THE TRUCE

8

The Coming of Christmas

Christmas is less than six weeks hence. This means that no time can be lost if sufficient money is to be subscribed to enable us to send one of our Christmas boxes to every Midland soldier and sailor. Perhaps you have read the appeals we have previously made, and while recognising the worthiness of the object have concluded that there was no need to send your share towards providing a soldier or sailor with a reminder of home this Christmastide. If you have had that idea we hope you will get rid of it at once. We shall need all the money that it is possible to raise.[1]

The public in Great Britain and Germany were in do doubt that Christmas was coming. They were exhorted through the press and local 'opinion-formers', not to forget their menfolk at the front. The newspapers carried numerous advertisements for funds, such as that being raised by the *Birmingham Gazette*, and for all manner of gifts and comforts to be sent overseas. The Commander-in-Chief's wife, Lady French, called for ladies to knit 250,000 mufflers; the Wincarnis drinks company pledged to send every man a French phrase book; the *Surrey Mirror* ran an appeal for a 'tobacco fund', with the aim of sending a plentiful supply of English smoking materials. The pubic responded with alacrity. No one who could afford it was prepared to let their men be forgotten, or go without their Christmas. The donating, collecting, making and packaging began to resemble a wartime industry in itself – and of course, in the middle of it all, was Princess Mary's appeal. The result of this tremendous charitable effort was the deluge of mail that left Britain for France in December 1914. There was a similar flow of goods from German firms, individuals and clubs to their men in the trenches. The Duke of Wurttemburg distributed gifts of cigarettes and a photograph of himself to troops of the German Fourth army. In their Fifth Army, the commander, the Kaiser's son, Crown Prince Wilhelm of Prussia, sent a commemorative pipe bearing his image.

The somewhat sentimentalised Christmas of the late nineteenth and early twentieth centuries – already on its way to becoming, but still a very long way from, the commercialised affair that it is today – was as much about home and family as it was about its religious underpinning. Over the decades of the nineteenth century, Britain had happily absorbed many aspects of the traditional German celebration of Christmas. Their decorated trees were as familiar to the men of the BEF as they were to their enemy across no man's land. The singing of carols, the cards and greetings, the sumptuous food, drink and revelry were all aspects that both sides recognised, as indeed were the concepts of good will to all men and that Christmas should be about peace and quiet. When soldiers did begin to sing carols in the trenches, or when lit trees appeared on German parapets, these were motifs immediately recognisable and as un-warlike a symbol as anyone might have imagined.

Many people readily understood the irreconcilable conflict between a war of nations on one side, and the atmosphere and traditions of Christmas on the other. There were voices that suggested Christmas should be cancelled, lest it affect a successful prosecution of the war. Pope Benedict XV saw it the other way – it was the war that should be cancelled, even if temporarily. On 7 December 1914, the Reuters news agency wired that 'the Pope is endeavouring to bring about an understanding whereby a truce may be possible during the Christmas season. It is thought, however, that there is little hope of its succeeding.' The Vatican had indeed appealed to the warring nations for a truce. It appears that while none of the nations really took this seriously as a proposition, most did send a formal acknowledgement that they would comply. Not unnaturally, none of the belligerents made their own overtures for a ceasefire. By 12 December, Reuters was reporting that the official organ of the Vatican, 'Osservatore Romano', was accepting that the idea had foundered:

> The august Pontiff in homage of faith and devotion to Christ the Redeemer, who is the Prince of Peace, and also out of the sentiment of humanity and pity, especially towards the families of the combatants, addressed an enquiry to the belligerent Governments to know how they would receive a proposal for a truce during the sacred and solemn festival of Christmas. All the Powers declared they highly appreciated the Pope's initiative, and the majority sympathetically adhered to his Holiness's suggestion, but some did not feel able to second it in practice, and thus, the necessary unanimity being lacking, it was impossible to reach the benevolent result which the paternal heart of his Holiness had promised himself.

The Times, of the same date, said that 'according to a wireless message from Berlin, Russia is the Power which refuses to accede to the proposal of the Pope.' There would be no peace sponsored by governments.

Above: 1. British infantry of the Expeditionary Force, marching through the French hilltop town of Cassel on their way to the front.

Below: 2. A hero of the Boer War, FM Sir John French (*left*) commanded the British Expeditionary Force until late 1915. (*George Grantham Bain Collection, Library of Congress*)

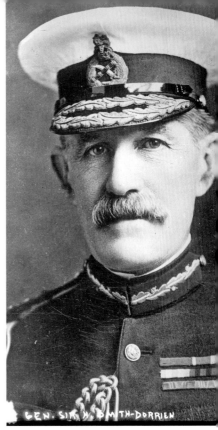

GEN. SIR H. SMITH-DORRIEN

Above: 3. Lt-Gen. Sir Horace Smith-Dorrien commanded II Corps. (*George Grantham Bain Collection, Library of Congress*)

Above left: 4. Officer commanding IV Corps, Lt-Gen. Sir Henry Rawlinson.

Left: 5. Lt-Gen. Sir James Willcocks (*seated*), and his personal staff, at the headquarters of the Indian Corps at Merville. (*Girdwood Collection, British Library, Crown Copyright*)

Above: 6. The battlefield today. House on the site of the Estaminet du Bon Coin. The trenches where the 2nd Essex Regiment fraternised with 181st Infantry Regiment, on 11 December, lay just beyond it.

Right: 7. Second-Lt Terence Brabazon, who went out of the trenches to meet the enemy. (*Essex Regimental Collection*)

Below: 8. Second-Lt Samuel Wade of the 1st Lincolnshire Regiment, killed at Petit Bois on 8 December. His last words were, 'Come on, my lad; it only wants one to lead.'

Above: 9. Pte Henry Robson, awarded the VC for bringing in wounded men from Petit Bois on 14 December.

Above left: 10. Second-Lt Alexander Pirie, 1st Gordon Highlanders, mortally wounded as he reconnoitred his trenches before the attack on 14 December.

Left: 11. Lt Billy Congreve VC, who observed the attack on Petit Bois and thought it little short of murder.

Above: 12. German machine gunners took a heavy toll on the British attacks. (*Author's collection*)

Right: 13. A soldier of the 181st Infantry Regiment, which fraternised with the 2nd Essex well before Christmas 1914. (*Brett Butterworth Collection*)

14. The battlefield today. Looking towards Maedelstede Farm from the 1st Gordon Highlanders' front line of 14 December 1914. (*Author's collection*)

15. The graves of the Gordon Highlanders in Irish House Cemetery. Their remains were not recovered until this ground was captured in June 1917. (*Author's collection*)

16. December 1914, German artillery, in the sector facing Armentières. (*Europeana*)

Above: 17. The small Fauquissart Military Cemetery contains the graves of men of the 2nd Rifle Brigade, including Sgt Goff and Pte Newman. (*Author's collection*)

Right: 18. French Gen. Grossetti, whose men fought on the British left in December 1914.

Below: 19. Lt Geoffrey Ottley, 2nd Scots Guards, died of wounds sustained during the attack near Rouges Bancs.

Above: 20. The arcaded memorial to the missing at Le Touret. The cemetery includes many graves of men of the Leicestershire Regiment, part of the Indian Corps. (*Author's collection*)

Left: 21. Two soldiers of the 55th Infantry Regiment, which defeated the attack by 22nd Infantry Brigade at La Boutillerie. (*Brett Butterworth Collection*)

Below: 22. Pte James Mackenzie VC, 2nd Scots Guards, killed after rescuing wounded comrades.

23. British wounded were quickly evacuated for treatment at base hospitals in France and at home.

24. A photo taken during training in early 1915, which gives a good indication of the uniform and equipment of the men who went into action in December 1914. (*British Library*)

25. German trenches in the Frelinghien-Ploegsteert area. (*Zehmisch Collection, in Flanders Fields*)

26. The battlefield today. A view from the German trenches of the 'Birdcage', towards Ploegsteert Wood.

27. Battlefield burials of officers and men of the 1st Somerset Light Infantry.

28. Ploegsteert Wood Cemetery – one of several in and around the wood that contains graves of men killed in December 1914.

29. The Memorial to the Missing, at Ploegsteert, includes names of men lost throughout the war, many of whom fell in December 1914.

30. Ghurkas in the trenches of the Givenchy-Festubert sector. (*Andrew Thornton collection*)

La Grande Guerre 1914-15. - Les restes de l'Église de GIVENCHY (P.-de-C.)
Visé Paris 528.
PHOT-EXPRESS

31. The village of Givenchy, devastated during the war and already badly damaged in this early postcard photograph. (*Author's collection*)

32. The battlefield today. View from Chapelle St Roch towards Le Plantin. The first German mines were exploded below these fields, and bitter fighting followed. (*Author's collection*)

33. The battlefield today. The site of the Orchard, defended by the 1st Seaforth Highlanders, looking along the lane towards Chocolat Menier Corner and the Jat Salient. (*Author's collection*)

34. Seriously wounded Sepoys and Ghurkas, at the Indian hospital in Brighton, in 1915. (*Girdwood Collection, British Library, Crown Copyright*)

35. Gorre British and Indian Cemetery. (*Author's collection*)

36. Graves of Jat, Ghurka and Muslim soldiers, all killed in December 1914. (*Author's collection*)

37. The men of Indian units who have no known grave are commemorated at the beautiful Neuve Chapelle Memorial. (*Author's collection*)

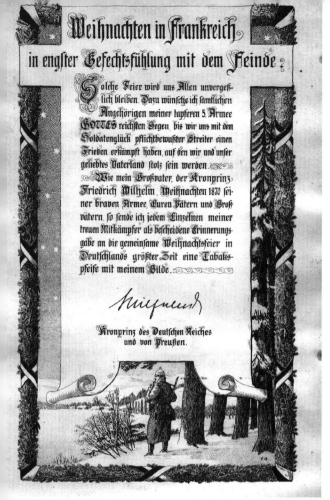

Left: 38. The Crown Prince Wilhelm sent this greeting, with the commemorative pipes given to the men of his armies.

Below: 39. A rather festive German card. (*Europeana*)

40. The German military cemetery in the village of Wicres. (*Author's collection*)

41. The extraordinary photographs taken in no man's land, at Christmas 1914, have become iconic.

42. Men on both sides died at Christmas 1914. (*Author's collection*)

Above: 43. Erected in 2008, this memorial in the park at Frelinghien bears the regimental crests of the 2nd Royal Welsh Fusiliers and the 6th Jaeger. (*Author's collection*)

Left: 44. Lt Kurt Zehmisch, who wrote in his diary that football was played with the English. (*Zehmisch collection, in Flanders Fields*)

Below: 45. In this centenary year of 2014, the truce will be remembered, but the football legend takes a centre stage. (*Author's collection*)

On 18 December 1914, *Kreigsfreiwilliger* (war volunteer soldier) Karl Aldag wrote home to Obernkirchen from his billet near Fournes-en-Weppes. It proved to be prophetic, and is especially noteworthy as he wrote it within earshot of the British guns firing in support of the attacks made by the 7th and 8th Divisions between Bois-Grenier and Neuve Chapelle:

> It is a strange kind of Christmas this year: so really contrary to the Gospel of Love – and yet it will be more productive of love than any other – love for one's own people and love to God. I honestly believe that this year the Feast will make a deeper impression than ever and therefore will bring a blessing to many, in spite of the war.[2]

Aldag was referring to the love of his 'own people', at home and his comrades in arms, not love for his enemy. It is almost certain that, if asked in advance, neither side would have trusted the other to hold to a locally-agreed truce. There had already been too much blood spilt and too many instances of treacherous behaviour. Tempered by our knowledge that there had already been a certain amount of exchange, as exemplified by the 2nd Essex Regiment earlier in the month, what developed over Christmas was nothing short of extraordinary. There was a literal atmospheric change, too. After days of almost ceaseless rain and flooding, the temperature dropped, bringing snow flurries and then a clearing of the skies that led to a hard freeze. This was a blessed relief for the men in the trenches and on the tracks and lanes behind them, for it meant that the ground could be walked upon without the risk of losing a boot in the mud. Well, a blessed relief for most. On Christmas Eve, Pte 1266 William Seed, a twenty-one-year-old from Stalybridge, who was serving with the 1/6th Cheshire Regiment, found his left foot frozen in the bottom of his trench. He had had trouble with his foot since he was twelve years of age and, on pulling his boot from the icy mud, wrenched it so badly that the injury led to his discharge on medical grounds in January 1915. While it may have ultimately saved his life, that frozen mud caused Seed to miss the event of his lifetime – the truce.

9

In Their Words

It is evident that before, and during, the bloody fighting of the period 14–21 December 1914, there had been a series of moments when the enemies came to tacit or explicit agreement to temporarily abandon hostilities. On 11 December, in the case of the 2nd Essex and 181st Saxon Regiment, this resulted from boredom, men's curiosity and the appalling wet and mud. An attitude of 'live and let live; they are in the same boat as us' prevailed. Other such armistices came as a result of German ceasefire offers to allow British units that had just attacked them to recover their dead and wounded, piled up on the barbed wire and in no man's land – a mix of humanitarian act and simple hygiene. The trenches were bad enough, who wanted dozens of dead lying about just yards away? These were all local affairs, not widely known, and certainly not undertaken in any spirit of rebellion against the war or what the men were being asked to do.

Then came Christmas, bringing the added factor of traditional holiday, a feeling for peace and goodwill, and thoughts of home and family. The localised armistices grew more widespread, but were far from a complete and stable truce. Collectively, they were possibly the largest such voluntary cessation of hostilities. A letter published in the *Cheltenham Chronicle* on Boxing Day written before Christmas hinted that men had the forthcoming season on their minds. It was from an unnamed local officer to his mother:

> … it cheers one to see the Germans baling water out of their trenches, too, and also having to dig new ones, like ourselves. However, they seem cheery enough, and sing all night and play mouth-organs. The ones opposite us are Saxons, a better brand than the usual Hun. They shouted across the other morning, 'How are you getting on ------?' Clever how they know who is opposite them. On Christmas Day I am going to put up a huge notice: 'Mann bitten ein Ruhe' [Let us rest]. It is splendid those German cruisers being sunk. I wish the German army had been on board as well.

This letter from an unidentified lieutenant, first published in the *Daily Mail* and then widely reproduced in the local press as early as 26 December, would have been the first intimation to those at home that any such event had actually occurred:

An extraordinary thing happened between us and the Germans yesterday. We are so close in our trenches that we can talk to the Germans, and yesterday we got quite friendly. After a lot of talking and shouting to each other, we arranged that one of our men should go out half way and meet a German and that there was to be no shooting meanwhile. Both men got up at the same time and went out, everyone in the opposing trenches looking out over the tops of them. The men met and shook hands amid cheers from both trenches. Our man gave the German some cigarettes and received in return some chocolate. Then I went out and met a German and did the same, and so did a few others. I went right up and stood on the parapet of their trench and talked to them. Several spoke English quite well. They said they were very sick of it, and added, 'Hurry up and finish this cursed war'. They told us they were in a bad state as regards water in the trenches but were fed fairly well and got letters about every five days. We had quite a long talk, and then one of their superior officers came long, so they said, 'Get back'. So back we got, and then they fired very high over our heads just to warn us that they were going on as before, evidently to satisfy their superior officers. They were very sporting, and played the game perfectly. We asked them whey the sniped such a lot, and said 'Why don't you chuck it? It's a terrible nuisance'. Funnily enough, they never fired a shot while we were relieving last night.

The letter would have been read with considerable interest, if not amazement or bafflement, by those who were not in the trenches. Along a considerable portion of the British-held front, the fighting stopped and there was contact with the enemy. By no means could all of this contact be described as fraternisation, but in certain areas the two sides came together. What happened is the stuff of legend, but legend now layered with myth and emotional recital. It began with the publication of such letters – tantalising and exciting, but shorn of verifiable fact. To understand what really happened, we must turn to the words of those who were there, focusing on texts where such facts are included or can be deduced. There is plenty of material of hearsay or hindsight, but it is of dubious value for anyone who wishes to get to the bottom of things. As a solid background, the operational records of the formations and units that were present are reproduced below. Some units were very terse and matter of fact in the way they recorded things, others more personal and descriptive. There are repeated themes: the sudden drop in temperature and light snowfall; the firing quietening down; of each side requesting to go out and bury its dead and the enemy agreeing to the request. Men heard the enemy singing and sometimes put up messages above the trenches. In many cases, that was as far as the truce went, with little or no actual meeting between the men of the two sides. But in others, we read of acts of a more genuine fraternisation, of shouts across the quiet, of meetings in no man's land, and of men talking and exchanging gifts and souvenirs.

In addition to the official accounts, we have the legacy of letters, some private and some made public by being printed in newspapers. We have diaries and memoirs, some of which were written decades after the event. These sources tend to bring out the smaller events and human stories, but we must be wary of their legitimacy. Letters written soon after the event are more likely to be honest and not so contorted by hearsay, but of course men do exaggerate and put themselves at the centre of things of which in truth they may only have been peripheral. It was not unknown for newspapers to pay for a good story. While too many reports match with the basic facts from official unit diaries and narratives for us to be overly suspicious, there are grounds for scepticism here and there – letters about involvement in a truce by a man whose unit was not in the front line at the time, for example. Of all of the various aspects of the truce, none is more difficult to pin down than the story of football being played. This very factor, that has assumed such importance these days, sees the truce rarely discussed without it being at the very centre, and almost to the exclusion of all else. We shall return to this subject, for the reader will note that it is almost entirely absent from official reports.

A widespread truce was not contemplated by either side, nor were there precedents or regulations for dealing with it. At 6.30 p.m. on Christmas Eve, British General Headquarters signalled to all of its corps that the Germans may be contemplating an attack at Christmas or New Year, and called for special vigilance to be observed. This was passed down to the divisions and brigades to the units in the field, some of which report receiving it at around 7.45 p.m.

The period of the truce is described below by looking at each British formation and unit in turn, going from the left (north) to right (south) of the front line it held over the Christmas period. A selection of letters and words from private papers and memoirs appear alongside some of the unit descriptions. They are certainly not all that exist, for there is a small mountain of such evidence, but they have been selected because they appear credible and of genuine interest. What becomes immediately clear is that the truce was not conducted all the way along the line, and that in many cases the truce did not include direct, close fraternisation with the enemy. The British II Corps barely participated at the northern end of the line and the I Corps at the southern end, but this may have been the effect of heavy and terrible fighting taking place in the area, and the I Corps having recently arrived there. The main centres were on the central fronts of III and IV Corps, but even there were patchy.

The 3rd Division (the II Corps in Wytschaete Sector)

Since their attack at Petit Bois on 14 December, the units of 8th Infantry Brigade had been withdrawn from the trenches and were now resting behind the lines. The fighting had resumed what was becoming recognised as a 'normal' pattern of trench warfare. On Christmas Eve, the 7th Infantry Brigade was ordered to move forwards to relieve the 9th Infantry Brigade. The diaries of the infantry battalions that moved into the trenches that day make no reference to a truce in this area.

The 9th Infantry Brigade
The 9th Infantry Brigade was in the process of being relieved. All the battalions of the brigade (1st Northumberland Fusiliers, 4th Royal Fusiliers, 1st Lincolnshire Regiment and 1st Royal Scots Fusiliers) left the front line on Christmas Eve and went into billets at Locre. The Lincolns and Royal Scots Fusiliers report that they were shelled in their trenches during the morning before the relieving battalions arrived. The brigade's fifth battalion, the 1/10th King's Liverpool Regiment (Liverpool Scottish) had already been in reserve billets in Kemmel, but moved to Locre during Christmas Eve.

The 7th Infantry Brigade
The battalions of this brigade (3rd Worcestershire Regiment, 2nd South Lancashire Regiment, 1st Wiltshire Regiment, 2nd Royal Irish Rifles and 1/1st Honourable Artillery Company) moved to the front line during Christmas Eve. None of them mention any friendly activity over the Christmas period. The Worcesters, South Lancashires and Wiltshires all reported a small number of casualties.

The 8th Infantry Brigade
The brigade's battalions (2nd Royal Scots, 4th Middlesex, 1st Gordon Highlanders and 2nd Suffolk Regiment) all spent the Christmas period in billets at Westoutre. The only diary entry of any note comes from the Royal Scots on Christmas Eve: 'footballs were issued to companies. Game of football stopped in afternoon by bombs from hostile aircraft.'

The 5th Division (II Corps in Messines Sector)

The 5th Division had not taken part in any significant offensive actions during December, but had remained active in improving their trenches, probing the enemy's position and 'demonstrating' by firing whenever divisions on either side were making their attacks. It reported to divisional headquarters that, 'on the afternoon of Christmas Day opposite Sector B a large number of Germans and our men meet half way between the trenches and fraternise. Badges show the Germans to belong to Schulenberg's Landwehr Brigade.'

Brig.-Gen. George Forestier-Walker replied to 5th Division in no uncertain terms on 28 December. 'The incident reported by you appears to be in direct contravention of instructions, and the Corps Commander desires that a fuller investigation of the circumstances should be made, and the names of officers present at, who should have been responsible for preventing, the meeting shall be forwarded.'

The division replied that it seems the incident 'seems primarily due to the Germans and our 4th Division meeting each other, the III Corps apparently not having issued orders similar to those of II Corps. The Germans opposite the Norfolks and Cheshires left their trenches, placing the company officers [of those battalions] in a position of some difficulty.' Smith-Dorrien professed himself satisfied with this response and the matter was considered closed. No disciplinary action was taken against the British officers or men of II Corps.

The 14th Infantry Brigade

On 22 December, the brigade had moved from corps reserve and took over the front line that had been occupied by 13th Infantry Brigade. It found the trenches in a very bad state, being some 9 to 12 feet wide and flooded to a depth of 2 feet of water. The brigade had two of its battalions in the front line over the Christmas period. During the night of 24–25 December, reports began to come into brigade headquarters, in Neuve Eglise, that the Germans were singing carols and ringing bells. All sniping ceased, and other than four German shells fired on Wulverghem in the morning, all remained quiet.

The 1st Devonshire Regiment

The battalion moved forwards and relieved the 2nd Duke of Wellington's of 13th Infantry Brigade in trenches near Wulverghem on 23 December. On Christmas Eve, eleven casualties were sustained, even though the diary reports that it was a 'quiet day except for some sniping'. Christmas Day was 'a particularly quiet day. Beyond a few shells fired at Wulverghem during the early morning, there was practically no firing in our section. Considerable progress was made in improving trenches etc. The day was frosty and misty. Wounded: other ranks 2; to hospital: other ranks 8.' The brigade's diary tells us that, in the thick fog of Christmas morning, the battalion, working with 59th Field Company of the Royal Engineers, took the opportunity to dig six saps out towards enemy lines.

The 2nd Manchester Regiment

The battalion took over trenches near Wulverghem on Christmas Eve and sustained a small number of casualties. That night, the battalion advanced its line by 150 yards by digging a new trench. Christmas Day was reported quiet and it remained so (other than for British artillery firing short onto the Manchesters trenches on Boxing Day) until the battalion was relieved on 29 December. Among the casualties were Second Lt Herbert Farrar, Sgt 4170 William Williams and Pte 6470 George Robinson. The brigade chaplain, Douglas Winnifrith, recalled presiding over their burial: 'Many of our comrades lie in the north-west corner of the churchyard [at Dranoutre], and on Christmas Day I buried [the three men] near the south transept, at the end of which there is a beautiful calvary'.[1]

The 1st East Surrey Regiment
This battalion was in billets in and near Dranoutre.

The 1st Duke of Cornwall's Light Infantry
This battalion was also in billets in and around Dranoutre. It reported that, on Christmas Day, 'the day being rather misty apparently prevented any fighting taking place.' The battalion played football against the 28th Brigade of the Royal Field Artillery in the afternoon.

The 15th Infantry Brigade
Reports submitted by this brigade headquarters, and the units under its command, are among the most detailed of any by a British unit. They appear, at least in part, to have been written in response to demands from II Corps to know what had happened, and with stern warnings for it to cease. This report by Brig.-Gen. Count Edward Gleichen summarised the situation:

> I beg to report that an informal meeting took place yesterday between the lines of trenches of ourselves and the Germans, at which about 200 of our men assisted, and an even larger number of Germans. It appears that on Christmas Eve there was a good deal of shouting and chaff between our right trenches (Norfolks) and the Germans about La Petite Douve Farm, each inviting the other to come over. Although there was a certain amount of firing on our part all yesterday morning and up to 2 p.m. (Christmas Day), there was no response of rifle fire from the enemy on our front (only a few shells in the early morning some distance to the north). About 2 p.m. a German officer or NCO appeared and walked over to our trenches holding up a box of cigars. He was not fired at, and one or two of our men went to meet him. Others, German and Englishmen, chimed in and soon there were large numbers in the space between the trenches nearer the German ones than tours, talking and fraternising and accepting each other's cigars and cigarettes, etc. Most of the Norfolks and some of the Cheshires (on their left) from the fire trenches took part in this informal gathering including several officers. I might add that the men sung Christmas hymns together each in

their own language. PS the Germans stated that they were not taking any action by fire or otherwise from 25th to 27th instant. I have however ordered hostilities to proceed as usual.

The 1st Cheshire Regiment
The war diary of this unit is so terse it is almost useless. It merely says that the battalion was in trenches near Wulverghem – and does not spell that correctly!

The 1st Norfolk Regiment
On 17 December, the battalion relieved the 1st DCLI (of 14th Infantry Brigade) in trenches near Messines and remained there for twelve days. The war diary merely records that the trenches were very bad, with a wet approach. A number of casualties were sustained. Given that the battalion appears to have been central to the truce in the brigade area, the complete absence of a mention of anything unusual is rather intriguing.

The 1st Bedfordshire Regiment
The battalion moved into the trenches during the evening of Christmas Eve.

> Christmas Day: quiet day. Germans semaphored over that they were not going to fire. Hard frost all day. Boxing Day: another quiet day. A little shelling by both sides. Some Germans came forward unarmed, apparently with a view to friendly intercourse. A few shots fired in their direction as a hint to withdraw. Later, enemy shelled trenches and Wulverghem: damaged several rifles but only wounded one man.

The battalion was relieved on 29 December and moved to Bailleul.

The 1st Dorsetshire Regiment
The battalion had been in the trenches south of the Wulverghem–Messines road since 17 December. On 19 December, it increased fire in support of other attacks, but the period was otherwise relatively quiet but for sporadic shellfire. On Christmas Eve, the battalion reported that enemy snipers and machine guns were active, and had to appeal through brigade for a correction to British shelling which was falling dangerously near the battalion's front line. Christmas Day was merely reported as quiet. Sounds of singing were heard late on Boxing Day.

The 1/6th Cheshire Regiment
This territorial battalion had only arrived in the forward area on 11 December, and came under brigade command six days later. It was split for instruction under the more experienced units. Two companies went to the 1st Dorsets

and one each to the 1st Bedfords and 1st Norfolks. During the period, up to 29 December, it lost 120 men to rheumatism and frostbite. The battalion reported to brigade that it had found during the truce:

> [The] Germans appear to be some Landwehr and some Landsturm age about 40 to 50, big and healthy men, well fed, well clad and clean. An officer said that he belonged to the 5th Konigslieber Landwehr Infantry Regiment number 20, Berlin. Several had number 20 on their shoulders, others 35.

Opposite the 15th Infantry Brigade, Josef Wenzl, of the 16th Bavarian Reserve Infantry Regiment, was in billets during Christmas Day and heard rumours of the truce. He was sceptical until his company moved into the line before dawn the next day:[2]

> That which only hours ago I should have thought was nonsense I now saw with my own eyes. A British soldier, who was then joined by a second man, came from our left and crossed more than halfway into no man's land, where they met up with our men. British and Bavarians, previously the worst of enemies, stood there shaking hands and exchanging items. The one star still in the sky above them was regarded by the men as a special sign from heaven. More and more joined in all along the line, shaking hands and swapping souvenirs. More than half of my platoon went out. Because I wanted to take a closer look at these chaps and obtain a souvenir, I moved towards a group of them. Immediately one came up to me, shook my hand and gave me some cigarettes; another gave me a handkerchief, a third signed his name on a field postcard and a fourth wrote his address in my notebook. Everyone mingled and conversed to the best of their ability. One British soldier played the mouth organ of a German comrade, some danced around, whilst others took great pride in trying on the German helmets. One of our men placed a Christmas tree in the middle, pulled out a box of matches from his pocket and in no time the tree was lit up. The British sang a Christmas carol and we followed this with 'Silent Night, Holy Night'. It was a moving moment; between the trenches stood the most hated and bitter enemies and sang Christmas carols. All my life I shall never forget the sight ... Christmas 1914 will be completely unforgettable.

The 13th Infantry Brigade
During Christmas, this brigade had been relieved and was moved to rest billets during 22 December.

The 2nd King's Own Scottish Borderers
The battalion was in billets in St Jans Cappel. Its diary is of interest, not only as a description of how Christmas was spent behind the lines, but for anecdotal reports it had heard from the front line.

Christmas Day: rest. Princess Mary's gifts of an ornamented box containing cigarettes and tobacco, and pipe and a card of good wishes given out to every man in France. Also a Xmas card, with a portrait of HM King George V and of the Queen and their good wishes is issued as a surprise to every man. Owing to the kindness of people at home, great quantities of warm clothing, tobacco and eatables are issued to the troops. It is reported from the trenches that at various points during Xmas Eve and on Xmas Day the officers and men of the Bavarian Landwehr opposed to us in this portion of the line made overtures of peace for a Xmas holiday. These were generally accepted. At one point a football match was played between the opposing sides. Food and tobacco were exchanged and the opposing sides visited each other's trenches. The Bavarians were reported to be looking well fed and in a good state, but in some cases in want of clothes. They are reported to have been in ignorance of the present state of affairs on the Russian border, to have been told that the Germans had won enormous victories there and that the war was to be over in a month. From hearsay evidence of officers and others.

Boxing Day – 28 December: Rest, reorganising. Large numbers continue to report sick with rheumatism and allied complaints. Superior authority expresses dissatisfaction at the fraternising with enemy on Xmas Day. It is forbidden in future. Also great dissatisfaction expressed by the II Corps commander at the work done, both offensive and defensive, in the trenches. Battalions are ordered to do much more spade work, and battalion commanders are ordered to take greater trouble in the trenches.

The 2nd Duke of Wellington's (West Riding Regiment)
The battalion was at rest near Bailleul.

The 1st Queen's Own (Royal West Kent Regiment)
The battalion was in billets in St Jans Cappel. Many men were ill on Christmas Day, suffering the effects of an inoculation against enteric fever that they had received on Christmas Eve.

The 2nd King's Own Yorkshire Light Infantry
The battalion was in billets in St Jans Cappel. Football matches were played in the afternoon.

The 1/9th London (Queen Victoria's Rifles)
This territorial battalion was also in billets in St Jans Cappel.

The 4th Division (the III Corps, Douve–St Yves–Le Gheer Sector)

After the 11th Infantry Brigade's attack on the 'Birdcage' on 19 December, things quickly quietened down on the 4th Division's front.

The 10th Infantry Brigade

This formation was holding the line throughout the period. It had supported the 'Birdcage' attack by firing, but had not directly participated. German sniping activity was noticeably reduced and shellfire infrequent thereafter, although small numbers of men were killed or wounded each day. It was evident that the enemy was using the time to strengthen the barbed-wire defences. On 22 December, the 2nd Royal Dublin Fusiliers saw that the Germans had put up a sign saying that prisoners would be kindly treated.

The 2nd Seaforth Highlanders

The battalion relieved the 1st Royal Irish Fusiliers on the brigade's left (River Douve) sector on 23 December.

> Christmas Eve: German ceased hostilities after dark and commenced celebrating Xmas by singing and shouting. Some of our men went right up to their trenches and obtained a certain amount of information. We put up a lot of wire during the night. Christmas Day: hard frost, misty. Not a shot fired, and we were able to walk about in the open, even after the mist rose. Had some trouble keeping the Germans away from our lines. Put some more wire out and did a good deal of work by day.

The battalion was relieved by the Royal Irish Fusiliers on 27 December.

The 1st Royal Warwickshire Regiment

The battalion relieved the 2nd Royal Dublin Fusiliers during the evening of Christmas Eve.

> Christmas Day: a local truce. British and Germans intermingle between the trenches. Dead in front of trenches buried. Not a shot fired all day. Boxing Day: truce ended due to our opening fire. German light gun reply on D Company trenches, 2 wounded. No sniping.

These conditions continued, with the battalion carrying out much work on its defences, until it was relieved on 28 December. The diary of 10th Infantry Brigade headquarters adds detail:

The Germans appear to think that an armistice exists for Christmas Day. An informal interchange of courtesies took place between troops in the fire trenches of both belligerents. Some valuable information was gleaned during the intercourse. The trenches seemed fairly strongly held, the enemy seemed cheerful and well fed. The numerals noticed on shoulder straps were 35. The 1st Royal Warwickshire Regiment reported that Germans and their men buried (1) 3 men of the Somerset Light Infantry (2) 3 Germans of 134th Saxons within 50 yards of barricade east of St Yves (3) 7 of Hampshire Regiment; 2 Germans (one of Russian infantry, one a Uhlan) found in an evacuated British trench 50 yards east of and parallel to road running N and SE of St Yves. The Germans helped in the digging, the 1st Royal WarwickshireRregiment supplying the tools, the Germans stating they had no spades. These Germans belonged to the 134th Saxon Regiment and 6th Jaeger Regiment, mainly reservists, old and quite young. They believed (?) Russia already defeated but that taken all together, Germany had undertaken too great a task. They were well fed in the trenches, with plenty of tea, cocoa and Swiss chocolate. However they were seen to almost fight for a tin of bully. Their letters and papers were four or five days old. They cooked in trenches in company kitchens. They stop in advanced trenches only one night. Digging and wiring in front of trenches was carried out in full view of the other.

This battalion has received much attention in previous works about the truce, not least due to the presence of its brilliant cartoonist and officer Lt Bruce Bairnsfather. He reported that some men met the enemy on Christmas Eve, and he himself went out to do so the next day, joining the fraternisation in a 'waterlogged turnip field'. In his book *Bullets and Billets*, which was published during the war, Bairnsfather captured the spirit of the moment, going some way to explaining how it was that men who would have murdered the other, a few days on either side of these extraordinary events, could possibly stop to shake hands now:

> This was my first real sight of them at close quarters. Here they were—the actual, practical soldiers of the German army. There was not an atom of hate on either side that day; and yet, on our side, not for a moment was the will to war and the will to beat them relaxed. It was just like the interval between the rounds in a friendly boxing match.[3]

Bairnsfather's sketches and photographs of the day have become symbolic – of fighting men, wearing whatever garb they could find to keep out the cold and wet, smiling as they met their enemy. The *Birmingham Daily Mail* of 5 January included a letter from Pte 200 Frank O'Dell of the battalion's 'B' Company, written to the Superintendent of the Norton Boys' School:

I can honestly say we enjoyed ourselves better than we expected. At midnight we heard the Germans shouting across in English to us, so at daybreak we watched them very closely, and after a little consideration we walked half way to their trenches for them to come and meet us, and they were only too pleased to welcome us. ... One of them gave me a German handkerchief issued to him by the Kaiser. I am sending it to my wife in Birmingham. On one side are the Kaiser's photo, the 'Goeben', two forts, the Iron Cross, and a mine layer that the British sunk a few weeks ago. They told us that every one of them holding this position was a Saxon and said they never wanted to fight from the beginning and though they were being imposed on by being made to fight the British soldier. We also found that they were mostly employed in London firms as bakers, waiters, etc. They said, 'It is better to be in London than in the trenches!'

The 1st Royal Irish Fusiliers

The battalion was relieved in the trenches by the 2nd Seaforth Highlanders on Christmas Eve, and moved to billets at Le Creche. Goatskin jerkins with long sleeves were issued to the men.

The 2nd Royal Dublin Fusiliers

The battalion was relieved by the 1st Royal Warwickshire Regiment during the evening of Christmas Eve and moved to reserve billets at Point 63. Lt Cyril Drummond, an officer of the 32nd Brigade of the 4th Division's Royal Field Artillery, found himself in the 10th Infantry Brigade's forward area, and became one of the few gunners to witness the scenes at first hand.

We subalterns used to take turn-about a couple of nights at a time at the cottage, spending the day on Forward Officer duty, and it so happened that I was to relieve Gordon Harborne on Christmas night. Johnny Hawkesley said he would walk part if the way with me through the wood. As we neared it, coming down the road towards us was our Battery Sergeant Major – and his eyes were nearly standing out of his head. He said 'There's Germans coming over to our trenches and our people going over to the Germans, and I have shaken hands with a German. According to the Sergeant Major there was to be a football match on Boxing Day between the Dublin Fusiliers and the Germans! There were two sets of trenches only a few yards apart, and yet there were soldiers, both British and German, standing on top of them, digging or repairing the trench in the same way, without ever shooting at each other. It was an extraordinary situation. One of the Dublin Fusiliers was killed one day by a bullet which came from the front of Ploegsteert Wood and the Saxons immediately sent over and apologised, saying it hadn't been anything to do with them, but [was] from those so-and-so Prussians on their left. [4]

When his battery was finally ordered to open fire on a farmhouse, Drummond now knew that the Germans gathered there for coffee. It was a target upon which a gunner would not normally hesitate to fire on, but he sent word across via the Dublin Fusiliers, ensuring no German was at the farmhouse when the guns opened up again.

The 11th Infantry Brigade

Battalions of this formation had taken part in the attack on the 'German Birdcage', east of Ploegsteert Wood, on 19 December. The brigade headquarters' war diary for Christmas reads:

> After a night entirely free from sniping, a kind of informal truce took place all day. The Germans, who were not allowed near our lines, met our men between the lines on most friendly terms, cigars, cigarettes and news being exchanged freely. The enemy belonged to the 133rd and 134th Regiments of the XIX Saxon Corps and stated that they came from Chemnitz; among their men were some very old and very young men. Several of our officers visited the German trenches, most of which were well made but partly full of water; a lot of the enemy however wore gumboots. The trenches were very thickly manned; 1 man per yard or 2 yards in most places. Much valuable information was gained with regard to the enemy's wire entanglements. Both sides collected and buried many dead.

Among those burying the dead was Capt. George Allman Bridge, an officer of the Royal army Medical Corps, serving with 11 Field Ambulance. His daughter later wrote down George's recollections of the event. He recalled burying nineteen British soldiers in Ploegsteert Wood on Christmas Day. He also remembered that Capt. Henderson was a man found dead in no man's land.[5]

The 1st Somerset Light Infantry

The battalion was still in the trenches and breastworks on the eastern edge of Ploegsteert Wood.

> Christmas Day: There was much singing in the trenches last night by both sides. Germans opposite us brought up their regimental band and played theirs and our national anthems followed by 'Home, sweet home'. A truce was mutually arranged by the men in the trenches. During the morning officers met the German officers halfway between the trenches and it was arranged that we should bring in our dead who were lying between the trenches. The bodies of Captain Maud, Captain Orr and 2nd Lieut. Henson were brought in, also those of 18 NCOs and men. They were buried the same day. The Germans informed us that they had captured a wounded officer and this was thought to be 2nd Lieut. K. G. G. Dennys who commanded one of the attacking platoons of B Company on the

19th. There was a sharp frost last night which continued during the day, and the weather was very seasonable. Not a shot or shell was fired by either side in the neighbourhood; and both sides walked about outside their trenches quite unconcernedly. It afforded a good opportunity for inspecting our trenches by daylight. The enemy's works were noticed to be very strong. A very peaceful day. Boxing Day: A day very similar to yesterday; but thaw started in afternoon. Truce still continued. No firing of any description. Spent the day strengthening defences and working at the new breastworks in supporting line.

The 1st Rifle Brigade

This battalion had also remained in the trenches of Ploegsteert Wood after its part in the attack on the 'German Birdcage'. An extract reads,

Christmas Day: Everything extraordinarily quiet. Germans came out of their trenches and met our people half way; all friendly and helped collect each other's dead; no shooting; 133rd and 134th Saxon Regiments, XIX Saxon Corps are opposed to us. Their Majesties Christmas card distributed. Starting on the 24th we now have one company London Rifle Brigade attached, so that each company does four days in the trenches, one day in support, four days in billets in Ploegsteert, one day in support breastworks, 4 days in trenches, one day in support and four days in billets in Armentières where they get baths! By 27 December: Still hostilities have not been properly resumed, though, finding their advances rather coldly received, and not encouraged, the enemy do not walk about quite so much; but peace still reigns. We got to such terms that they sent over to warn us that hostilities were to recommence and we several times walked out to tell their patrols to keep further away, instead of warning them in ruder fashion.

The 1st East Lancashire Regiment

The battalion was in the middle of an exceptionally long unbroken spell in trenches at Le Gheer, having moved into this position late in November. The diary only reports that 'Christmas Day was quiet with no shots being fired and an informal truce being held.' Sniping did not recommence until 31 December.

The 1st Hampshire Regiment

The battalion was in trenches between Le Gheer and Frélinghien. The diary only reports that, between 20 and 31 December 1914, 'nothing of importance occurred', but does add that, 'On Christmas Day an informal truce began with 133rd Saxons, XIX Corps, opposite us and continued until the New Year.'

The *Bath Chronicle* of 16 January 1915 carried a letter written home by the battalion's Bandsman 8951 Peter Williams. It is more illuminating than the official battalion's account.

I am glad to say we had a peaceful Christmas [he wrote on 27 December]. The Huns played the game well. It was my turn in the trench as stretcher-bearer. I took over my duty about six o'clock and to my surprise I walked right into the trench without hearing a single shot fired. I had not been in the trench long before I heard one of the Germans shout 'Gentlemen, a Happy Christmas to you all', and our boys answered 'the same to you'. They even wanted us to go over and drink their health but, of course, this was not allowed. All night they were signing, which was grand to hear. I tried to get to sleep but couldn't, so I stood up and had a look at what was going on. One of them gave us a few cornet solos. Some of them were 'Home, sweet home', 'Nearer my God to thee' and 'God save the King'. One of them shouted 'What would the Kaiser say if he heard us playing this?' and this is how they carried on all night. I came out of the trenches at about five o'clock on Christmas morning and got back to headquarters in time to have Christmas dinner, which was very nice, and we had a good old time. We had roast pork and beef, and plenty of Christmas pudding, which we have to thank the people of England for. Princess Mary sent us a good present, a most splendid box, and the contents were tobacco, cigarettes, pipes, photograph and a card.

The newspaper added soberly, 'it seems a pity to spoil the story of the German soldiers who played God save the King on the cornet, but the fact is, of course, that the tune of the English National Anthem and the German song '*Heil dir im Siegerkranz*' are precisely the same.'

The 1/5th London Regiment (London Rifle Brigade)

On 23 December, one company of this battalion was attached to each of the four regular battalions. Its own diary for Christmas merely says, 'Freezing. Very quiet day. Practically no firing.' Several letters from its officers and men did soon appear in the press. The *Liverpool Echo* of 2 January 1915 included this letter from Pte 123 Charles Welton.[6]

It is Christmas and I am writing this in the trenches after having the most exciting time of my life. Last night I was on listening patrol in front of the trenches and the Germans, who were about 200 to 300 yards away, were singing all night, mostly in English. They sang comic songs, hymns and carols, and at twelve o'clock they sang 'God save the King' in English, and then their own national anthem, in German. Then someone made a speech, and others kept breaking in with cheers. This morning a good many of us went out in the front, and the Germans came and met us halfway. I spoke to a good many of them (by signs) and shook hands with a German officer, who gave me a gold-tipped cigarette. I managed to get a German helmet and one or two things which I hope to send home if they will let me.

The same newspaper printed a letter from an unidentified private of the London Rifle Brigade on 31 December (it had apparently been in the London press the day before).

> The Germans started singing and lighting candles about 7.30 on Christmas Eve, and one of the challenged any one of us to go across for a bottle of wine. One of our fellows accepted the challenge, and took a big cake to exchange. That started the ball rolling. We went half way to shake hands and exchange greetings. There were ten dead Germans on the ditch in front of the trenches, and we helped bury these. They were trapped one night trying to get at our outpost trench. The Germans seem very nice chaps, and said they were awfully sick of the war.

Capt. Arthur Bates, commanding the battalion's Number 4 Company, took the opportunity to write home to his sister Dorothy:

> Just a line from the trenches on Xmas Eve. A topping night with not much firing going on and both sides singing. It will be interesting to see what happens tomorrow. My orders to the Company are not to start firing unless the Germans do![7]

J. Selby Grigg is most important to the London Rifle Brigade's account of the truce, not least because he took photographs that are now in the Imperial War Museum collection.

> Number 3 Company went into the breastworks (which have in most places round here superceded the flooded reserve trenches) on Wednesday night and had quite a quiet time. Soon after dusk on the 24th the Germans put lanterns on top of their trenches and started singing, and their shooting practically ceased. From where we [were we] couldn't distinguish all the tunes but we understand from the regulars then in the advance trenches that, in addition to their own songs, they played 'Home, sweet home', 'God save the King' and 'Tipperary' on a cornet.
>
> After daybreak on Christmas Day small parties on both sides ventured out in front of their trenches all unarmed and we heard that a German officer came over and promised that they would not fire if we didn't. Apparently dueing the morning small parties of German and English fraternised between the trenches which at this particular spot are some 200 yards apart. ... When Turner and I and some of our pals strolled up from the reserve trenches after dinner, we found a crowd of some 100 Tommies of each nationality holding a regular mother's meeting between the trenches. We found our enemies to be Saxons. I don't know what their status is, but they are certainly not first-line troops – mostly under 21 or over 35 – very few men in their prime and some very weedy specimens. Turner took some snaps with his pocket camera.

Near where we were standing a dead German who had been brought in by some English was being buried ... [they] said 'we thank our English friends for bringing in our dead'. They stuck a bit of wood over the grave – no name on it, only 'Fur Vaterland und Freiheit'.[8]

Grigg mentioned that the British artillery fired the next day, and the infantry yelled across 'we didn't do it!' J. Selby Grigg:

I understand but only from an unreliable source that on Friday in another part of the line the Germans played us a football between the trenches. I don't know which side won.[9]

The 12th Infantry Brigade

It will be recalled that this brigade had given a 'no further parleying' order on 13 December, after the 2nd Essex Regiment had been involved in an informal truce two days before. The headquarters' war diary for Christmas reads,

Practically no sniping and no artillery fire all day. In left section, both sides sent parties out to bury dead between lines by daylight. At Le Touquet a German came into our lines to ask permission to bury dead. Having been allowed to see into our lines unarmed he could not be allowed to return. Normal relations were resumed on Boxing Day although the situation remained quiet.

The 1st King's Own (Royal Lancaster Regiment)

This battalion was relieved from the trenches at Le Touquet late on Christmas Eve and went into billets at Le Bizet. They were replaced by the 2nd Lancashire Fusiliers, whose diary says of period that there was no firing on Christmas Day, states, 'practically none 26th but one man killed.'

The 1/2nd Monmouthshire Regiment

This territorial unit says that,

Between 14 and 29 December the battalion continued to occupy the same line of trenches, relieving the 2nd Essex Regiment every four days (and on one occasion five days). Most of its spare time and available men were employed in keeping trenches dry. Vast quantities of brush wood, planks and several hand pumps were sent into the trenches for this purpose. The enemy's machine guns were sometimes very active. It was found, however, that they were temporarily silenced by our men firing controlled volleys at them. Christmas Day was spent in the trenches, the relief of the Essex having taken place on the evening of Christmas Day. The communication trenches still continued to be almost impossible to use and reliefs and ration parties had therefore to walk up unprotected and in the open to the trenches. Curiously no casualties occurred on relieving. On Xmas Day practically no firing took place on either side by mutual agreement. The opportunity was made use of to ascertain what German regiment opposed us. The losses in killed were five and wounded were six during this period.

The Monmouths' private, 1250 Arthur Gill, had a letter published in the *Birmingham Gazette* on 12 January 1915. He had expressed satisfaction at the amount of chocolate and Christmas pudding he had eaten, and had exchanged some with the enemy. 'The Germans don't get looked after like we do. The one to whom we were talking put out his hands the way they hold a rifle and said "English damned good!"'

The 2nd Essex Regiment
The battalion left its billets at Warnave and relieved the 1/2nd Monmouths in the trenches in the early evening of Christmas Day. It reported the situation quiet for next few days, but made no mention of fraternising.

The 2nd Royal Inniskilling Fusiliers
The battalion remained in brigade reserve at Wisques.

The 6th Division (the III Corps, Frélinghien–Bois-Grenier Sector)

The 19th Infantry Brigade
The 6th Division had been holding the trenches that skirted the town of Armentières since the fighting had settled down here in October 1914. Their line ran down from Frélinghien, past L'Epinette, Porte Egal, Chapelle d'Armentières, Rue du Bois to Bois Grenier.[10] During the period of November and December, it had a fourth brigade under its control. This was the 19th Infantry Brigade, a formation that had gone to France in August, but which had acted as an independent command until joining the division in October. The brigade had been placed on the division's left front.

The 2nd Royal Welsh Fusiliers
The battalion had been almost a month in the flooded trenches west of Frélinghien when it was finally relieved by the 2nd Durham Light Infantry at 5 p.m. on Boxing Day. From there, it moved to billets at Erquinghem-Lys. A patrol from C Company had found a number of dead of the 133rd Saxon Regiment in no man's land on 22 December. Three days later, after the temperature had dropped and some light snow fallen, there was:

Practically a truce all day. Both sides walked about on top of their trenches –
allowed the Germans to bury their dead. The following telegramme was sent to
His Majesty the King: All ranks 2nd Royal Welsh Fusiliers which their Colonel-
in-Chief and Her Majesty a Merry Christmas and a Happy New Year'. The
following reply was received: 'The Queen and I thank all ranks for their Xmas
and New Year greetings, which we heartily reciprocate'.

The battalion's captain, Clifton Stockwell, who during the war would go on
to become a highly respected commander of a brigade, wrote:

I think I and my Company have just spent one of the most curious Christmas Days
we are ever likely to see. It froze hard on Christmas Eve and in the morning there
was a thick ground fog. I believe I told you the Saxons opposite had been shouting
in English. Strict orders had been issued that there was to be no fraternizing on
Christmas day. About 1 p.m., having seen our men get their Christmas dinners,
we went into our shelter to get a meal. The sergeant on duty suddenly ran in and
said the fog had lifted and that half a dozen Saxons were standing on their parapet
without arms. I ran out into the trench and found that all the men were holding
their rifles at the ready on the parapet, and that the Saxons were shouting, 'Don't
shoot. We don't want to fight today. We will send you some beer.' A cask was
hoisted onto the parapet and three men started to roll it into the middle of no man's
land. A lot more Saxons then appeared without arms. Things were getting a bit
thick. My men were getting a bit excited, and the Saxons kept shouting to them to
come out. We did not like to fire as they were all unarmed, but we had strict orders
and someone might have fired, so I climbed over the parapet and shouted, in my
best German, for the opposing Captain to appear. Our men were all chattering and
saying, 'The Captain's going to speak to them.' A German officer appeared and
walked out into the middle of no man's land, so I moved out to meet him, amidst
the cheers of both sides. We met and formally saluted. He introduced himself as
Count Something-or-other and seemed a very decent fellow. He could not talk
a word of English. He then called out to his subalterns and formally introduced
them, with much clicking of heels and saluting. They were all very well turned
out, while I was in a goatskin coat. One of the subalterns could talk a few words
of English, but not enough to carry on a conversation. I said to the German captain,
'My orders are to keep my men in the trench and allow no armistice. Don't you
think it's dangerous, all your men running about in the open like this? Someone
may open fire'. He called out an order and all his men went back to their parapet,
leaving me and the five German officers and the barrel of beer in the middle of no
man's land. He then said, 'My orders are the same as yours, but could we not have
a truce from shooting today? We don't want to shoot, do you?' I said, 'No, we
certainly don't want to shoot, but I have my orders to obey'. So then we agreed not
to shoot until the following morning, when I was to signal that we were going to

begin. He said, 'You had better take the beer. We have lots'. So I called up two men to take the barrel to our side. As we had lots of plum puddings I sent for one and formally presented it to him in exchange for the beer. He then called out, 'Waiter', and a German Private whipped out six glasses and two bottles of beer, and with much bowing and saluting we solemnly drank it amid cheers from both sides. We then all formally saluted and returned to our lines. Our men had sing-songs, ditto the enemy.

Stockwell reported that on Boxing Day He played the game. Not a shot all night and never tried to touch his wire or anything. There was a hard frost. At 8.30 I fired three shots in the air and put up a flag with 'Merry Christmas' on it and I climbed on the parapet. He put up a sheet with 'Thank You' on it, and the German captain appeared on the parapet. We both bowed and saluted and got down into our respective trenches, and he fired two shots into the air, and the war was on again.[11]

Second Lt Mervyn Richardson's account, which is attached as an appendix to the battalion war diary, differs only in detail. On 31 December 1914, he wrote:

I will tell you of the extraordinary day we spent on Christmas Day. On Christmas Eve we had a sing-song with the men in the trenches (this applies to our company – A). We put up a sheet of canvas, with a large 'Merry Xmas and a portrait of the Kaiser painted on it, on the parapet. The next morning there was a thick fog, and when it lifted about 12 [noon], the Germans (Saxons) who were only 150 yards in front of us saw it, they began to shout across, and beckoning tour men to come half way and exchange gifts. They then came out of their trenches, and gave our men cigars and cigarettes, and two barrels of beer, in exchange for tins of bully beef. The situation was so absurd, that another officer of ours and myself went out, and met seven of their officers, and arranged that we should keep our men in our respective trenches, and that we should have an armistice till the next morning, when we would lower our Christmas card, and hostilities would continue. One of them presented me with the packet of cigarettes I sent you, and we have them a plum pudding, and then we shook hands with them, and saluted each other and returned to our respective trenches. Not a shot was fired all day, and the next morning we pulled our card down, and they put up one with 'thank you' on it.[12]

The battalion appears to have fraternised with men from the *Jäger-Batallion No. 6 (Schlesiches No. 2)*, as well as the Saxon infantry.

The 1st Cameronians
The battalion returned to the trenches of the Pont Ballot sector on 11 December. The war diary makes no remarks with regard to a truce,

saying, on Christmas Day only 'Enemy very noisy during the night. One man wounded.'

In his detailed private diary, Capt. James Jack of C Company wrote that his battalion heard music being played across in the enemy trenches and at one point a German with evident knowledge called out, 'When are you going back to Maryhill barracks?' He twice wrote that his unit did not take part in any truce. 'Their merry making continues till the small hours of the morning, but C Company, physically cold and mentally dour, maintains a stiff reserve except when, as with the Imperial Toast, particularly irritating remarks are made by the Huns.'[13]

Old soldier Harry Archibald Taylor, a 1903 recruit who had seen garrison service in India and South Africa, and now of the battalion transport, witnessed the truce at a distance:

> On Christmas Eve a corporal and I escorted the rations up the line. We made the usual distributions to companies including the rum issue and found that we still had a jar of rum left. We have our driver a good issue and sent them back to our lines. We sat, of all places, outside the cemetery of Houplines having a tot or two, listening to the singing of the troops. It was a beautiful night, moonlight and serene. We heard someone approaching. It proved to be our new Regimental Sergeant Major. He enquired what we were doing there, we explained that we were listening to the singing. We offered him our jar of rum, meantime I told him that his batman had drawn his issue. By the time he left we were all merry. Wishing us a Merry Xmas he made his way to headquarters and we strolled to billets, which was a large school building.

After two hours rest, Taylor was ordered to the divisional railhead at Steenwerck, where he helped collect the boxes of 'Princess Mary' tins for his battalion. But that was not all.

> At the railhead were three trucks loaded with large bundles of gifts for Scottish troops at the front, just that, with no specific regiment being mentioned. Our Quartermaster Sergeant marked twenty of these bundles '1st Batt, the Cameronians' and ordered us to load them onto our wagon. Inside them after opening, were everything from shaving soap to socks, balaclava caps, sweets and a host of things including cigarettes and plenty of well-wishing notes from the donors. Many a romance commenced through these innocent notes. After this episode the corporal and I were named the 'scroungers'.

The 2nd Argyll & Sutherland Highlanders

Late on 20 December, the battalion left its billets in the asylum at Armentières and took over the front line trenches at Houplines. 'Christmas was a very quiet day. Germans came out of their trenches unarmed in afternoon and were seen to belong to 133rd and 134th Regiment. The position was reconnoitred by Lieutenant Anderson. The Germans asked for leave to bury dead. This was granted.' On Boxing Day, after a number of German shells fell in the battalion area, the Argylls were relieved for the brigade was now going into divisional reserve.

The *Angus Evening Telegraph* of 31 December reported a letter from Jack Peters, previously a footballer with Arbroath Football Club, who was now serving with the battalion.

> We exchanged caps and cigarettes, and a German officer asked one of our officers to let a football match be played on Boxing Day, but our officer said, of course, that it couldn't be done, and the German officer understood.

The same newspaper included a letter from Sgt 905 John Minnery on 17 February 1915:

> We are lying facing the Saxons, and I think they are about fed up with this war. They have behaved as they are doing now ever since the Christmas Truce. They walk about on top of their trench, and we do likewise. They are only about 200 yards from us. They don't snipe at us and we don't snipe at them, but the Prussians who are on our right are sniping pretty constantly. The Saxons have a large French flag flying in front of their trench, and I am going to try to get it as a souvenir.

Minnery's bold and fearless nature is quite clear, and goes some way to explaining the fact that he was awarded the Distinguished Conduct Medal (DCM) and the Military Medal, before being commissioned as an officer in 1916. His DCM was gazetted in June 1915, with a citation that described the award as being, 'For conspicuous gallantry and ability on patrol work. Corporal Minnery has done valuable work and his boldness has set a fine example to other patrol leaders.'

The 1st Middlesex Regiment
The battalion was relieved from the trenches on 20 December, and was in billets in Armentières throughout the Christmas period.

The 17th Infantry Brigade
The brigade headquarters reported that there was an informal truce on Christmas Day, except on the left of the Leinsters, and that both sides left their trenches and talked together.

The 1st North Staffordshire Regiment

The battalion was in a lengthy spell of holding trenches near Rue du Bois that they called the 'Death Trap'. After two days of a good deal of firing in both directions, things quietened down on 23 December.

> Christmas Eve: Germans ask for armistice. Sing songs in turn from opposite parapets. Germans win prize at this [that is, they are better]. Christmas Day: not a shot fired. Germans bury their dead, our men go and help. Baccy and cigars exchanged and Germans and our men walk about in the open together! Return to trenches at 4 p.m. Peace reigns till midnight.

The peace continued next day, but it rained in torrents and, by 27 December, the battalion reported that its trenches were waist deep. The battalion was eventually relieved on New Year's Eve and moved to billets at Chapelle d'Armentières.

The *Staffordshire Sentinel* of 14 January 1915 published two letters written by the battalion's machine gunner Cpl 9488 Fred Cornes, to his parents in Chesterton. The first bemoaned his condition, but suggests that fraternisation was not entirely unexpected:

> It is Christmas Eve in the trenches and the Germans are going mad shouting and singing and giving a big drum socks. I am afraid something will happen before morning for we are expecting them to attack any night. But we are ready for them, and the sooner they come the better so that we can let them see what we are made of. Our trenches and the Germans are only about 50 yards apart and they keep shouting across to us to ask for cigarettes, Christmas pudding and other things. I am sure if they dared some of them would come over to us for they are properly fed up, and so are we, having to spend Christmas in the trenches nearly frozen to death, and the trenches up to the knees in sludge. We have been in the trenches thirteen days now and have got to remain until the 31st. The weather is terrible and I find myself lying in about six inches of water, for while I had slept the water had oozed up out of the ground and everything I had on was saturated. We have all received a box of chocolates from the *Staffordshire Sentinel* and a present from Princess Mary. Hello? What's the matter with the Germans? What? They are re-advancing. All right, stand to the guns. Finish my letter later.

Pte 9929 Thomas Harper's letter was published in the *Tamworth Herald* on 9 January 1915:

> I would be very pleased if you would allow me a space in your valuable paper to let you know how we are going on at the front. I received the kind and

welcome latter and tobacco from the Chamber of Trade, which was also a very nice Christmas box, and I also thank you for the *Herald* which I receive every week. I was surprised when I woke up from out of my 'funk hole' in the firing line to see all the Germans out of the top of the trenches with our fellow, exchanging fags for German cigars, and giving them corned beef, which we call 'bully beef', for rum and coffee. They told us they were fed up with the war, and would be pleased when it was over. A lot of the German fellows had worked in England, and they asked us if the places were still working where they used to be employed. We told them 'yes', and you should have seen the laugh when we said 'yes'. Some of them took our addresses, and said they would write when the war was over. We parted from them at 5 o'clock on Christmas night, but before we parted we sang 'Auld Lang Syne' and shook hands with each. Firing is as usual today, Boxing Day. They are letting us have bags of Jack Johnson today.

Cornes wrote again on New Year's Day:

On Christmas Eve we ran to our guns ready to send a few Germans to the happy hunting grounds if they attacked, but it was not so, for I put my head over the top of the trench to see if they were attacking. What I saw surprised me as it did the others, for the Germans were putting lighted candles and fires on top of the trenches and our fellows were knocking them down as fast as they put them up. Then we heard a lone voice in English asking us not to fire and as they were not firing we stopped. The same voice asked that one of our officers went and met the man whose name was Fritz, a German interpreter. They shook hands and there was much cheering and clapping of hands. At the same time arrangements were made that no firing should take place until Christmas Day was over. The Germans asked permission to bury their dead, and this was granted. The Germans then began singing German songs and we sang one or two English ones. Early next morning they were out burying their dead, and when we saw how many then had we went out and helped them. Each German we approached shook hands and wished us a Merry Christmas and gave us plenty of cigars and other things for which in return we gave them bully beef. They seemed very hungry. One fellow showed us what he had for Christmas Day rations, and all it consisted of was half a loaf of brown bread and half a hunk of sausage. They said that they should not fire at us again as long as we did not fire at them and they added that if their officers made them, they should fire up in the air. So we spent another six days in peace. It was not like being on a battlefield at all, we could do nearly anything we liked. They were all Saxons from the 179th Regiment, 79th Regiment, 102nd Regiment and 132nd Regiment. A good many of them came from London. Well we are out of the trenches now for a few days.

The 2nd Leinster Regiment

The battalion was in a lengthy spell holding the front line of L'Epinette. On Christmas Eve, it reported hearing a German band playing hymns and, at 8 p.m., saw several strong lights or flares in the enemy's trenches. Next day...

> without previous arrangement, but apparently by mutual consent, this has become a day of peace. No shots have been fired on our right or centre, but on the left there has been a little hostile sniping. Our men have been digging outside in front of their trenches whilst the Germans have buried their dead that lay between the two lines. Later, some consultations between the two sides took place in the open, both officers and men of each side being concerned. The enemy opposite us are the 139th Saxon Regiment and consist largely of Landwehr and young soldiers. They appeared more numerous in the trenches than we are, and an artillery officer and some artillery privates were with them. For the most part the man are small but of good physique and remarkably content and confident of victory. Christmas cards from HM the King and HM the Queen, and presents from HRH Princess Mary received and issued to the troops today. One man killed and three wounded opposite our left.

After a reportedly very cold Boxing Day, the battalion was relieved at 8 p.m. by the 1st West Yorkshires (18th Infantry Brigade) and moved to billets at Chapelle d' Armentières. It stood-to in the early hours, as a result of the alarm that an enemy attack was expected.

The 3rd Rifle Brigade

On 5 December, the battalion had moved into the front line of the Porte Egal sector south-east of Chapelle d'Armentières and was still there. Its diary reports only that one non-commissioned officer and two riflemen went missing on Christmas Day, believed to have been taken as prisoners of war. The *Liverpool Echo* of 2 January 1915 included a letter from Acting-Cpl 8434 Frank Edwards, formerly a policeman in Birkenhead.

> After a time some of our fellows shouted to tell them that if they would come half-way unarmed we would meet them and have a chat. A couple of our fellows left the trenches and, sure enough, a couple of Germans came to meet them ... several more of us went, myself included, and had a bit of a chat and afterwards smoked side by side, and buried two dead Germans who had been lying there for fully two months. You may guess that was by no means a pleasant job. However we were on the best of terms with the Germans, and for the greater part of the day cigars, cigarettes and chocolates were freely exchanged between friend and foe. At 3 p.m. a German officer called his men in. The fellow I had exchanged a cigar off said as they parted, 'Today [Christmas Day] nice; tomorrow, shot'. As he left me he held my hand, which I accepted, and he said 'farewell, comrade'. With that we parted,

and in all probability in the course of a day or so we shall be doing our utmost to kill each other. I know this sounds like a fairy tale, but I assure you it is perfectly true. If I had not participated in it I should feel rather inclined to disbelieve it myself, as I have witnessed some very treacherous acts on the part of the Germans, but I think this will go to prove that there are honourable Germans.

The same edition included this letter from Rfn 3256 Frederick Mallard of the battalion's machine gun section, a native of the Isle of Wight [the newspaper incorrectly gives him as C. Mallard]:

At 4.30 p.m. on Christmas Eve we heard music, and gathered that the Germans had a band in their trenches, but our artillery spoilt the effect by dropping a couple of shells right in the centre of them and you can guess what became of the band, for we heard it no more. We were wondering if the Germans would agree to a couple of days' truce and as soon as it was dark we were surprised to see Christmas trees stuck up on top of their trenches lighted with candles, and men sitting on the trench. So we got out of our trench and exchanged a few cigarettes with the Germans and invited them to come over and have a drink and a smoke, but we did not trust each other at first. After a while three of our officers started to go over to meet three German officers who were approaching them, their way being directed by a searchlight in the German lines. It made a fine picture to see those six officers meet between the two lines, shake hands, and smoke each other's cigarettes in the glow of the searchlight, and all of the boys became quite excited over it. Then it was the turn of the troops, and they swarmed over to each other. Our going over to them quite altered their opinion of the British soldier and now they think a lot more of us.

Mallard was killed in action near Ypres, on 4 September 1915.

The 1st Royal Fusiliers
The battalion was in billets at Chapelle d'Armentières, but relieved the Queen's Westminster Rifles of 18th Infantry Brigade in the front line at 4 a.m. on Boxing Day. During the day, Capt. William Ford Coates found time to write a letter: one of considerable historical significance, as it turned out. He had only joined the battalion two days before, after conducting a draft of Second-Lt Sidney Bunker and fifty men.

Dear old John,

Have been sent back from the trenches for a court of inquiry job at the headquarters [of the] Field Ambulance, and now having got it finished have to wait here till dark before I can rejoin. 'Here' is a house on the outskirts of a town about 900 yards from the German trenches [Chapelle d' Armentières]. They've been knocking hell out of it all the morning with small Jack Johnsons. When I came back I couldn't find my servant (hope he hasn't been sniped on his way to headquarters) and so had to make myself a small meal. A few scraps of wood and some tea mixed with sugar and onions and a few more things and some bread and butter were all I could find, but having had nothing 'cept a basin of tea since 7 p.m. last night and now 1.30 p.m. today it went down like fresh milk. War is undoubtedly the greatest game in the world – but it's no game for a gentleman. I had a shave and a wash a few days ago but I am already unrecognisable! The Bosches here have just removed the spire from the local church an about 20 minutes ago removed a corner of the house roof, causing me to spill part of my 'tea' over my boots and I really thought I'd have to take to the cellar – cos just previously while enjoying a peaceful if uncomfortable nap an Xmas present from the Bosches messed up the nap window. However one of our heavies got on the job and the shelling has cased pro tem and beyond the rattle of rifle shots which goes on day and night there's nothing doing at the moment. It's bloody cold here –freezing hard and water everywhere. Frostbite about too. However in the ordinary way one is quite well fed here so one can carry on – on special jobs one feeds when one can – or doesn't as the case may be. I am at present 2nd in command of one Curme of B Company. Quaint old bird but some soldier. When I arrived here I had to trek 12 miles at night in full kit through seas of mud and snow after 2 days troop trains! Bloody what! However on arrival I received a warm welcome from the Adjutant and shared his bed for the night and his razor for the morning so that was all right. They have been in billets then 'resting' (so called – really consists of digging like hell but it's a change from the trenches and one gets one's valise and is under cover).

Yesterday – Xmas Day – was priceless. Our men arranged signals with the Bosches to have no firing from dawn till midnight, to celebrate Noel and came out of the trenches! They produced a football and kicked it across from our entanglements to theirs and they kicked it back! Some game. Officers were present to see that no one crossed the half way line between the trenches and some of the men went up, shook hands and exchanged cigarettes for cigars and souvenirs etc. They're not a bad lot really – they aren't Prussians which makes all the difference. The French were quite sick about it all – didn't see the sporting side at all – and their lines made a hell of an attack about 2 a.m. Xmas Day. It is most damnably cold.

Coates deleted his own short paragraph here, and added a note 'the censor wouldn't approve!'

War is a great game (tho' as I say, not for gentlemen) if only our people didn't get killed so frequently. Our 4th Battalion has lost 62 officers and 1900 men since the show started – roughly 200 per cent of its original strength! The local kirk is somewhat bent now and they've made a hell of a mess of this house – lets the draught in so damnably and it's something cold. This is some regiment! The senior people are sahibs to the marrow – the 2nd in command Major Roberts was blown over arse over tip out of the 2nd storey window of a farm last week but is now back again with a black patch over one eye. Doesn't worry him much as with a monocle he sees twice as much out of the surviving eye that most people with two. He is immensely popular and is known all over the Division as Bobby!

The letter continues and ends with an appeal to be sent a sou'wester oilskin hat as soon as possible.[14]

The 16th Infantry Brigade

The brigade reported that, on Christmas Eve, 'the Germans appeared to be very jovial in their trenches. Two came into our lines and were made prisoners. They belonged to the 179th Regiment of the XIX Saxon Corps. Several bombs were thrown in the Yorkshire & Lancashire Regiment lines.' The next day, 'Christmas [was] celebrated as far as practicable. The receipt of the Xmas card from the King and Queen gave great pleasure to the troops. The day was frosty and foggy. We had more casualties today than for some time past.'

The 1st Leicestershire Regiment

The battalion was holding trenches in the Rue du Bois–La Grande Flamengrie Farm sector. No truce is mentioned. Two men were killed and one wounded on Christmas Day.[15]

Pte 9654 Harold Startin, describing himself as a 'Mid-Somerset Old Contemptible', later wrote,

> On Christmas Eve, as we were standing-to, the Germans started to sing Christmas Carols, the first one being 'Holy Night', and then as though a preconceived plan we joined in. There we were, the fighting men of the two forces, who had previously been at one another's throats, joining together having a real Carol Concert. Next morning ... dawned unnaturally quiet and still, broken only by the squelch of boots in the everlasting mud. Soon a few were bold enough to scramble over the top of the trench and it became evident that both sides had somehow inexplicably decided to honour the season of goodwill ... Everything was spontaneous and sincere. Perhaps never before, and probably never again, will the world witness such a demonstration of the 'brotherhood of man' between opposing warring forces.[16]

The 1st Buffs (East Kent Regiment)

The war diary only reports that the battalion was in trenches near La Grande Flamengrie Farm between 9 and 29 December.

The 1st King's Shropshire Light Infantry

The battalion was relieved by the 2nd York & Lancaster Regiment on 23 December, and moved to billets at Rue de Lettres. It moved back into the trenches on Boxing Day but makes no mention of a truce.

The 2nd York & Lancaster Regiment

The battalion relieved the 1st King's Shropshire Light Infantry on 23 December. The war diary reads, 'situation unchanged – advances for armistice for Christmas Day from enemy – no notice taken. Usual sniping and a few bombs thrown at our line.'

The 18th Infantry Brigade

With the exception of one battalion that was already there, the brigade moved from reserve into the trenches late on Christmas Day.

The 1st West Yorkshire Regiment

The battalion was in billets at Erquinghem-Lys, until it moved forwards to relieve the 2nd Leinster Regiment (17th Infantry Brigade) at L'Epinette in the evening of Christmas Day. The diary is one of the least verbose of all, and only gives casualty figures for each day after that.

The 1st East Yorkshire Regiment

The battalion was in billets in d'Armentières for several days, including Christmas Day. On 22 December, it had been forced to move, when a jute factory it was occupying was accidentally set on fire. It relieved the Cameronians of 19th Infantry Brigade late on Christmas Day, taking over the stretch of line between a point 500 yards north of L'Epinette, to 300 yards north of Pont Ballot. Reporting this portion of the line fairly dry, by two days later, the battalion was suffering from severe flooding. No hostile activity or truce is mentioned.

The 2nd Sherwood Foresters (Nottinghamshire & Derbyshire Regiment)

The battalion moved from Nieppe to Armentières on 23 December 1914, and was there on Christmas Day. 650 of its men attended a voluntary divine service. It relieved the 2nd Argyll & Sutherland Highlanders (19th Infantry Brigade) in the afternoon of Boxing Day, and held a 1,500-yard long stretch of line.

The 2nd Durham Light Infantry

The battalion moved from Pont de Nieppe to Armentières on 23 December 1914, and was there on Christmas Day. It relieved the 2nd Royal Welsh

Fusiliers (19th Infantry Brigade) in the afternoon of Boxing Day, taking over the line near Frélinghien, with its left on the River Lys.

1/16th London Regiment (Queen's Westminster Rifles)

The battalion returned to the trenches near Houplines on 23 December, to find conditions worse than ever. Things were relatively quiet, although on this day and Christmas Eve, enemy snipers picked off seven men, killing one of them. The war diary reassures us: 'we can always silence them when they get annoying.'[17] It continues on Christmas Day:

> No war today. Much conversation with enemy between trenches. 107 Regiment opposite us. Trenches strongly held. Their men of good military age for the most part, though a few very young ones. Seemed happy and healthy and well-fed. Some however were despondent. Some said they were just outside Paris, having been brought up to the line in closed railway carriages. They also believed that the Germans were occupying London. Casualties: other ranks, missing 3.[18]

Walter Mockett, the stretcher bearer who thought his pals' attempts at raisin puddings might have made good trench mortars, wrote to a friend on 28 December.

> My dear Charlie, I am writing to let you know that I am alive and well. We are in billets at present. We came out Boxing Day, so that we spent part of Xmas out of the trenches. Xmas Day was spent by us in a most remarkable way. The Germans and our own fellows got out of their trenches and shook hands with each other. The Germans said 'you no shoot, we no shoot' so we agreed and all day long we walked about on top of the trenches, where in the ordinary course of events it would have been instant death for us. I went over and talked to some of them. They said they were fed up with the war and ready to go home. I have a coat button, a hat badge and some cigarettes from one of them. Some of them come from London and so speak fairly good English. Opposite to us they are Saxons, who are not so bad as the Prussians. The Kaiser presented his men with cigars Xmas Day.[19]

Rfn 2115 Ernest Morley wrote to a soldier pal on 29 December 1914:

> The last time was not so bad as regards weather, it was chiefly frosty, and as regards the war [it] was a perfect scream. We had decided to give the Germans a Christmas present of three carols and five rounds rapid. Accordingly as soon as night fell we started, and the strains of 'While shepherd' (beautifully rendered by the choir!) came upon the air. We finished that and paused preparatory to giving the second item on the programme. But lo! We heard answering strains arising from *their* lines. Also they started shouting across to us. Therefore we stopped

any hostile operations and commenced to shout back. One of them shouted 'A merry Christmas English, we're not shooting tonight' ... and from that time until we're relieved on Boxing morning at 4 a.m., not a shot was fired. I exchanged a cigarette for a cigar with one of them (not a bad exchange, eh?) and as some of them spoke English had quite a long conversation. One fellow said as soon as the war was over he was 'going back to England by express'. He had a wife and two children in the Alexander Road! [20]

The press published several letters from men of the battalion, almost to the extent that one wonders whether there was a concerted effort for publicity. The Queen's Westminster Rifles, along with the London Rifle Brigade and several other territorial units, was rather select and had good connections. An unnamed officer of the battalion, quoted in various newspapers in early January 1915, but apparently originally published in the *London Daily News* on 30 December, reported that his company had been carrying wood to the trenches on Christmas Eve.

> Next day would have made a good chapter in Dickens's Christmas Carol. It was, indeed, a tribute to the spirit of Christmas. Many of our chaps walked out and met the Germans between the lines. I went over in the afternoon and was photographed in a group of English and Germans mixed. We exchanged souvenirs; I got a German ribbon and a photo of the Crown prince of Bavaria. The Germans opposite us were awfully decent fellows – Saxons, intelligent, respectable-looking men. I had quite a decent talk with three or four and have two names and addresses in my notebook. It was the strangest scene you could imagine – going out to meet our enemies, also unarmed. After our talk I really think a lot of our newspaper reports must be horribly exaggerated. Of course – these men were Saxons, not Prussians.

The *Liverpool Echo* of 2 January included a letter from an unnamed private of the battalion, writing to a friend in Leighton Buzzard.

> Two of them with whom I happened to get in conversation were quite decent fellows and a cut above the others. They were brothers in the 107th Saxons, and being reservists were called up. One had a ticket for London with him, and told us that he was going to London for a holiday when he was called up. Both said they were personally very sorry to have to fight against us. The rest of the regiment were of a rather lower class, and looked as if a good feed would benefit them. Taking them all round, they were of medium age and rather well built. One fellow had an iron cross, which he kept in his purse. One thing that made us envious was their jackboots, which are just the things we want.

The same newspaper said that L/Cpl 1147 Reginald Hines had written to his brother, in Chester, on 27 December.

On Christmas Eve, when it got dark, we heard the beggars shouting across to us: 'Lustige Wiehnachten', and of course our boys returned the compliment. There was no firing at all, as we had decided not to as well. A crowd of us got out of the trenches and walked up and down singing carols. It was a glorious night, freezing hard, and a white cast over everything, and a cloudless sky to crown it all. Next morning we repeated the programme, and before it was light. After breakfast it was misty, and we took the opportunity of going out and repairing the wire entanglements. Later on the mist cleared away and we could see several Germans moving about on the top of their trenches. Then the strangest thing of all happened. As if by some mutual agreement, both sides clambered out of the trenches and met in the middle of no man's land. We exchanged cigarettes, etc and had a general conversation. One of them came up to an officer, and said in broken English: 'Good morning, sir; I live at Alexander Road, Hornsey, and I would see Woolwich Arsenal play Tottenham tomorrow'. In the afternoon the same scene happened again. Near their lines there was a tumbledown farm, and German and English Tommies were rummaging about together for wood, etc to improve their respective trenches. Next day another regiment relieved us before dawn. We were rather sorry, as we might have still further good relations with the enemy. We are now billeted in a spinning factory – a weird kind of home, lying down between the looms and bobbin frames.

Reginald Hines was killed in action on 9 August 1915.

An anonymous letter from a rifleman appeared in the *Hull Daily Mail* on New Year's Eve:

As things seemed to be going very well, we thought we might as well get out on top, so four of us got on top of the parapet and struck matches, which was received by a cheer form the other side, so we all got out and held a concert and dance in the open. After this a few thought it would be just as well to shake hands and exchange cigarettes, etc, with them, so we called to them, and mat a few halfway between the trenches and they were jolly good sports, too. On Christmas Day we had a football out in front of the trenches, and asked the Germans to send a team to play us; but either they considered the ground too hard, as it had been freezing all night, and was a ploughed field, or else their officers put the bar up. Anyhow, we had a chat with each other in the afternoon, and one of them produced a camera, and we have a group [photograph] taken, about twelve QWR and twelve Germans. I expect you think this is a bit of a yarn. In fact the regulars, who were in reserve here, would not believe, and some of them came up to see for themselves.

The 7th Division: (the IV Corps, Bois-Grenier to the Rue du Bois)

The division had taken part in the attacks during mid-December and continued to hold the same blood-soaked ground.

The 22nd Infantry Brigade

The brigade reported that it spent Christmas Eve clearing the Layes river to prevent its water flooding the trenches. Next day there was 'practically no shooting of any kind throughout the day. Armistice in front of No 5 Sub-sector to bury dead who fell on the 18th ... lasted till 3 p.m.'

The 2nd Queen's (Royal West Surrey Regiment)

The battalion, which had taken part in the attack near Well Farm on 18 December, returned to the trenches late on 23 December. It reported that on Christmas Eve it was:

Enemy quiet and not much sniping. In the evening enemy were evidently keeping Xmas – many flares going in rear of their lines. Weather fine and frosty. Christmas Day: at 11 a.m. an armistice began. It stated opposite the left of the Wiltshire Regiment, the regiment on our right. Many Germans, officers and men, came out of their trenches to midway between the two lines –parties were sent out to collect and bury the dead who had been killed on the 18th – graves were dug in the centre between the lines. 71 bodies were collected, chiefly Warwicks. The body of Lieut Ramsey, previously reported missing, was found near the German trenches and [was] later [taken] back to the dressing station to be buried in the churchyard. The Germans were nearly all belonging to the 55th Regiment. Several staff officers also came over. These were quite a different class to the infantry officers, who were of a very low class, and professed themselves as confident as to their being able to end the war in their favour. They had no opinion of the Russians, who they considered already beaten. All gave the appearance, however, of being fed up with the war. Armistice concluded at 4 p.m. with agreement to resume it at 9 a.m. following morning, as dead all not buried. Boxing Day: armistice recommenced as arranged at 9 a.m. A large number of staff officers appeared during the day. All were immaculately dressed without a speck of mud on them, mostly in fur lined coats. They furnished us with a list of officers they had taken prisoner and asked that their relatives might be informed. They also promised to try and obtain the release of 2nd Lieuts Rought and Walmisley, who had been taken prisoners during the armistice on 19th inst. Owing to frost the ground was very hard and the graves were not completed till 1 p.m., when the chaplain read the burial service in the presence of the digging party, some officers of the Queen's and 8 or 10 German officers. The body of 2nd Lieut. Bernard, Royal Warwicks, was found and buried. In addition to the 55th Regiment, men of the 7th, 15th and 22nd Regiments were noticed. Armistice concluded at 3.30 p.m.

The 1st Royal Welsh Fusiliers
The battalion had been in reserve during the 18 December attack. It relieved the 1/8th Royal Scots in the trenches on 20 December, but returned to billets during Christmas Eve after being relieved by the 2nd Queen's. The diary does not mention a truce.

The 1/8th Royal Scots
The battalion had been in the firing line during the 18 December attack but had only provided support. After relief by the 1st Royal Welsh Fusiliers, they returned to the trenches on Christmas Eve, but there is no mention of a truce.

The 1st South Staffordshire Regiment
This under-strength battalion was at Merville, where it was employed on guard duties and fatigues.

The 2nd Royal Warwickshire Regiment
The battalion came out of the attack of 18 December with only 149 men left. It was relieved and went into billets on Rue Biache early on Christmas Eve. Drafts of two officers and 310 men arrived that day and the next.

The 20th Infantry Brigade
In the days prior to Christmas, the brigade reported that the Layes river had risen 1 foot, and consequently units in the front line had to remove men from there as they were in places up to their waists in water. Reports from a scout of the Scots Guards (below), who had gone into no man's land on Christmas morning, heard a voice from the enemy trenches shouting that they would like to parley. A soldier came out and said they wanted a quiet Christmas Day; all their men were sick of the war. Twenty-two of their comrades had been killed fending off the recent British attack. As an officer approached, the man changed the conversation to Christmas. Arrangements were made and the day passed without a shot being fired after 9 a.m. Much time was spent in burying the many dead, 'silent witnesses to the fierce contest which must have taken place in the darkness' of 18–19 December. The Germans remarked that most of their wounds were caused by British bayonets. Brigade remarked that this was accounted for by the fact that the men's rifles had been so clogged with mud at the time of the attack. The truce lasted through Boxing Day. It was only on the third day that,

the Germans tried to come over and enjoy another day's so-called armistice, but were informed that they must keep to their trenches. They seemed quite indignant, and said they wouldn't fire if we didn't, but if we had orders to fire to signal them with three volleys first fired into the air.

On the night 27–28 December, the Germans enticed four Scots Guards to go over to them, whereupon they were taken prisoner.

The 2nd Scots Guards

The day after the battalion had taken part in an attack on 18 December, it moved to reserve billets at Sailly-sur-la-Lys. The battalion returned to the trenches on 23 December. Its RF Company took up the position from the 'left of 8th Division to tall poplar trees'. LF Company took on the line from the trees to the Fromelles road, G Company from the road to the south east end of the newly dug grenadier communication trench. Two men of the battalion were killed on Christmas Eve. During the fine and frosty night, another man was wounded.[21] The battalion's war diary is unusually descriptive and personal.

On the night of Christmas Eve, the German trenches opposite those occupied by the battalion at Fromelles were lit up with lanterns and there were sounds of singing. We got into communication with the Germans, who were anxious to arrange an armistice during Xmas. A scout named F. Murkin [actually Pte 8497 Peter Murker] went out and met a German patrol and was given a glass of whisky and some cigars, and a message was sent back saying that if we didn't fire at them, they would not fire at us. There was no firing during the night.

Early on Xmas morning a party of Germans 158 Regiment came over to our wire fence, and a party from our trenches went out to meet them. They appeared to be most amicable and exchanged souvenirs, cap stars, badges etc. Our men gave them plum puddings, which they much appreciated. Further down the line we were able to make arrangements to bury the dead who had been killed on December 18–19 and were still lying between the trenches. The Germans brought the bodies to a half way line and we buried them. Detachments of British and Germans formed in line and a German and English chaplain read some prayers alternately. The whole of this was done in great solemnity and reverence. It was heartrending to see some of the chaps one knew so well, and who had started out in such good spirits on 18 December lying there dead, some with terrible wounds due to the explosive action of the high velocity bullet at short range. Captain Taylor's body was found amongst them. His body was carried to the Rue-Pétillon where we buried him in our little cemetery. I talked to several officers and men. One officer ,a middle aged man, tall, well set up and good looking, told me that Lieut. Hon F. Hanbury Tracey had been taken into their trenches very severely wounded. He died after two days in the local hospital and was buried in the German cemetery at Fromelles. He also said that another young officer had been buried. He was fair. We think this would be Lieut. R. Nugent who was reported missing. Captain Paynter gave this officer a scarf and in exchange an orderly presented him with a pair of gloves, and wished to thank him for his kindness. The other officers were rather inclined to be stand-offish and of the burgers class. Another officer who could not speak English or French appeared to want express his feelings, pointed to the dead and reverently said 'Les braves', which shows that the Germans do think something of the British Army.

The men I spoke to were less reticent. They appeared generally tired of fighting, and wanted to get back to their various employments. Some lived in England. One man told me he had been seven years in England and was married last March. Another said he had a girl who lived in Suffolk and said it had been impossible to communicate with here through Germany since war began.

Their general opinion of the war was as follows. France is on her last legs and will soon have to give up. Russia has had a tremendous defeat in Poland and will soon be ready to make terms of peace. England is the nut which still has to be cracked, but with France and Russia out of the way she Germany would be too powerful. The war they thought might be over by the end of January. This shows what lies are circulated amongst the German troops and the hatred which exists between Germany and England.

Discipline in the German Army is of the most rigid character. The men seemed to hate their officers but nevertheless are afraid of them. A photo was taken by Lieut. Swinton of a group of Germans and English. Both sides have played the game and I know that this regiment anyhow has learnt to trust an Englishman's word. They appeared to be a smart-looking lot of men, possibly only the best were allowed to come out of the trenches. As far as I could see the officers don't wear any distinguishing badge of rank.

The battalion remained in the trenches until 28 December but makes no further observations regarding relationships with the enemy. Four men including Peter Murker were declared missing: they had been the men enticed across to the Germans, and had been captured and were now prisoners of war.

Pte 7792 Harold Bryan recalled:

As usual an hour before daybreak we stood to arms in case of attack. Presently we could hear the Germans singing carols and songs. Not a shot had been fired yet. We had had our breakfast and were enjoying smoke, when the lookout man shouted down that an officer and two men were approaching from the German lines. They were entirely without firearms and carried a white flag. We told him not to shoot but see what they intended doing. On any other occasion we should have treated the white flag with scant ceremony owing to their trickery on past occasions, but it being Xmas Day we thought we would wait and see what they wanted. They came just over halfway and halted, calling out to us, asking if an officer of ours [could] go out and speak to them. Without a moment's hesitation one of our officers, a Captain, jumped the trench and advanced to meet them, also unarmed. We saw them exchange cigars and then our officer came back and told us the Germans wished to keep up Xmas Day with them and that we were to meet halfway between the trenches. We agreed like a shot ... it may seem strange but the first thing we did was to shake hands all round, then followed an exchange of eatables.[22]

The Times of 11 January 1915 printed a letter from a 'piper in the Scots Guards':

We had a glorious time of it on Christmas Day. There was a keen frost and snow falling slightly. On Christmas Eve the Germans shouted from the trenches, which are only 100 yards from ours, in these terms: 'A merry Christmas, Scottie Guardie. We are not going to fire tomorrow; we will have a holiday and a game of football'. Our fellows agreed. Next morning, sure enough, the Germans came out of their trenches, and began to saunter over to ours unarmed. At this, our chaps went over halfway to meet them. They greeted one another like the best of friends and shook hands. You would have thought the war was at an end. We exchanged cigarettes for cigars, tobacco, etc. They brought over any so many things as souvenirs. A German officer gave me a button off his coat for my capstar. We were chatting all day. I was talking to a German who was four years in London. He could speak fine English. I asked him when did he think the war would be over. He said in six months' time. I remarked that they were getting the worst of it now; and he said that if they were beaten it was taking four countries to do it. They said they were getting tired of it. Them seem to be as well off as we are, and have plenty of everything. One German gave our officer a letter to post to a lady he knows in Essex. I had such a funny feeling talking to our enemy, who would seek to shoot us on the morrow; but there was another surprise in store for us. Next day they came over and stood up on the trenches. We could walk and go anywhere we liked ... I must say some of them were very nice fellows, and did not show any hatred, which makes me think they are forced to fight. I wrote you a letter telling you we made a bayonet attack. We lost a few men. The Germans helped us bury them on Christmas Day.

One of the longest and most detailed accounts of fraternisation is the latter, written by Captain Sir Edward Hulse to his mother on 28 December. It was reproduced in full in his posthumous book *Letters Written From the English Front in France*. Hulse describes a party-like atmosphere, conversations with the enemy and the exchanging of souvenirs.

Just after we had finished 'Auld Lang Syne' an old hare started up, and seeing so many of us about in an unwonted spot, did not know which way to go. I gave one loud 'View Holloa,' and one and all, British and Germans, rushed about giving chase, slipping up on the frozen plough, falling about, and after a hot two minutes we killed in the open, a German and one of our fellows falling together heavily upon the completely baffled hare. Shortly afterwards we saw four more hares, and killed one again; both were good heavy weight and had evidently been out between the two rows of trenches for the last two months, well-fed on the cabbage patches, etc., many of which are untouched on the no-man's land. The enemy kept one and we kept the other.

Few could ever have imagined a reasonably senior officer of a regiment of Guards, at war with an implacable enemy, engaging in such a way. After returning to the trenches for an excellently-provided Christmas lunch, Hulse went out again as the truce lasted throughout the day.[23]

The 2nd Border Regiment

After the battalion's part in the attack on 18 December, it was partly moved to billets at Sailly-sur-la-Lys. A and C Companies moved from Sailly and relieved B and D in the trenches on 22 December. The battalion diary for Christmas Day reads,

> In the morning the enemy in front of A and C Companies trenches signalled for an officer. One was sent over to their trenches and an armistice agreed upon till 4 p.m. for the purpose of burying the dead lying between the trenches from the night of 18 December. There was no firing on either side on this day, and the bodies were buried near the trenches.

The diary for Boxing Day said that B and D Companies relieved A and C, and that the armistice was still recognised, with no firing and the troops walking about on top as the communication trenches were so bad.

The *Sunderland Daily Echo* on 9 January included a letter from Sgt 9050 Charles Dobson:

> We had three days' rest in billets and then went back into the trenches for another four days. So while you were enjoying Christmas I was in the trenches. There was a vast difference during those four days, for instead of keeping sniping at one another we had a very peaceful Christmas. Somehow or other there was an armistice arranged and we were talking to the Germans, who met us halfway between the trenches. This gave each side an opportunity to bury the dead, who had lain there since the time of the attack. It seemed peculiar to be talking to the Germans, for some of them could talk English. We listened to them signing on

Christmas night, and some good singers they have. On Boxing Day it was still the same; they were out of the trenches again and some of them even gave our men chocolate and cigarettes. We got out [for our relief] without a shot being fired.

Dobson transferred to the Machine Gun Corps when it was formed in 1915. He ended the war as a company sergeant major.

The 2nd Gordon Highlanders

The war diary of this battalion appears not to have been delivered to headquarters, and the existing diary was compiled by reference to other units of the brigade. The entry for Christmas is of a very general nature, stating that not a shot was fired and that the dead were collected and buried side by side. Capt. Bertrand Gordon, however, submitted this report to divisional headquarters:

I beg to report for your information the following. The Commandant of the German forces immediately in front of my sub-section came out of his trench this morning at 10 a.m. I met him half way between the two lines of trenches. We agreed to bury the dead – any bodies of our men over the half way line should be carried across by their men and vice versa, so there was no possibility of viewing the trenches. This was done and all the dead have now been buried. I would like to point out that the Borders who made their night attack were intermingled with the German dead and would appear that they (Germans) made a counter attack. I observed the following: the regiments holding the points of the line immediately in front of my sub-section belong to the 15th Saxon Corps, 59th and 159th Bavarians [this was inaccurate information and was questioned by Division]. The men are mostly young but of good physique. I noticed that the majority of them carried hand grenades at their sides. Several of them showed me the 'Iron Cross' which they had received, which would make it appear that they had been fighting in other parts before coming here. I obtained information about Captain Askew, 2nd Border Regiment. He was in their trench firing his revolver when he was killed. Captain [Hanbury] Tracey, Scots Guards, was captured by them (wounded) and lived for six hours. His effects were taken off him and are being sent home to his wife by them (the Commandant gave me this information about the two officers). He said only seven prisoners were taken during the night attack on 18th. I am quite confident that none of the Germans approached our trenches and men were on observation in the trenches all day.[24]

The 1/6th Gordon Highlanders

This territorial unit only joined the brigade on 5 December. Based at billets in Sailly-sur-la-Lys, it spent Christmas Eve and Day digging. Two men were killed and three wounded on Christmas Eve.[25] Second Lt Spence Sanders recorded his experience in a diary. He had gone to France with the battalion as a Lance Sergeant and 'found he had been commissioned' on 18 November 1914. On Christmas Eve, he wrote:

> We left at 11.30 p.m. yesterday. At the dressing station a Borderer offered to guide us to our place on their left. He did but when we got there we found it impossible to enter as the German trenches were so close that it wasn't safe to get over the parapet. We about-turned and went along the communication trench. It took us hours to get into position. We had to come through a bad piece of trench with water in it and several man stuck. Spent a rotten night in a miserable little dug-out. This morning a man in Number 1 Section was hit in the shoulder – a nasty wound. It quite upset Petrie Hay – he was as white as a sheet and had to have some brandy. The poor devil [the wounded man] was suffering badly and will probably have to lie in the trench till night. The German trenches are only about 50 yards away and between are a lot of dead Germans and I believe Borderers through I haven't seen the latter. The General has just been along to tell us that we must leave an officer and men to mend the wire when we go out. That will be a rotten job for me, I fear.
>
> Christmas Day and a jolly queer Christmas too. Last night we had orders to move along to the right at 4.30. Some moved, then C and D Companies on the left said they were not ready as the 2nd Gordons had not come. A tremendous lot of trenches were left empty. I posted a few men here and there to keep up the fire and finally about 10 o'clock we got to our positions. It was a hard frost last night so we had a miserable cold time in our dug-out. The casualties yesterday were bad. Two men killed – one in D Company and one in F; several wounded, one in E badly in the shoulder. This morning the Colonel came down and the Padre – the latter was going to bury the F Company man. While talking to them an order came along not to shoot. Very shortly we found the Germans were getting out of the trenches and our men were doing the same. They walked across and met and talked to each other. I went over and talked to some. A tremendous lot of dead were lying about. Very soon an order came to return to the trenches but then another came to send our parties to bury the dead. The Germans did the same and we all mixed up and chatted. The dead were a horrible sight – nearly all Borderers left after the charge. The German dead had been there much longer I believe and were quite rotten. The Germans were a nice lot, though – as fed up as we are. There is to be no firing for an hour after the burying and unofficially I believe it is agreed that there will be none either today or tomorrow. I only hope there won't be – I have seen enough horrors for one day.[26]

Pte Edward Duncan of the battalion's E Company wrote home to Inverurie on 28 December. His rather lighter observations about the events were published in the *Aberdeen Evening Express* on 1 January 1915:

We spent Christmas Day in the trenches and it was one long to be remembered for a reason that you can hardly credit. We had a day off with the Germans, and had fun along with them in chasing a hare, and giving as well as receiving souvenirs. It seemed to be a mutual truce along our part of the line. Certainly, it was not official. The first that we knew about it was a few Germans putting their heads up above the trenches and some of the boys saying that they were out to bury their dead. A few of the enemy soon appeared clear of the trenches and before you could say 'Jack Robinson', they all came out and over the trenches without their rifles. Our boys were soon swarming up to meet them, and hand shaking ensued. We were not allowed to go near their trenches, so we carried their dead halfway across, and they carried our dead the same distance. Soon a hare made its appearance between our trenches and all joined in the chase. Not a man could refrain from laughing at the sight, as the Germans mixed with us in the scramble. Spontaneous laughter re-echoed all around, and the hare got clean away, so there was no trouble over who was to have the soup. A good few of them could speak English, and one of them was once a Sunday school teacher in Blackpool. He said they got bulletins issued to them every day, and they were told of a great German victory in Poland, and that they were to get 160 guns which had been captured from the Russians, up to help them. They had been waiting patiently, but no guns had come their way, so they are now fearing it was a bulletin of falsehoods. They are all fed up, and wishing it was over. Some of them were exceedingly smart looking chaps, and gave our boys cigs and chocolate, as well as drinks of gin. They said that if we did not fire, they would not, and the agreement was carried out. The day after Christmas, they cried across if we would play them at a game of football, but as no football was forthcoming, there was no match. The first night we were in the trenches they were crying across to us and singing Christmas carols, and taking spasmodic turns of shouting 'are we down-hearted? No!'

The 1st Grenadier Guards

The battalion moved forward on 18 December and held the line on the right of Scots Guards. They were relieved by the latter on 23 December, and moved to billets on Rue de Quesnes. Maj.-Gen. Capper and the Prince of Wales visited the battalion on Christmas Eve. The diary for Christmas only mentions the arrival of a draft.

The diary of 7th Divisional headquarters includes a note describing how Lt Oldfield of the Royal Artillery, a fluent German speaker, also went out into no man's land in the area of 20th Infantry Brigade:

He personally saw several men of the 139th Regiment and actually spoke to others of the 69th Regiment. He also saw men of the 22nd and 68th Artillery. The former he thought were Field Artillery and the latter Foot Artillery. Only officers and NCOs of artillery were seen, and he gathered the impression that they were observation parties. One NCO told him he was a telegraphist. They came out of the German trenches opposite the 'D' of 'Cordonnerie' [a crude way of identifying the location on a map]. In the course of conversation with an officer, Lieut. Oldfield learnt that the Germans lost about 50 men killed in a counter attack during the night 18–19th, either on left of the Scots Guards or on the Border Regiment. Lieut. Oldfield, who has lived in Germany for some time, met an acquaintance – a Feldwebel in the 22nd Regiment of Artillery. This man stated that they considered our shrapnel very deadly but that our 18-pounder high explosive shell was a joke and hurt nothing. He deplored the shortness in [that is, the lack of] artillery in this neighbourhood, and also said they were limited as to expenditure of ammunition. The health and morale of officers and men appeared to be excellent. They said they were well fed, and were convinced that Germany was playing a winning hand. They were very pleased with the news from Russia – they believe the Russians were running out of ammunition, and although they recognised that there were vast undeveloped resources in the country, they thought Russia would get such a blow in the present operations that they would not come again. They were confident that as soon as the winter was over they would be able to drive us back into the sea.

The 21st Infantry Brigade

The 2nd Bedfordshire Regiment
The battalion had left its billets in Fleurbaix and returned to the trenches on 22 December.

On the evening of 24 December at about 8 p.m. the Germans were singing in their trenches. There were numerous lights on their parapets, apparently on Christmas trees. A voice shouted from their trenches and could be distinctly heard, 'I want to arrange to bury the dead. Will someone come out and meet me'. 2nd Lieut de Buriatti went out with three men and met five Germans, the leader of whom spoke excellent English but was not an officer. He said he had lived in Brighton and Canada. This German said they wished to bury about 24 of their dead but would not do so at night as they were afraid of their artillery might open fire and they could not stop them and this would not be fair to us. No arrangement was made at the time. During the conversation the German said he belonged to the 15th regiment and gave Lt de Buriatti a postcard with the following information: the addressee was in the 3rd Battalion, 15th Infantry Regiment, 26th Infantry Brigade, VII Army Corps. The men also had 15 on their shoulder straps. The red band round their caps was covered with grey cloth.[27]

This morning, 25th inst, at 10 a.m., a German officer and two men unarmed came out of their trenches with a white flag and were met by Captain

H. C. Jackson and asked to be permitted to bury their dead, so we said we would not fire till 11.30 a.m. to give them time, and this was done. My men had already buried some on night of 24/25th. It was noticed that the German trenches are strongly held, their being a large number of men sitting on the parapet during the time the bodies were being buried. The men were a young lot from 19–25 years, well turned out and clean. I had given strict orders that none of my men were to go towards the enemy's lines without definite orders and that no one except those on duty were to be looking over their parapet. No Germans were allowed to come near our trenches. The German wire was closely inspected as previously reported. During the period that no firing was taking place, one of my Company Sergeant Majors was speaking to a German when an elderly officer passed. The German said he was the 'Divisioner'. This German also said they were very comfortable in a very nice village behind and he did not give the name! He seemed surprised that our troops were not an elderly reserve class. The general impression was that the Germans had had enough and were anxious for the war to come to an end.

The 2nd Wiltshire Regiment

This unit relieved the South Staffords and Royal Warwickshires of 22nd Infantry Brigade in the trenches on 19 December. It returned to the Fleurbaix billets on 21 December but then relieved 2nd Royal Scots Fusiliers in the front line on Christmas Eve. The diary reads,

> Christmas Day: No firing. An unofficial armistice took place and troops of both sides met and buried the dead. The battalion fixed up a board with 'A Merry Xmas' written on it in German, midway between the trenches, and was evidently much appreciated by the enemy. Boxing Day: No firing. Another unofficial armistice took place and Captains Makin and Beaver met some German staff officers and had a few minutes conversation.

The 2nd Royal Scots Fusiliers

The battalion relieved the 2nd Wiltshire Regiment in the trenches on 21 December but was relieved by the same unit early on Christmas Eve, whereupon it moved to billets in Fleurbaix.

The 2nd Yorkshire Regiment

The battalion spent the Christmas period in divisional reserve billets at Sailly-sur-la-Lys.

The 8th Division:
The IV Corps, the Rue du Bois to Port Arthur

The division had taken part in one of the attacks during December and continued to hold the line of the Neuve Chapelle sector.

The 24th Infantry Brigade

The brigade took over the division's A and B Lines on 19 December. After taking part in firing and actions in support of the Indian Corps' fighting to the south, the brigade began to report unusual activity on 23 December:

> About 4 p.m. Germans showed themselves over their trenches. No firing by mutual consent. Our men also showed themselves and finally small parties of both sides met and conversed in the space between trenches. After a very quiet night, on Christmas Eve, yesterday evening's conversation repeated in B Lines. Information obtained that enemy opposite belonged to 53rd Regiment, 27th Brigade, 14th Division, VII Corps. Once again the night was quiet, with the men rising to fine, frosty Christmas Day. Water reported to be rising on right of A Lines and flooding our trenches. Cause believed to be a German pump 150 yards south on La Bassée road. At end of A Lines a temporary truce established. Both sides buried dead and conversed between trenches. Captain Watts in B Lines was shot dead by the Germans when exposing himself.

A certain amount of shellfire fell on part of the brigade line during the night.

The 2nd Northamptonshire Regiment

The battalion left billets at La Gorgue and moved into the trenches of the division's B Line, in the afternoon of 22 December.

> On Xmas Eve, the Germans and our men got into conversation, eventually meeting in no man's land between the trenches. Cigarettes and buttons (non-regimental) were exchanged and one of our men even got to their parapet and looked in. The German private soldiers seemed very friendly and said they did not wish to fight us, eventually even cheering the English. Most of them seemed very young as was also an officer who also came and spoke to one of ours. They wished to have no firing on Xmas Day to which we agreed as far as concerned the two companies of ours (A and B) immediately opposite them on this part of their line. The cessation was to be form midnight to midnight. The next morning, 25th, acting on instructions from our brigadier, we again got into conversation with them and they admitted that they had suffered heavily from our artillery fire on the previous evening. They also sent over some cigars and bread. We sent them some papers. Further intercourse was stopped by superior orders, not, however,

before two of their officers sent us a letter* which was far from complimentary. The truce was, however, observed honourably by both sides. In the evening, the Germans decorated the trenches with lights and there was a good deal of singing on both sides. One of our Captains was killed in another part of the line about 8 a.m. on the 25th, but there seems no reason to suspect treachery. The battalion was relieved about 5.30 p.m. and went into its billets at the Red Barn.[28]

Transcript of German letter:

You asked us yesterday to temporarily suspend hostilities and to become friends during Christmas. Such a proposal in the past would have been accepted with pleasure but at the present time when we have clearly recognised England's real character, we refuse to make such an agreement. Although we do not doubt that you are men of honour, yet every feeling of ours revolts against any friendly intercourse towards the subject of a nation which for years has, in an underhand way, sought the friendship of all other nations, that with their help they might annihilate us; a nation also which, while professing Christianity, is not ashamed to use dum-dum bullets; and whose greatest pleasure would be to see the political disappearance and social eclipse of Germany. Gentlemen, you are not, it is true, the responsible leaders of English politics and so you are not directly responsible for their baseness, but all the same you are Englishmen whose annihilation we consider to be our most sacred duty. We therefore request you to take such action that will prevent your mercenaries, whom you call 'soldiers', from approaching our trenches in future. Signed, Lieutenant of Landwehr.

The 1st Worcestershire Regiment
The battalion had moved to La Gorgue when it was relieved by the 2nd Northamptons on the afternoon of 22 December. It returned to relieve the same battalion at 5 p.m. on Christmas Day.

No firing during relief at all. The 2nd Northamptonshire Regiment had arranged an unofficial armistice with the Germans till midnight, which we also kept. There was a certain amount of shouting, remarks between the Germans and ourselves and the Germans sang English and German songs most of the night which were applauded by our men. In spite of the armistice our sentries were kept much on the alert as usual. Next day there was practically no firing although the British guns fired a few rounds in the morning.

The 2nd East Lancashire Regiment
This battalion relieved the 1st Sherwood Foresters holding the A Lines trenches west of Neuve Chapelle, on 22 December. The war diary does not mention anything unusual on Christmas Eve except for the 'usual interchange of rifle

fire', and that the Germans were pumping water into the La Bassée road ditch, with water rising in the battalion's support trenches. Next day,

> The German began shouting Christmas greetings in the early morning and there was no firing throughout the whole day. During the afternoon some of our men and the Germans went into the open outside No. 1 Section to bury some German dead which had been lying there for some time. Battalion was relieved in the trenches at 5 p.m. by 1st Sherwood Foresters and marched to billets.

One was killed and two wounded on Christmas Day.[29]

The 1st Sherwood Foresters

After being relieved by the 2nd East Lancashires on 22 December, the battalion moved to reserve billets in the Red Barn near Richebourg. A draft compiled of an officer and 165 men also arrived. As it was under orders to return to the trenches on Christmas Day, the battalion celebrated on Christmas Eve instead. It reported that it consumed 1,100 plum puddings sent out by the county and city of Nottingham. The men began to move forward again at 4.15 p.m. on Christmas Day. By 8.20 p.m., the relief was reported complete:

> The quickest relief we have yet had due to entire lack of fire and to severe frost of night 24–25 December [making it easier to move]. An informal armistice was arranged between some of the Germans opposite 'A Lines' and the 2nd East Lancashire, and during this time both sides collected the dead in front of the trenches. Lieutenant Maclean Dilworth (killed 20 November] and L/Cpl Walters brought in and buried near battalion headquarters. The 2nd East Lancashires had also found body of Private 16768 John Clarke of the Sherwood Foresters, previously reported missing.[30]

The 23rd Infantry Brigade

The brigade took over the division's C and D Lines on 19 December. At 7.45 p.m. on Christmas Eve, it received a notice from the divisional headquarters that special vigilance was required, as it was thought the enemy may attack during the Christmas season.

The 2nd Devonshire Regiment

This battalion had returned to billets after the attack of 18 December. Knowing it was due to return, it held its Christmas celebrations on 23 December. The battalion returned to the D Lines' trenches between 5 p.m. and 7 p.m. on Christmas Eve, relieving the 2nd Scottish Rifles. It was in the front line until it was relieved on 27 December.

Informal armistice during daylight. Germans got out of their trenches and came towards our lines. Our men met them and they wished each other a marry Xmas, shook hands etc. About 7.30 p.m. sniping began again. We had one man killed and one wounded. Hard frost.

The man killed was 8316 Pte Richard Gregory.

A letter from Pte 4812 John Dymond was published in the *Western Times* on 14 January. He referred to an earlier letter in which he said he had been through a most terrible bayonet charge on the German trenches, which were captured, and that he had now lost all of his chums on the Western Front.

We have been having it fairly quiet the last few days, but we have had awful weather here. When in the trenches it is up to our knees in mud and water, and very cold: but we don't mind. We know we have got to do it, so we stick it with a joke and a smile. We spent Christmas Day in the trenches. We made an agreement with the Germans not to fire that day, and it was a sight that you would never believe unless you saw it yourself. First one German came out of the trench shouting out 'A merry Christmas to you English' and then one of our chaps went out to him, and they shook hands with each other. Of course, when the boys saw this they must all go out, until there was about fifty of each side out there exchanging articles with each other. We asked them what they thought of the war and they said they were fed up with it and will be glad when it is all over. They said 'it is not our fault we are fighting; we are the same as you, we have got to do what we are told'.

Dymond survived the war, in which he was awarded the Meritorious Service Medal for his actions.

The 2nd West Yorkshires

This battalion had also taken part in the 18 December attack, and in the meantime had some rest in billets. It moved forwards to relieve the 2nd Middlesex in C Lines at 6 p.m. on Christmas Eve. The diary only reports 'all quiet'.

The battalion's sergeant, 8878 Arthur Self, recorded his recollections in a paper that was printed in 1974, entitled 'A gunner in a ring side seat'. He said:

Just after breakfast in the front line a white flag appeared in the German trench. A bit later we responded and all firing ceased. A German office left his trench and met one of ours in the centre of no man's land. Speaking English he offered an armistice so that an unarmed party (stretcher bearers) could bury our dead lying behind the German front line. A Sergeant and six men wearing red cross armlets crossed over and carried out this task, which took about two hours. During this period I was able to bury the Lance Sergeant in a grave about four yards behind our front line. This was in full view of the German front line – no mourners, no chaplain, just myself – in a shallow grave and a small wooden cross. The task finished, I jumped down into the trench thankful that Fritz had kept faith to the truce. Later on, the burial party returned to our lines. There were no planes overhead, no observation balloons, no bombs, no rifle fire, therefore no snipers, just an occasional lark overhead. Just watching ... and watching, it was so quiet, it was uncanny, two forces facing each other in the muddy trenches, sentries posted at each periscope, which were put up without being shot at. The truce ended at 10 p.m. with a burst from a Maxim.[31]

The 2nd Scottish Rifles

The battalion was relieved by the 2nd Devons on Christmas Eve, and went to billets at La Flinque. The dairy makes no comments about the period.

The 2nd Middlesex

The battalion was relieved by the 2nd West Yorkshires in C Lines at 6 p.m. on Christmas Eve, and moved to billets at Pont du Hem.

The 25th Infantry Brigade

The headquarters of this brigade also received the 7.45 p.m. Christmas Eve warning order for special vigilance to be maintained. Fifteen minutes later, it was recording that the Germans had come out of their trenches and were saying that they would not fire on Christmas Day, as long as the units of the brigade did not fire. The Germans illuminated their trenches and lit some big fires behind them. Unsure as to the meaning of this, the brigade issued orders forbidding men to hold any communication with the enemy. Brigade reported that the next two days were quiet, with men getting out of their trenches and going to within 100 yards of the enemy.

The 1st Royal Irish Rifles

This battalion was only indirectly involved in the attack of 18 December. Four days later, its war diary said that 'after five weeks desultory trench operations and little to show for it', it had still suffered a cumulative ninety-five casualties. On 23 December, the battalion left its billets and relieved the Lincolns in E Lines; a draft of sixty-four men arrived and joined the battalion in the trenches. The Christmas diary is one of the most detailed of all the battalions that were in the trenches at the time.
Christmas Eve:

Nothing of importance occurred up to 8 p.m., when heralded by various jovialities from their trenches. The Germans placed lamps on their parapets and commenced singing. Various remarks such as, 'If you're English come out and talk to us'. Both British and Germans met halfway between respective trenches and conversed.

Message to the brigade at 8.30 p.m.:

Germans have illuminated their trenches, are singing songs and are wishing us a Happy Xmas. Compliments are being exchanged but am nevertheless taking all military precautions. Brigade reply: It is thought possible that enemy may be contemplating an attack during Xmas or New Year. Special vigilance will be maintained during this period.

Message to brigade at 11.45 p.m.:

Germans before my regiment state they will not fire until midnight 25/26th unless we fire. No shot has been fired since 8 p.m. A small party of one company met Germans half way and conversed. 158th Regiment, fine men and well clothed. They gave us a cap and helmet badge and a box of cigars.

Message from brigade at 12.35 a.m. on Christmas Day: 'No communication of any sort is to be held with the enemy, nor is he to be allowed to approach our trenches under penalty of fire being opened.' Judging by the battalion's diary, and the words of some of its men, this order had little effect.

Battalion diary: 'At dawn the Germans shouted out 'Merry Xmas' from their trenches and danced and sang in front of their parapets.' A message was received from division not to snipe unless sniped at, and that guns would not fire unless called for or if Germans fire. The line settled down, both sides doing work and singing but apparently not communicating directly with each other.

It is very doubtful how one should regard this curious soldier's truce. The German soldiers themselves are probably simple-minded enough about the thing but only time will show whether there is not something behind all this and whether we have not made a mistake in permitting this to take place. Captain O'Sullivan of B Company will fire his revolver at midnight, at which signal the truce ends.

This took place. It remained quiet during 26 December, but there was occasional firing. The battalion was relieved by Lincolns later in the day. A German deserter indicated an attack was due, and the battalion was turned out of its billets, only to be stood down again next morning. 'The deserter who caused the alarm *unfortunately* did not fall into the battalion's hands.'

During the month, the battalion sustained the loss of one officer, one NCO, and five men. The officer was Capt. Robert Patrick Miles, attached from the 1st King's Shropshire Light Infantry, who was shot dead on 30 December. He was taken for burial in Estaires Communal Cemetery. He had written home, just days before.

> We are having the most extraordinary Christmas Day imaginable. A sort of unarranged and quite unauthorised but perfectly understood and scrupulously observed truce exists between us and our friends in front. The thing started last night soon after dusk when the Germans started shouting 'Merry Christmas, Englishmen!' to us. Of course, our fellows shouted back and presently large numbers of both sides had left their trenches unarmed, and met in the debatable, shot-riddled no man's land between the two sides. Here the agreement – all of their own – came to be made that we should not fire at each other until after midnight tonight. There was a half-moon and the ground was covered with hoar-frost, and one could see dim shapes wandering about or standing round in groups, English and Germans, where it would have been death to have shown a whisker an hour or two before. The men were all fraternising in the middle (we naturally did not allow them too close to our line) and swapped cigarettes and lies in the utmost good fellowship. Not a shot was fired all night. He reports going out and seeing the German trenches ... I was disappointed to see such a cheery lot of fellows, as I had hoped to see a collection of living skeletons half covered with rags – animated toast-racks in uniform. The funny thing is that while we are fraternising here, swapping bully beef for bread and 'fags' for most execrable cigars (perhaps the gift of a box of these is a symbol of hate), one can hear the dull booming of guns and a certain amount of rifle fire going on in the same old sweet way on our right and left.[32]

The Tacoma Times, an American newspaper which printed Miles' words, said that, 'Of all the letters printed in the English newspapers none had breathed such a spirit of optimism none portrayed with such humour and intimate detail the life in the trenches as those of this officer.'

The Royal Irish Rifles commanding officer, Lt-Col George Brenton Laurie, wrote home, giving us not only a view of the truce but of the veritable feast of good things sent from home:

> Here we are, on Christmas Day! We have had a curious time of it. Last night, about eleven o clock, the enemy (100 yards only from us) put lanterns up on the parapet and called out: 'Do not shoot after twelve o clock, and we will not do so either.' One of our men ventured across; he was not fired upon, and was given a cigar and told to go back. A German officer came out next, and asked for two days truce from firing, but we said, 'Only one day.' Then we saw both sides, English and German, begin to swarm out to meet each other; we thought it wiser to keep our men in, because we did not trust the Germans, so I rang up the General to tell him this. We had to station sentries on the trenches to keep the men back; they were so

eager to talk to the Germans. Then I offered to go across myself and learn what I could, and finally the German General asked me to send one of our officers over to them. This I did, and gave the latter as an ostensible reason the Daily Telegraph of December 22nd, which I had got hold of, and which contained a very fair account of the troubles in Austria-Hungary and Berlin. He went out with this paper, met some German officers, and discovered a certain amount. They were very anxious to know if the Canadian Division had arrived, whether our trenches were very muddy, and told him that our rifle fire was good. We said that our rifle fire in general was our weak point, etc., etc. So now this is the queer position of affairs: we fire a pistol shot off at 12 midnight to-night by arrangement, and they reply with some shots over our heads, after which things continue to hum as before. You have no idea how pleasant everything seems with no rifle bullets or shells flying about. I need hardly tell you that we have kept our men ready in the trenches all the same, as we do not trust our friends further than we can see them.

As to other matters. (1) The pheasants and the partridges arrived in time, and we lunched off them sumptuously today; many thanks. (2) The chocolate arrived, and was distributed this afternoon to the men. (3) I enclose three Christmas cards. They are very hard to get, and you had better keep them as mementoes of this war. I am sending one to my mother. (4) Only 500 lbs of plum pudding arrived for our men this afternoon. If more does not turn up tomorrow, I will write to the A.D.C. of General Rawlinson to find out what has happened to the remainder.

Whilst we are peaceable, the guns are booming out now and then some miles away on our left and right where the French are fighting. I suppose we all thought from the Germans behaviour that they had something up their sleeves and are looking out for squalls. They said that their army was in Moscow, and that the Russians were beaten, and, moreover, that the war would be over in two, or at most three weeks, so we are expecting a push.

He continued in another letter on 27 December:

Our strange sort of armistice continued throughout yesterday. The Germans told us they were all Landwehr men, and therefore not obliged to fight outside Germany except as volunteers, and that they did not intend to fight at present. Sure enough, though we shelled them and fired at them with rifles, they paid not the slightest attention. Whilst the shelling was on, they dodged down in their trenches, and popped up again when it was over. We hit one with a rifle, but as they would not reply, we felt rather mean and fired over their heads. The relieving regiment [Lincolnshire], of which Mr. Brown of South Collingham is a member, said they would not go on like this. Curiously enough, they have done so. Leaving our trenches, we marched away gaily, getting in here about eight o clock, or a little later.

1/13th London Regiment (Kensington)

This territorial battalion had relieved part of 1st Royal Irish Rifles on 21 December, but only half of the unit was in the line and this was reduced to 600 yards in extent by handing over a portion to the 2nd Scots Guards on Christmas Eve. The diary for next day is uninformative, only saying that the situation was quiet. One officer wrote:

Being in the line at Christmas was an extraordinary experience. The evening of Christmas Eve was very quiet, after the first really fine day for a month. After spending the day at the Aid Post with violent diarrhoea, I and my batman went up and as it was very quiet, just dusk, and the communication trench very wet, we decided to go in over the top which we did. I found my platoon and had to move immediately. My batman collapsed soon afterwards and later we had to move again, so I carried him on my back, crossing a stream over a fallen tree being no easy matter. Shortly after settling in we heard a voice 'Englishman, Englishmen, Happy Christmas to you' and in answer 'same to you and many of them'. Soon Christmas trees all lighted up appeared in the German parapet and they started singing carols to which we replied. Later we heard that there was to be no firing till 5 p.m. on Christmas Day. Next day after stand-down we saw Germans walking about no man's land in groups, and as I saw some of our men out too and also the men of the Scots Guards on our left, I allowed my men to go in pairs and reconnoitred my own line 'on the top' finding that my only piece of habitable trench was separated by 150 yards of impassable trench on one side, and two hundred yards od deeply flooded trench on the other. I doubled sentries and one of our RE officers came down and examined the wire but the Bosche told him we could do what we liked behind the wire but if we did anything to the wire they would fire. So I constructed a new trench to the left of my company (which was 3 feet deep in water in 48 hours). The truce lasted all day and from the fraternisation we identified the enemy as 13, 126, 158 German Infantry. We were relieved by D Company the next night and went to billets at Laventie. Lieutenant Maltby had caught a deserter, who said that the enemy were going to attack that night.

The deserter was the cause of a widespread order for the British Expeditionary Force to go onto the alert during the night of 26–27 December.

The 2nd Royal Berkshire

The battalion spent Christmas in the trenches at Fauquissart.

At 7 p.m. [Christmas Eve] enemy ceased fire and an informal truce commenced. Communications by word of mouth taking place between our men and the enemy. Xmas Day. Men got up on parapet and advanced half way towards German trenches, and in some cases conversed with them. Orders given at 11 a.m. prohibiting our men from going beyond parapet. Much work done in improving trenches during this day. The enemy protested against barbed wire being repaired, and we stopped enemy from repairing theirs.

The next day, there was little or no rifle shooting although artillery opened fire. The battalion was relieved at 5 p.m. Boxing Day, but had its rest disturbed by the alert during the night of 26–27 December. Second-Lt Albert Raynes, an officer of the Royal Sussex Regiment, who was attached to the battalion at the time, wrote home to his parents in Nottingham on 27 December:

> I would not have missed it for anything. Xmas Eve was cold and frosty, with a lovely moon (ideal Xmas Eve). Soon after dark, we heard someone in the German trenches shout, 'Hullo, English, a Merry Xmas'. Soon all along the line of the German trenches, we heard 'English, we're friends tonight'. 'Don't shoot, we won't shoot'. We shouted back we would not fire. They then fixed small fires like toy lamps all along the top of their trenches and sat on the parapet. Most of them could speak English and shouted all sorts of things, asked for the latest football results, asked if we would like a song. We shouted back 'yes', whereupon they struck up the 'Watch on the Rhine'. The whole of the German line for a considerable distance took it up, and sang it with great gusto. When they had finished we struck up, 'Tipperary', then they sang an Austrian hymn and we replied with 'Rule Britannia'. Several Germans came half way, but none of our fellows went out to meet them during the night. [Next day] '… when a German walked towards us, one of our men went out, then another German carrying a bottle of something came out, whereupon another of our men went out to meet them. Both sides watched the four men approach each other, in silence they met and shook hands heartily. That broke the spell, the remainder of the men in the trenches jumped out and each side waved their caps and cheered wildly.

Raynes went on to describe the exchange of gifts and souvenirs, remarking upon how quiet things were until the battalion was relieved – with an exception of a shot accidentally fired on Boxing Day for which the battalion apologised. He makes no mention of the order prohibiting further dialogue.[33]

The 2nd Lincolnshire
The battalion spent Christmas in at Fort d'Esquin, Rue Masselot and Picantin. It had been relieved by the 1st Royal Irish Rifles on 23 December and relieved them in the front line four days later.

The 2nd Rifle Brigade
This battalion was in billets at Laventie. It had been relieved by the 2nd Royal Berkshire in the trenches at 4 p.m. on Boxing Day. 'An informal truce reigned.

No firing on either side. The opportunity was taken to do a lot of work in the open and mending wire.' As did most units, the battalion stood-to late in the day, on warning of the impending German attack. At 11.40 p.m., the British artillery opened a heavy fire. It was quiet for the next few days, and the battalion did more work on its trenches and wire. The enemy recommenced sniping at 10 a.m. on 28 December. A divisional order forbidding any further truce was received.

The 45th Brigade, Royal Field Artillery

A letter home from former Aston Villa football player, now gunner, 58071 Herbert Smart was reported in the *Birmingham Evening Despatch* of 4 January 1915.

'Come over', said one German soldier, 'I want to speak to you'. We didn't know how to take it at first, but one of the 'nuts' went over, and as no harm befell him others followed. But our commanding officer would not let more than three go at a time. I went myself on Christmas Day and exchanged some cigarettes for cigars. The German I met had been a waiter in London, and could use our language a little. He says they do not want to fight. Fancy a German shaking your flapper as though he was trying to smash your fingers, and then a few days later trying to plug you! I hardly know what to think, but I fancy they are working up a big scheme. But our chaps are prepared.

Smart's brigade fired 270 rounds at 11.30 p.m. on Boxing Day night, as part of the alert caused by the deserters' information. The guns of the brigade were located south of Laventie and south-east of Rouge de Bout.

An unnamed German officer, who began his statement by saying, 'My regiment was entrenched at Neuve Chapelle' and was facing the 8th Division, said:

On the 24th in the afternoon the activities on both sides died down and after nightfall cased completely. We had received mail, parcels and some Xmas trees from home. The choir of my company tuned up some Christmas songs. In the dugouts the men were awake, gaily talking, eating, reading and playing games. At dawn the officer on duty reported everything alright but strange, he mused, not a single shot was fired.

About noon a Sergeant rushed in. 'Captain, come out.' The British have started waving in their trenches, but no shooting and our men do the same. On both sides the trenches had come to life. The duty-free soldiers [that is, men with no specific duties that morning] stood upright on top of their trenches without arms, waved and shouted Merry Xmas. I ordered half the company back into the trenches, arm and reinforce the sentries, on the alert but no shooting and avoid any menacing movement. Meanwhile some soldiers had slowly advanced into no man's land.

Intensely we watched the strange sight when the soldiers met in the middle of no man's land, shook hands, talked and strolled about. Then a man of my company came running back and reported the British officer wanted to talk to me. Thus I gave my command to the officer on duty and marched off 150 yards to the middle of no man's land where I met two English officers, one Indian officer and one German officer of a neighbour company. We shook hands, wished Merry Xmas, agreed that both sides would abstain from any hostile activity until next day at noon, then we exchanged small presents like plum puddings, cakes, whisky, brandy and thus did our men. Finally some photos were taken for both sides. When daylight began to fade away, everybody returned to the trenches.

Next morning there has been no more meeting but also no shooting. After noon we lifted a helmet on top of our trench. It took quite some time before a bullet came – far and wide – as a warning. And thus we knew that the war had begun again.[34]

The 7th (Meerut) Division (the Indian Corps, from Neuve Chapelle to near Festubert)

The division, headquartered at Locon, was in the process of being relieved by I Corps. Two of its brigades were now in the rear area, and only elements of the 20th (Gharwal) Brigade remained in the line. On Christmas Day, it reported that all was generally quiet and that the Germans threw cigarettes into the brigade's trenches. At 3 p.m., an unauthorised truce took place and lasted about thirty minutes.

The 20th (Garhwal) Infantry Brigade

Headquartered in Lacouture, the brigade was relieved during the night of 27 December. On Christmas Day, after several days of intensive activity, it reported:

A quiet night, followed by a quiet day. During the afternoon the Germans and some of the 1/39th and 2/39th [Garhwalis] left their trenches and met in the intermediate space. It was found that the 76th Infantry Regiment occupied the trenches opposite and the 142nd was opposite the left of the 2/39th. The dead that were lying between the trenches were collected and buried: one Jemadar and four men of the 2/3rd [Ghurkas] and one Jemadar and one man of the 1/39th. Captain Robertson-Glasgow's body was also recovered from the German parapet. It was found that the Germans had three machine guns opposite the 'gaps'. Loopholes and wire entanglement of 1/39th were repaired.

The next day remained quiet.[35]

The 2/39th Gharwal Rifles

The battalion had been in the trenches for several days and faced the 16th (3rd Westphalian) Infantry Regiment. On Christmas morning it reported,

A cold misty morning, hard frost, water reported not rising. About 9 a.m., gunner observing officer came, and 4th Howitzer shortly afterwards stared shelling enemy's [water] pump. After three or four blind shells [that is, they failed to explode] he reported that he had dropped shells, as far as he could see, within five yards each side of the pump, and one shell a good deal nearer, and about ten shells within 15 yards radius, but it was impossible to estimate the damage. At 11 a.m. the Officer Commanding 5th (British) Brigade and the Commanding Officer and officers [of the 2nd] Worcesters came to see the trenches with a view to relieving us, though no actual orders had been received for relief. About 3 o'clock the Germans, who had since the morning been shouting and singing in their trenches, made signs to our trenches that they wished to communicate with us, and eventually they began to climb out of their trenches. We did the same, as did also the regiments on our right and left. Both sides fraternised for about an hour, several Germans coming over to our trench and talking and conversing by signs with officers and men. They gave our men tobacco, cigarettes and newspapers, and for about an hour both sides walked about freely outside their trenches and in the open space between the lines. Opportunity was taken to search for the bodies of the officers and men who were missing after the night attack on the enemy's trenches on the night of 13 November. Captain Burton found Captain Robertson-Glasgow's body lying on the parapet of the enemy's trench. The bodies of several men were also found near the trench, but the situation did not admit of a careful search sufficient to identify them. About 3.45 p.m. both sides retired again to the trenches, but little or no firing took place for the rest of the day, except an occasional shot.

The battalion reported that things remained quiet through most of the next day.

The 2/3rd Ghurkas

This battalion remained in the trenches at the beginning of the Chrismas period, in the area of Rue du Bois and Rue du Berceaux. There are only mentions that the officers of the British 5th Infantry Brigade came to reconnoitre before they relieved the battalion, and that the battalion stood-to in the general alert after the German deserter said that an attack was imminent.

The 2nd Leicestershire Regiment

The battalion was in reserve billets in Richebourg St-Vaast throughout the Christmas period.

The 21st (Bareilly) Brigade

The units of this brigade had been relieved, and were now in billets in the area of Paradis and Richebourg St-Vaast.

The 19th (Dehra Dun) Infantry Brigade

The units of this brigade were relieved by the 1st Guards Brigade during Christmas Eve and the early hours of Christmas Day. They were now in billets in the area Croix Marmuse–Cornet Malo.

The Indian Corps' 3rd (Lahore) Division had been relieved, with headquarters at Lozinghem and the battalions billeted in Allouagne, Lapugnoy, La Beuvrière and Auchel, and was not present in the front line over the Christmas period. The detachment of the Secunderabad Cavalry Brigade had also been withdrawn from the battlefield, and the men rejoined their respective regiments.

The 1st Division: the I Corps but temporarily under orders of Indian Corps, from Chocolat Menier Corner to Festubert

The 1st Guards Brigade

This brigade had also gone into the counter-attack between Givenchy and Festubert on 21 December and, on the evening of Christmas Eve, relieved the Dehra Dun Brigade and extended its line up to Chocolat Menier Corner. Its diary for the Christmas period is terse, with the entry for 25 December merely saying 'Quiet. No shelling.'

The 1st Royal Highlanders (Black Watch)

During the evening of 22 December, the battalion had moved from reserve at Cuinchy to take over trenches that had been occupied by the 1st Coldstream Guards and 1st Cameron Highlanders. Under much sniper fire, work was undertaken to bring in the wounded from recent fighting. The diary for Christmas only mentions that the royal cards were distributed before the battalion was relieved late on Christmas Day.

The 1st Cameron Highlanders

The battalion was withdrawn into billets half a mile south of Pont Fixe on 22 December. It was joined there by a draft of an officer and 161 men. At 8 p.m. on Christmas Day, most of the battalion moved to relieve the 1st Black Watch from north-west of Givenchy church, extending north to join up with the 1st Gloucesters of 3rd Brigade. The diary makes no comment about the situation.

The 1/4th London Regiment (London Scottish)
Elements of this territorial unit were holding the front line of Givenchy, with others in reserve trenches and redoubts. The diary makes no comment about the situation.

The 1st Scots Guards
The battalion moved into billets in Cuinchy on 22 December, describing the village as being 'in bits, but habitable in places'. At 7 p.m. on Christmas Day, half the battalion moved forwards to trenches 'at a farm, and north west of it, on the north side of Givenchy village. A bad place – some of the men having to be in farm building (nasty of shelled) and the trench in prolongation of it being very narrow and shallow. No casualties.'

The 1st Coldstream Guards
The battalion spent Christmas in brigade reserve billets at Cambrin.

The 3rd Infantry Brigade
The brigade had gone into the counter-attack between Givenchy and Festubert on 21 December, and reorganised the disposition of its units during 23 December. The Christmas period was spent attempting to improve the trenches, with the situation being relatively quiet other than occasional sniping. Work also began on pushing out a number of zigzag saps towards the enemy lines. On Christmas Day, the men of the brigade received their royal Christmas cards and tins. Pte 9790 Peter Fitzgerald, of the brigade's 2nd Royal Munster Fusiliers, was the lucky recipient of a unique tin, for it included a card saying that it had been packed by Princess Mary herself.[36]

The 2nd Royal Munster Fusiliers
The battalion was in reserve west of Festubert. It sent its A and B companies to relieve the South Wales Borderers – on the left of the brigade front – during Christmas Eve. The diary reports that Christmas and Boxing Day passed quietly.

The 2nd Welsh Regiment
The battalion remained in its front line, in the central sector of the brigade front. Its war diary for the Christmas period is missing, but some feeling for the situation can be gained from this message:

> On 25 December under instructions from the GOC [divisional commander] I sent Lieutenant Hollingsworth and 70 men to try to [illegible] the corner made by the road 150 yards west of the Lone Tree and establish himself there in the communication trench. His force came under a heavy fire crossing 300 yards

of open ground, losing four killed and one wounded. He almost reached his objective and established himself in a curve of the communication trench, but was himself wounded at this point. This valuable position was taken and maintained by Lieut. Hollingsworth and Company Sergeant Major Hays personal example and effort. The position so taken is very valuable. Private 10954 Hogan brought back a report from Lieut. Hollingsworth under a sharp fire. Captain H. C. Rees, commanding 2nd Welsh Regiment.[37]

The 1st Gloucestershire Regiment
The battalion was in the new front line – on the right of the sector held by the brigade – and remained in position throughout the Christmas period. The war diary only comments on inter-company relief movements.

The 1/4th Royal Welsh Fusiliers
This territorial battalion moved into reserve trenches near Festubert on 23 December, remaining there during Christmas. The diary reports Christmas morning as particularly quiet, but Festubert was shelled during the afternoon.

The 1st South Wales Borderers
The battalion remained in the front line until relieved at 6 p.m. on Christmas Eve, whereupon it moved to billets in Festubert. Next day, the battalion had the usual 'stand to arms at 6.30 a.m. Many men are sick with frozen and rheumatic feet. Day passes without incident. Royal Xmas cards, puddings and Princess Mary's gift issued to battalion. Quiet day.' Boxing Day was much the same until, at 5 p.m., the battalion moved to relieve the Royal Munster Fusiliers in the front line.
The division's 2nd Infantry Brigade had been withdrawn to Corps Reserve, and was in billets in the Essars–Le Hamel area during the Christmas period.

The 2nd Division (Festubert to Cuinchy)

The 4th (Guards) Brigade
The brigade headquarters moved from Béthune to Le Touret early on 23 December, and its battalions moved to relieve units of the 3rd (Lahore) and 1st Divisions. They found an enemy that could hardly be described as being in a festive mood.

The 2nd Grenadier Guards
The battalion relieved the 2nd Royal Sussex Regiment of 1st Brigade in trenches at Rue de Cailloux, after dark on 23 December. Before this could be

completed, some men of the outgoing battalion had to be dug out from the mud, and the guards found their new position to be waist-deep in water. On Christmas Eve there was

considerable sniping and bombarding with heavy trench mortars during early morning. Enemy sapped to within 10 yards in two points. About 11 a.m. they blew in the end of No 2 Company's trench and attacked at the same time. Numbers 2 and 3 Companies retired from trenches and occupied second line which was attacked. Attack driven off with loss. Communications between trenches difficult owing to deep water and mud. During night, dug new line of trenches. Lost: Captain Sir M. A. R. Cholmeley, Bart, and Second Lieutenant J. H. G. Nevill killed; Second Lieutenant C. G. Goschen wounded and missing; Second Lieutenant Mervyn Williams slightly wounded, and following NCos and men: 15 killed, 27 wounded, 5 wounded and missing, 2 slightly wounded, 4 missing. Total 4 officers 53 NCOs and men. During the night and into Christmas Day, very severe frost during night. Great deal of shooting all day. Relieved about 7 p.m. by 3rd Coldstream Guards and marched back to Le Touret and billeted.[38]

Given the ferocity of events on Christmas Eve, it is perhaps unsurprising that the battalion was not in a Christmas mood. Maj. 'Ma' Jeffreys writes in his diary:

Hard frost and ground as hard as bricks. Dykes frozen over. At daybreak a few Germans put their heads up and shouted, 'Merry Xmas'. Our men, after yesterday, were not feeling that way and shot at them. They at once replied and a sniping match went on all day.[39]

The 2nd Coldstream Guards

The battalion merely reported the trenches wet and the weather cold. Snipers caused a few casualties on Christmas Eve; the next day was quiet.

The 1st Irish Guards

The battalion was ordered to move forward and relieve the 41st Dogras (Bareilly Brigade), 1/9th Ghurka Rifles and part of the 6th Jats (Dehra Dun Brigade) on Christmas Eve. Supplies like plum puddings were provided to the men before relief began at 6 p.m. During the night, German flares and rockets lit the scene for their snipers who were active. On Christmas Day,

A patrol from Number 1 Company made a good reconnaissance under Sergeant Lynch up a disused British trench running straight towards the enemy and brought back some valuable information – enemy's trenches are about 250 yards off. The whole ground in front is a network of trenches as it has been fought over for some time with failures and successes on each side. There are many cross trenches and communication trenches which run straight into those held by the battalion. Fortunately it was a hard frosty night so the men, though cold, kept dry. Telegram wishing the battalion a Merry Christmas was sent by the Colonel. A letter was received from General Monro, and a message from the brigadier to the same effect. A quiet day was spent as regards shelling by the enemy, although they were bombarded by heavy artillery. Lieutenant G. P. Gough and Lieutenant F.H. Witts were wounded while digging trenches, the former in the hand and the latter, slightly, in his leg. There were also six men wounded. During the day Christmas cards were issued to the battalion from their Majesties the King and Queen.

The situation remained quiet on Boxing Day, although a further four men were wounded. Despite the weather, which worsened considerably next day, the battalion was not relieved until 2 January.

The 1/1st Hertfordshire Regiment
This territorial unit landed in France on 6 November 1914 and joined the brigade two weeks later. The battalion acquired the nickname of the 'Hertfordshire Guards', through their association with this prestigious formation. It left its billets at Les Facons Farm during the evening of Christmas Eve, and relieved part of the 6th Jats south of the Rue du Bois. The war diary for the period is brief, only remarking that Lance Sergeant 2301 Thomas Gregory and Pte 2701 Percy Huggins were both killed on Christmas Day.[40]

The 3rd Coldstream Guards
On Christmas Day, the battalion moved from billets at Rue de l'Epinette and relieved the 2nd Grenadier Guards in the trenches. No comments are made in the diary.

The 6th Infantry Brigade
The units of this brigade were resting at Caestre, before being moved by bus to Béthune and then by march, via Beuvry, taking over the southernmost sector previously held by the Indian Corps, on 22 December. All units reported continual sniping but little shellfire before they were relieved. No unit mentions any friendly arrangements.

The 1st Royal Berkshire Regiment
The battalion moved into the trenches east and north east of Givenchy. It reported the situation quiet until it was relieved on Boxing Day, although Captain George Wyld was killed near the battalion's support trenches by a stray bullet.[41]

The 2nd South Staffordshire Regiment
The battalion relieved the 57th Wilde's Rifles and a company of the French infantry, on a 1,000-yard frontage of the trenches east and south-east of Givenchy.

The 1st King's Royal Rifle Corps
The battalion relieved the 1st Connaught Rangers in the trenches east of Cuinchy (south of the La Bassée Canal) on 22 December. It was relieved on Christmas Day by the 1st King's (Liverpool Regiment), but only after suffering the loss of four men killed and thirteen wounded. Rifle and mortar fire continued unabated, and there is no mention of any friendly arrangements.

The 1st King's (Liverpool Regiment)
The brigade diary shows that, when the battalions took over this sector, the King's was held in reserve behind the 1st King's Royal Rifle Corps, on the Béthune–La Bassée road. The battalion diary for December does not appear to exist, but there is an extract from the private diary of Lieutenant-Colonel Charles Steavenson, who in December 1914 was a Major. The entry for Christmas Day reads:

> Hard frost at night. Very cold foggy morning. Church parade at 10 a.m. in the open. Orders to relieve the KRRC in the trenches, starting at 1 p.m., so had our Xmas dinner at noon. Lord Derby sent out an enormous hamper for the officers and one for the sergeants. The first company moved off at 1 p.m., the last with Major Steavenson at 4.30. Very good trenches, all of them paved with bricks of which there were plenty as the support trenches were in a brickfield. The communication trench with headquarters – 600 yards long – was paved the whole way. Very good dugouts for officers and men. All the men, especially those in support, had very good cover and were really more comfortable than they had been in billets. The KRRC were quite annoyed at being relieved.

The 5th Infantry Brigade
This brigade moved to the Locon–Lacouture area and relieved the Gharwal Brigade after Christmas.

Football in No Man's Land

Readers will have noted that football is scarcely mentioned in the official accounts. Some of the men who were there did not believe it happened at all. The practicalities of taking footballs into the front line and having somewhere one could play anything that resembled a game made many veterans sceptical. Pte 6618 Thomas Goodwin of the Northumberland Fusiliers had a letter published in the *Staffordshire Sentinel* on 6 January 1915. He was quite certain about it, but he also seems to deny that fraternisation had taken place, so is perhaps not the most reliable commentator:

> We had a rough time out there. We lost 1,200 men and 40 officers. My chum got a shrapnel straight into him. Don't believe all the letters you see about playing football in the trenches and shaking hands with the Germans. You dare not show your head out of the trenches or else you would get one through it.[42]

Many letters, diaries and memoirs bear witness to football having been played at Christmas, but not between the two enemy sides. These examples are typical: the *Yorkshire Evening Post* of 2 January 1915 carried a letter from an unnamed officer of the Rifle Brigade:

> We had an inter-platoon game of football in the afternoon, a cap-comforter stuffed with straw did for the ball, much to the Saxons' amusement. In the evening we said 'good night', and our men lit large fires in the trenches and sang songs, though I took good care to double my sentries, as I trust these fellows devil an inch [sic].

Pte 1125 William Farnden of the 3rd Rifle Brigade, writing to his parents in Leyton, talked in the *Chelmsford Chronicle* of 15 January 1915 of meeting the 139th Saxon Regiment: 'On Christmas Day we were out of the trenches along with the Germans, some of whom had a song and dance, while two of our platoons had a game of football.' Units behind the lines often reported Christmas football as one of the activities undertaken over the holiday period. One German soldier noted in his diary that the British opposite were grateful for the truce as they could play football again. This is all entirely to be expected, for the game was at a height of popularity and encouraged by the army.

But what of football with the enemy? In their masterly 1984 work *Christmas Truce*, historians Malcolm Brown and Shirley Seaton concluded that there was no question that football between the German and British had been at least discussed. A weight of evidence bears this out, but only to show that things rarely, if ever, progressed to the football match of truce mythology. On 2 January 1915, the *Hull Daily Mail* and other papers reproduced letters carried in the *Daily Telegraph*. One included the line, 'They [the Germans] wanted to play us [at football], but unfortunately we hadn't got one.' The *West Briton and Cornwall Advertiser* of 4 January included a letter from a colonel of an infantry regiment: 'For an hour I stood there: afterwards their captain and two subalterns came but, but I had left and did not see them. I said if they would have an armistice on New Year's Day we would play them at football between our lines – so that remains to be seen.' There are mentions of offers to play, refusals to play, orders not to play, men who wanted to play but could not get a ball, and more. Pte Frederick Mallard of the 3rd Rifle Brigade, whose letter describing the truce we have already seen, went on to describe how 'On Christmas Day we agreed to play a football match and we got a football, but their colonel would not let them play, so we had a bit of a game between us.' This is hardly the stuff of legend.

Company Sergeant Major, 1008 Frank Naden of the 1/6th Cheshire Regiment, gave an account that appeared in the *Cheshire Observer* on 9 January 1915, describing the extraordinary events that 'included football in which the Germans took part'. None of the British war diaries or German regimental histories, or even his own regiment's published history, mention anything, although the official accounts of both sides in this area are curiously short on detail.[43]

By 2 January 1915, British newspapers had reported that a football match had been played, with a score of 3-2 to the Saxons – a theme that comes up frequently thereafter, but almost certainly through men having read or heard that very headline. The information is said to have come from an unnamed officer of the Royal Army Medical Corps. There is no hard British evidence to substantiate it. The most persistent statement we have that something happened comes from the German side; in particular three officers: Johannes Niemann, Hugo Klemm and Kurt Zehmisch.

Niemann, who wrote on his unit's war and appeared as a veteran guest in BBC television programmes in the 1960s, was adamant that a game had taken place and that his side were the victors, winning 3-2. Klemm was from the same unit, the 133rd Infantry Regiment. At least one other letter from a man of this unit also mentions a game: 'We played ball with Tommy.' The regiment was holding the line in the area between Frélinghien and Houplines, facing the British 19th Infantry Brigade.

About midday Seiss, my batman, came rushing down into the dugout and reported that out there, between the trenches, friend and foe were mingling ... I thought briefly, then decided to go forward ... and was soon in the middle of the crowd. Everywhere hands were shaken. The soldiers opposite us were Scotsmen. We then exchanged everything we had with us - tobacco, chocolate, schnapps, insignia and many other things ... then a Scotsman produced a football ... and a regular football match developed, with caps put down to mark the goals. There was no problem, because the meadow was frozen hard. One of us had a camera with him ... Quickly the footballers formed up into a single colourful group with the football at the centre ... The game ended 3-2 for Fritz. During the football our soldiers soon discovered that the Scots had no underpants beneath their skirts [*sic*], so that rear views were clearly visible when the skirts flared up...

In other accounts, Niemann makes a point of reminding us that he saw kilted Scots. There were indeed Scottish troops in the 19th Infantry Brigade – the 1st Cameronians and the 2nd Argyll & Sutherland Highlanders. The former were not a kilted unit. Photographs of the battalion in the trenches during the winter of 1914/15 show them not only in standard trousers and puttees, but more often than not with gum boots, leather and goatskin jerkins. It is hard to believe that Niemann would have mistaken a Cameronian for a kilted soldier. The men of the Argyll & Sutherland Highlanders, on the other hand, only wore khaki aprons over their kilts, even in the flooded trenches of the Houplines sector. This does lend some credence to Niemann's account, but it is curious that the reports by the British unit and its men do not tally. We have seen (above) that even former footballer Jack Peters could only report forlornly that the thought was there, but that no football was actually played. James Jack, commanding a company of the 1st Cameronians, which were next to the Argylls in the trenches, wrote in his diary,

> It seems that on Christmas Day the 2nd Argyll & Sutherland Highlanders actually arranged to play a football match versus the Saxons … in no man's land that afternoon. Indeed, someone in my trench told me of the proposal at the time, but I scouted so wild an idea. In any case, shells prevented the fixture.

In other writing, Niemann mentions the 2nd Seaforth Highlanders, but this unit was some distance away.

Lt Kurt Zehmisch, of the 134th Infantry Regiment, made some notes in his extensive diary. It was only transcribed many years later, and is now held in the documentation centre at the In Flanders Fields museum in Ypres. In addition to his account of the singing, lighting of trees and tentative meetings in no man's land, he too referred to a game between the erstwhile enemies:

> Soon a couple of Englishmen brought a football out of their trench and a game started. This was all so wonderful and unusual. That's also how it seemed to the English officers. That's indeed the effect of Christmas, the festival of love, that the hated enemy should for a short time become a friend.

The diary also suggests that hopeful arrangements were made for a game the following day, but this did not take place as Zehmisch's unit was relieved. It was located opposite the British 10th Infantry Brigade, in the sector between the River Douve and St Yves (we have already seen that this was an epicentre of fraternisation, particularly around the 1st Royal Warwickshire Regiment). It may be significant that, in his diary, the battalion's Pte 8970 William Tapp wrote, 'we are trying to arrange a football match with them for tomorrow, Boxing Day.'[44] It would appear that this is the only instance where the mention of any kind of game of football is independently mentioned by men of each side. While it is inconclusive, it does suggest that something may have taken place, albeit far short of the mythology of football as the driver and centrepiece of truce.

There is a 1960s footnote to the way that football developed as a legend of the truce. In that decade, the BBC produced their important and enormously popular television series, *The Great War*. Dozens of veterans came forward in response to an appeal for anyone who had a story to tell. Among them was one Capt. Peter Jackson, an officer of the Wiltshire Regiment who recalled the tale of the truce including football. He said he had been a junior lieutenant at the time. With only a few minutes of screen time to be devoted to the truce, Jackson's piece was not used in the finished product. A few years later, another programme was produced, titled *Christmas Day Passed Quietly*. Jackson was invited to participate. This time so did Johannes Niemann, and after providing notes and being interviewed, they met with a film crew in France. Something did not add up. Niemann pointed out inconsistencies in Jackson's account and the latter was reluctant to be filmed. The BBC put it to him that all was not quite right, and that some background checking of facts had resulted in concern, and they wouldn't be using the film. Jackson confessed – he had not been an officer but an NCO. He had not enlisted under the name of Peter Jackson, but as 10932 A. E. Jackson. Nonetheless, he maintained that he had been there and his story was credible, but the situation was irretrievable and his story cut from the programme. These days, such statements can be checked in a matter of seconds: L/Cpl 10932 Albert Edward Jackson joined the 2nd Wiltshires in France on 11 December 1914. He was wounded in early 1915. It seems he was there during Christmas, but to what extent his truce and football story can be believed is a matter of conjecture.

10

Aftermath and Retrospect

Although truce conditions and general quiet remained for some days in certain areas, fighting had to all intents been resumed by 27 December. That night, a bad storm brought untold suffering and practical difficulties for the men in the trenches, and on the tracks and roads behind them. The River Lys rose by more than 3 feet, bringing serious flooding. It broke its banks along a 400-yard stretch between Frélinghien and Deulemont, making the area almost untenable for both sides. The Douve and Warnave also rose, and men now spent more effort on simple human survival than they did fighting the war. The 1st South Staffords, as an example, reported water 4 feet deep in their trenches near Well Farm.

The British Expeditionary Force carried out an important organisational development on 26 December, with the creation of a new level of command between general headquarters and the various corps. The new First Army was given to Sir Douglas Haig. One of his first actions was to order that no formal or informal truces would be arranged with sanction from his army headquarters. Further orders were given to those units not already doing so, to recommence artillery fire and heavy sniping on 28 December. The Second Army went to Sir Herbert Smith-Dorrien, whose attitude to the truce we have already seen. It is fair to say that hostilities had recommenced. On 30 December 1914, there was another significant German attack near Givenchy, in which trenches were lost by the British but later regained.

The extraordinary truces of Christmas were not isolated to the British–German front, but it appears to have been the sector in which such behaviour was most widespread. Similar truces took place on the Belgian and French fronts. No truce of noteworthy scale took place in later years, although localised incidents did occur – there was no repetition of 1914 and there never has been, possibly never will. There were signs of celebration at New Year. The 1st Rifle Brigade reported that, on 30 December 1914, they received a communication from the Germans regarding burial of the dead. A four-hour armistice was proposed for the next day to begin at 10 a.m. One officer from each side would agree a boundary line, which under no circumstances was to be crossed – there would be no fraternisation. The British dead were to be carried over the central line by German soldiers. There would be no firing or shelling between St Yvon and Le Gheer, and all of this must be agreed in writing by 8 a.m. on 31 December or it would not take place. In other words, this was a formality, and a far cry from the spontaneous truces that stemmed from men's curiosity and a Christmas spirit.

The lessons of December 1914 were clear enough to the front-line soldiers, as if these things were not already clear. The Germans held the initiative. They were on the defensive, taking every advantage of ground and trench-fighting technology to make life very difficult for any would-be assailant. The way to overcome them was not by making isolated attacks of pinprick size on narrow fronts where fire could be poured onto the attackers. It was certainly not to send unprotected infantrymen into an advance over deep, cratered mud and into barbed-wire defences that had not been swept away by artillery. It was definitely not a good idea to attack while one's army had a severe shortage of ammunition. The little it did have was shrapnel, and very little effort was made to destroy or neutralise the enemy's heavy firepower before the whistles blew. The deaths of over 3,000 men and the failure to make the slightest inroad into enemy-held territory, or provide meaningful assistance in diverting his resources, was testimony to this. Individual courage, of which on both sides there was never a shortage, was not enough. French and Foch already knew these lessons. They said as much before they went onto the offensive. Sadly for the British soldier, it took an awfully long time for the lessons to be learned and the political–military situation to develop to the point where Britain could resist requests from a key ally to do things that were not in its own interest. In January 1915, Sir John French still believed that operations to break through the German front in France and Flanders were feasible, given the sufficiency of high-explosive shells and of guns. He was right, but that point was not reached until 1918 when the military, production and political machinery was all working. By this date, the British nation and its hitherto immense financial strength was all but broken. Germany and France were of course also broken; their allies – Russia, Austria-Hungary and the Ottoman Empire – had ceased to exist. Millions of lives had been spent. One wonders whether, had the men who shook hands in no man's land that frosty Christmas morning had the gift of foresight, whether they would have ever returned to the trenches and opened fire once more.

APPENDICES

The British and Indian Dead of a Flanders December

The most reliable statistics regarding British and Commonwealth deaths in the Great War are those derived from the registers of the cemeteries and memorials in the care of the Commonwealth War Graves Commission. In the vast majority of cases, the date of death and regimental details are accurate. The numbers are of the men who died between 12 and 31 December 1914, inclusive.

No known grave	2,372
Identified graves	971
Total	3,343

The majority of those who died in the period have no known grave. Some of these men lie in the cemeteries listed below but could not be identified; the remains of many were destroyed in the battles of 1917 and 1918. Some still lie in the fields of Flanders, yet to be found.

Those officers and men with no known grave are commemorated on the following memorials:

Le Touret	989
Neuve-Chapelle Indian Memorial	650
Ploegsteert	376
Ypres (Menin Gate)	356
Arras Flying Services Memorial	1
Total	2,372

Those officers and men who are buried in identified graves lie in the following cemeteries:

Bailleul Communal	Hospital cemetery	71
Boulogne Eastern	Hospital cemetery	67
Lillers Communal	Hospital cemetery	44
Cabaret-Rouge	Post-war clearance	41
Bethune Town	Hospital cemetery	35
Le Touret	Battlefield plot	34
Ploegsteert Wood	Battlefield plot	29
Lancashire Cottage	Battlefield plot	28
Rifle House	Battlefield plot	27
Guards Cem, Windy Corner	Battlefield plot	27
Estaires Communal/Extension	Hospital cemetery	24
Calvaire (Essex)	Battlefield plot	22
Meerut, Boulogne	Hospital cemetery	21
93 other cemeteries	Various	470
Total		940

A large number of men died after they were evacuated to Casualty Clearing Stations or Base Hospitals. Those who died on the battlefield and who have a known grave are scattered into a great many locations. The single largest number lie at Cabaret-Rouge, a cemetery created when the battlefields were cleared after the war, and which is a considerable distance from the area held in December 1914. The men buried there were from the 7th Division (the Bois–Grenier front) and the 3rd (Lahore) Division (the Festubert–Givenchy front). The officers and men who died served with the following regiments:

Highland Light Infantry	189
Gordon Highlanders	144
Royal Warwickshire Regiment	141
4th Ghurka Rifles	140
Manchester Regiment	139
Scots Guards	124
1st Ghurka Rifles	115
Coldstream Guards	112
Loyal North Lancashire Regiment	100
Devonshire Regiment	87
Royal Munster Fusiliers	71
Royal Scots (Lothian Regiment)	70
Cameron Highlanders	69
West Yorkshire Regiment	65
Seaforth Highlanders	60
South Wales Borderers	60
Border Regiment	58

Middlesex Regiment	57
Rifle Brigade	56
129th Baluchis	55
Gloucestershire Regiment	52
2nd Ghurka Rifles	52
Northamptonshire Regiment	50
59th Scinde Rifles	50
131 other regiments	1,226
Total	3,342

The author is grateful to the Commonwealth War Graves Commission for the work of digitisation of the records, which has made such analysis and finding individual details so straightforward. As yet, the same cannot be said for the German dead. The *Volksbund Deutsche Kriegsgräberfürsorge e. V.*, a splendid, largely voluntary organisation, that takes responsibility for the registration of war dead and the care of German military cemeteries around the world, does not yet provide a similar database for public use. There are fewer German cemeteries within the area of relevance, but this is principally because the dead have been concentrated into fewer, larger cemeteries. Visitors to the battlefields described may want to visit the cemeteries at Illies, Aubers and Wicres.

Bibliography

British Official History, *History of the Great War Based on Official Documents: Military Operations, France and Belgium 1915*, volume 1

French Official History, *Les Armées Françaises dans la Grande Guerre*, Tome Deuxième

German Official History, *Der Weltkrieg 1914–1918 die militärischen Operationen zu Lande: Band 6. Der Herbst-Feldzug 1914: der Abschluss der Operationen im Westen und Osten*

Arthur, Max, *Forgotten Voices of the Great War* (London: Ebury Press, 2002)

Bottger, Karl, *Das Kgl. Sachs. 7. Infanterie-Regiment 'Konig Georg' Nr. 106*

Brown, Malcolm and Shirley Seaton, *Christmas Truce* (London: Leo Cooper, 1984)

Congreve, Billy, VC DSO MC *Armageddon Road: A VCs diary 1914–1916*, Norman, Terry (ed.) (London: William Kimber, 1982)

Cook, Arthur Henry, *A Soldier's War: Being the Diary of the Late Arthur Henry Cook*, (ed.) Lt-Col. G. N. Molesworth (Taunton: E. Goodman & Son, 1958)

Craster, J. M. (ed.), *Fifteen Rounds a Minute: the Grenadiers at War* (London: Macmillan, 1976)

Dunn, Captain J. C. (ed.), *The War the Infantry Knew* (London: P. S. King, 1938)

Falkenhayn, Gen. Erich von, *General Headquarters 1914–1916 and its Critical Decisions* (London: Hutchinson & Co, 1919)

French, Field-Marshal Viscount of Ypres, *1914* (London: Constable & Co. Ltd, 1919)

Foch, Marshal Ferdinand, *The Memoirs of Marshal Foch*, (ed.) Colonel T. Bentley Mott (London: William Heinemann, 1931)

Grieve, Capt. W. Grant and Bernard Newman, *Tunnellers* (London: Herbert Jenkins, 1936)

Hamilton, Andrew & Alan Reed, *Meet at Dawn, Unarmed: Captain Robert Hamilton's Account of Trench Warfare and the Christmas Truce of 1914* (Warwick: Dene House, 2009)

Hulse, Sir Edward Hamilton Westrow, *Letters Written from the English Front in France Between September 1914 and March 1915* (privately printed, 1916)

Juergs, Michael, *Der kleine Frieden im Grossen Krieg* (Munich: Goldmann, 2005)

Laurie, G. B., *Letters of Lt-Col. George Brenton Laurie* (privately printed by Gale & Polden, 1921)

Merewether, J. W. B. & the Rt-Hon. Sir Frederick Smith, *The Indian Corps in France* (London: John Murray, 1919)

Niemann, Johannes, *Das 9. Königlich Sächsische Infanterie-Regiment Nr. 133. im Weltkrieg, 1914-18*

Reith, John (the Rt Hon Lord Reith of Stonehaven), *Wearing Spurs* (London: Hutchinson & Co., 1966)

Sheffield, Gary & John Bourne (eds), *Douglas Haig: War Letters and Diaries, 1914–1918* (London: Weidenfeld & Nicolson, 2005)

Solleder, Fridolin, *Vier Jahre Westfront: Geschichte des Regiment List RIR 16* (Munich: Schick, 1932)

Terraine, John (ed.), *General Jack's Diary* (London: Eyre & Spottiswoode, 1964)

Verney, David (ed), *The Joyous Ptriot: The Correspondence of Ralph Verney, 1900–1916* (London: Leo Cooper, 1989)

War Office, *The Manual of Military Law 1914* (London: HMSO, 1914)

War Office, *The Statistics of the Military Effort of the British Empire During the Great War 1914–1920* (London: HMSO, 1922)

Winnifrith, Douglas P., *The Church in the Fighting Line: With General Smith-Dorrien at the Front, Being the Experiences of a Chaplain in Charge of an Infantry Brigade* (London: Hodder & Stoughton, 1915)

Wittkop, Philip (ed.) *German Students' War Letters* (Philadelphia: Pennsylvania Press, 2002)

Anonymous, *Historique du 142e Régiment D'infanterie Pendant la Grande Guerre* (Paris: Berger-Lavrault, undated)

The war diaries of the British and Indian units and formations are all held at the National Archives, Kew, London in the document series WO95. In addition to the specific works mentioned above, the published regimental and battalion histories of all units mentioned in the text have also been consulted. In the majority of cases, they rely very heavily on the information given in the war diaries.

Endnotes

Prologue

1. 'War Christmas at the Post Office', *The Times*, 22 December 1914, p. 5.
2. National Archives, WO161/114, *Organisation and Development of the Army Postal Service*.
3. Reported in the *Daily Mirror* and many other newspapers,1 January 1915.
4. Private papers of Pte 1681 Walter 'Wally' Mockett, stretcher bearer with the Queen's Westminster Rifles (1/16th London Regiment). Liddle Collection, GS/1121. He was taken prisoner of war in the battalion's attack at Gommecourt on 1 July 1916.
5. Total of names listed by the Commonwealth War Graves Commission for British Army deaths in France and Belgium between 12 and 31 December 1914. *Statistics of the British Effort* shows that, in addition to the deaths, over 6,500 men were wounded in the month of December 1914.

Chapter 1

1. Lt John Reith, later Lord Reith, the first director general of the BBC, in his memoir *Wearing Spurs*. Reith was present throughout the events described in this book.
2. There is a small enclave of the Belgian province of Hainault in the Ploegsteert area, and in the area of relevance to the fighting of December 1914. For simplicity's sake, we will also refer to this as being part of Flanders.
3. First Ypres was fought by the British I and IV Corps, with the French IX Corps joining soon after the start. French XVI Corps, cavalry and various other divisions joined in the later stages.
4. A copy of the order is included in the war diary of III Corps.
5. Sir John French, *1914*, pp. 303–304.
6. French, *1914*, p. 306.
7. French, *1914*, p. 301.
8. Ferdinand Foch, *Memoirs*, pp. 204–5.
9. War Diary, III Corps General Staff.
10. The British official history mentions that eight German infantry divisions and four cavalry divisions had left for the East by early December 1914.

11. Foch, *Memoirs*, p. 213.
12. French, *1914*, p. 307.
13. Liddle Hart Centre for Military Archives, Howell Papers IV C 3 11527, February 1915. The GHQ staff was based in Saint-Omer, with the operations section at 15 Rue Henri Dupuis, and intelligence in nearby Rue Victor Hugo. It also had a report centre (or field office) closer to the fighting at Bailleul, but apparently only open from 9 a.m. to 4.30 p.m., with the staff returning to St-Omer each evening. The quote about Murray is from Brig.-Gen. Philip Howell to his wife.
14. Copy in war diary of III Corps General Staff, National Archives WO95/668.
15. Paul-Francois Grossetti was born in Paris in 1861, but of Corsican background. He was the product of the military college of St-Cyr and veteran of campaigns in Africa, Algeria and Tonkin. In command of 42nd Division in the early months of the war, including at the Marne and Yser, Grossetti died of dysentery aged fifty-six on 7 January 1918. He had a reputation as a front-line commander and a fireball. Foch said of him in 1915, '*Mes généraux: d'Urbal, de Maud'huy, des héros. Grossetti: invulnérable! Toujours sous la mitraille, au milieu des balles. Elles ne le touchent pas. Quel homme!*' (My Generals d'Urbal, de Maud'huy: heroes. Grosseti: invulnerable! Always under fire, where the bullets are [flying]. They do not touch him. What a man!)
16. WO95/668, handwritten draft, 15 December 1914 and memorandum dated 11 December 1914. Brig.-Gen. John du Cane, of III Corps General Staff, drafted an order for an attack to be carried out by 4th Division in the direction of Warneton from St Yves, with the intention of assisting the II Corps attack on Messines and protecting its southern flank. He also stressed that while III Corps was in a holding role until Messines fell, it must act with vigour. His commander, Lt-Gen. Sir William Pulteney, would not let du Cane issue the order, on the basis that it was not what Sir John French had specified.

Chapter 2

1. Present when the December offensive began were the 1st, 2nd, 3rd, 4th, 5th, 6th, 7th, 8th Divisions, organised into the I, II, III and IV Corps; the 3rd (Lahore) and 7th (Meerut) Divisions of the Indian Corps; the 1st, 2nd and 3rd Cavalry Divisions of the Cavalry Corps; and the 1st Indian Cavalry Division. 27th Division and 2nd Indian Cavalry Division arrived later in the month. On 19 December 1914, the force comprised 9,610 officers and 260,101 men, according to *Statistics of the Military Effort of the British Empire*.
2. The standard term of engagement for a man joining an infantry regiment of the regular army was twelve years. They would spend the first seven years on full-time service and then go onto reserve. He would only be obliged to attend annual rifle training. A man could then extend this reserve service by four more years (this was Section D Reserve). Such reservists were called up at the declaration of war, and some of them had been out of full-time service for as long as nine years.
3. An extreme case is thirty-one-year-old married stonecutter Pte S/7569 John Tait, who lived at Causeway Head in Stirling. He had some prior experience, in that he had served in the regiment's 2nd Volunteer Battalion, but this was a part-time activity in a unit that ceased to exist in 1908. John re-enlisted on 22 November 1914, went to France with a draft on 3 December and was dead eleven days later. His wife was pregnant with their second child when John was killed.

4. A subaltern is a second lieutenant or lieutenant. In many regular battalions, they were regarded by other officers as the lowest of the low, and although they were in command of Platoons, they were not usually given the degree of battlefield responsibility, authority and latitude than would be the case by 1918.

5. The battalions that had arrived were the 4th London Regiment and 4th Royal Welsh Fusiliers (allotted to 1st Division); 1st Hertfordshires and 9th Highland Light Infantry (2nd); 1st Honourable Artillery Company and 10th King's (Liverpool Scottish) (3rd); London Rifle Brigade and 2nd Monmouthshires (4th); 6th Cheshire (5th); Queen's Westminster Rifles (6th); 6th Gordon Highlanders and 8th Royal Scots (7th); 5th Black Watch and 13th Londons (Kensington Battalion) 8th Division.

6. National Archives, WO95/1650.

Chapter 3

1. Reports were received of a German attack against the French at Ecurie, north of Arras, that took place on 27–29 November 1914. They had used saps, small trenches running forward into no man's land, to get their infantry as far forward as possible before the assault. The German sapped under the barbed wire entanglements, within 5 yards of the French trenches.

2. The incident is mentioned in the war diary of 20th Infantry Brigade and the man traced from the records of the Commonwealth War Graves Commission. Twenty-six-year-old married man Waring, who lived in Sheffield, is buried in Rue-Pétillon Military Cemetery.

3. By 21 December, commanders were being asked to consider their options should further abnormal rainfall render the entrenched area completely untenable. It was considered that the Ploegsteert front, Romarin, river Layes and Lawe were particularly problematic. Brig.-Gen. John du Cane, of III Corps General Staff, suggested that 4th and 6th Divisions consider abandoning the continuous trenches in favour of a line of defended posts and cottages some distance behind the existing line.

4. National Archives WO95/1501, War Diary of 12th Infantry Brigade Headquarters. The 2nd Essex Regiment on the left, 1st King's Own on the right.

5. National Archives WO95/1501, War Diary of 12th Infantry Brigade Headquarters. 2nd Essex Regiment on the left, 1st King's Own on the right.

6. National Archives, WO95/1506. The Monmouthshire War Diary reports that this was a long stretch of line, 1,100 yards in extent, 'between the Warnave stream and the railway line on the road running NW from Frélinghien'. This centers the line on grid map reference C.4.a.4.8 (map 36NW2), a crossroads at Estaminet du Bon Coin, between the hamlets of Le Touquet and Le Gheer.

7. The German unit was fifteen. *Königlich Sächsisches Infanterie-Regiment Nr. 181*, raised in Chemnitz and, since 6 October 1914, under command of Oberst Freiherr von Welck. It had played a central part in capturing the city of Lille in October 1914 and, in later years, saw action against British and Commonwealth forces at High Wood on the Somme (1916), Wytschaete (1917) and Cambrai (1918).

8. Lumley Owen Williames Jones was later promoted to brigadier-general. He died of pneumonia in September 1918.

9. Walter Percy Spooner had gone to France with the original contingent of the battalion in August 1914. He was later awarded the Military Cross and survived the war. Terence A. C. Brabazon was wounded in May 1915, and

subsequently saw service in Gallipoli before returning to France. He was wounded on 1 July 1916. He succumbed to his wounds on 3 August. Sgt 8530 Richard Valentine Flin was commissioned as an officer in January 1918.

10. The Army Act 1913, sections 4 and 5, quoted in the Manual of Military Law 1914.

Chapter 4

1. The fifty-two-year-old Haldane had only taken command of 3rd Division on 21 November 1914. He replaced Maj.-Gen. Hubert Hamilton, who had been killed in action and was promoted to divisional command at that time, having begun the war leading a brigade of 4th Division. A very experienced soldier who had seen action in earlier wars, Haldane was often reported to be a rather hard and unforgiving character.

2. William Hely Bowes, aged fifty-five, had been born in France. Commissioned into the Royal Scots Fusiliers in 1879, he was an experienced regimental and staff officer. Bowes began the war in the Directorate of Staff Duties at the War Office, but took command of 8th Infantry Brigade on 23 October 1914.

3. Ranging was a process of firing a number of shots at a known target. The fall of each shot was observed from ground and air, and suitable corrections made until the shots were hitting the target. Once this was achieved, the gun settings were known for firing from the current position onto that target. Ranging usually gave away all pretence at surprise, for the enemy knew that the target was the subject of ranging.

4. The casualties included ten men killed and eight wounded from the 1st Loyal North Lancashire Regiment, which was resting in billets miles behind the lines at Hazebrouck on 6 December. A German aeroplane dropped three bombs onto the billet of C Company. The explosion also killed eight civilians, of whom two were children.

5. Second-Lt Samuel Shorten Arthur Wade is listed at the Le Touret Memorial. He had been ill and had been ordered to go to hospital, but a man who had returned from the attack brought back a cap that was identified as his. It was riddled by a bullet. The courageous thirty-eight-year-old Wade had chosen to go into action rather than seek treatment in hospital. A private of his battalion wrote to Wade's widow: 'Mr. Wade said to me, "Come on, my lad; it only wants one to lead", and Mr. Wade and I set off, getting well in front of the company. We got to a German dummy trench, and I jumped in, and lying down turned round looking for the officer. I heard he was wounded, and asked if he was attended to they said, "No," and I got up and retired to the officer, and got him out of the trench and dressed him, seeing that he was hit in the head, and in my idea the officer was dead when I left him.' Samuel Wade had enlisted in 1895. A veteran of the Boer War, he was commissioned from the ranks in November 1914. From *The Bond of Sacrifice: A Biographical Record of all British officers who Fell in the Great War.* Vol. 1. 1917. Reprint.

6. Pirie is buried in Bailleul Communal Cemetery. He had recently been commissioned, having previously been a company sergeant major.

7. Capt. Hon. H. L. Bruce has no known grave and is commemorated at the Ypres Memorial (Menin Gate). According to one report (The Bond of Sacrifice) he was shot in the forehead by a German concealed in a dugout, while he was climbing out of a trench to lead his men on to the next trench. Wing would also lose his life in the war, killed while commanding 12th (Eastern) Division in 1915.

8. Gary Sheffield and John Bourne (eds), *Douglas Haig: War Letters and Diaries 1914–1918*, p. 85.

9. A quotation from a statement made about the attack by the Royal Newfoundland Regiment on 1 July 1916: 'It was a magnificent display of trained and disciplined valor, and its assault only failed of success because dead men can advance no further'. The sentiment applies perfectly to the 8th Infantry Brigade's attack on 14 December 1914.

10. The battalion war diary reports that they undertook this work 21–29 June 1917.

11. Dobie had joined the battalion with a draft on 5 December. MacWilliam had joined the battalion on the Marne in September 1914, and had only just returned to action after recovering from a wound he sustained on 12 October. He had been promoted to lieutenant three days before he died.

12. The same is true of the 1st Lincolns, who had attacked Petit Bois on 8 December. Only one man who died of wounds has a known grave. Fifteen others are listed at the Ypres Memorial (Menin Gate) and Wade at Le Touret.

13. The 32nd Division, raised in Perpignan, has an obelisk memorial on the lane that runs past Godezonne Farm cemetery. It records the division's exploits in this area between late October 1914 and early January 1915.

14. The letter was reproduced in the *Aberdeen Journal* on Saturday 26 December 1914. George Gleghorn had arrived in France on 27 November 1914. He was killed in action on 27 May 1915.

15. It is instructive to compare the 'guns per yard' ratio of this attack with that employed in the Battle of Neuve Chapelle in March 1915. For the Wytschaete action, II Corps had 103 guns and howitzers firing on a front of 1,250 yards, or 0.08 guns per yard. At Neuve Chapelle, IV Corps had 0.17 – twice as many. The attack succeeded.

16. Commissioned from the Royal Military Acadamy in 1912, Hew Ross Kilner was awarded the Military Cross in the 1916 King's Birthday Honours, ending his service as a major. He was knighted in 1947 and was, at that time, deputy chairman and managing director of Vickers-Armstrong.

17. National Archives, WO95/1390.

18. A. Clutterbuck, *The Bond of Sacrifice, Vol. 1*.

19. Reports vary. The battalion war diary says sixty Germans were captured; the official history reduces it to forty-two. II Corps sent a message of congratulations.

20. Henry Howey Robson was born in South Shields in May 1894. His Victoria Cross was gazetted in 18 February 1915. He was the first soldier to be made a Freeman of the Borough of South Shields. Robson later emigrated to Canada, where he died in 1964.

21. The full title of this unit is *Königlich Bayerisches Infanterie-Regiment Nr. 18 'Prinz Ludwig Ferdinand'*. It was under command of the 6th Bavarian Infantry Brigade of 3rd Bavarian Division, of II Bavarian Corps. The regiment was raised in Landau-in-der-Pfalz and, in December 1914, was commanded by Generalleutnant Otto Ritter von Breitkopf.

22. Sheffield and Bourne, *Haig Letters and Diaries*, p. 84. Haig's note reminds the author of the entry for 1 July 1916, when Haig recorded his belief that 'few of the VIII Corps had left their trenches'. In fact, they had died in their thousands that day.

23. Rupprecht's Diary, *In Treue Fest Vol 1*, p. 276.

24. French, *1914*, p. 322.

25. Billy Congreve and Terry Norman [ed.], *Armageddon Road: a VC's Diary, 1914–1916*. Congreve was an exceptional regimental and staff officer who

earned the Victoria Cross, Distinguished Service Order and Military Cross before being killed, in 1916, at the age of twenty-five.

26. National Archives, WO95/668. Copy in war diary of III Corps General Staff.
27. French official history, *Tome II*, p. 255.
28. National Archives, WO95. Copy in IV Corps General Staff war diary, Army Operation Order Number 40, issued 17 December 1914.

Chapter 5

1. Capper was accidentally wounded by a 'jam tin' bomb in April 1915 and was killed in action during the Battle of Loos in the September of that year.
2. The British called it the Aubers ridge.
3. It is marked on early maps as Ferme Vanbesien.
4. Neame had already been recommended for his work on the night of 15–16 November when laying out barbed-wire defences under fire.
5. The war diary of divisional headquarters states that the man was Pte Heinrich Schmidt of 1 Battalion of the 15th Infantry Regiment, 26th Brigade, 13th Division.
6. Lawford had been in the same Sandhurst intake as Douglas Haig, but was apparently not of quite the same calibre. Haig passed in first place with Lawford trailing in at 40th. Nonetheless, during his First World War service, he proved to be a very capable general. It appears that a nickname used for him was 'Swanky Syd'. He was the father of actor Peter Lawford.
7. *Infanterie-Regiment Graf Bülow von Dennewitz (6. Westfälisches) Nr. 55*, which was raised in the Detmold –Bielefeld area. A few days before, the Queen's had taken a prisoner of the *Königin Augusta Garde-Grenadier-Regiment Nr. 4*, who had been attached to the 55th.
8. National Archives, WO95/1664.
9. Almost all of the men of the two battalions have no known grave today, and are listed at the Ploegsteert Memorial. Lt-Col. Brewis, Second-Lt Benjamin Standring, and two men of the 2nd Royal Warwickshire Regiment, are buried in Sailly-sur-la-Lys churchyard. Just one of the 2nd Queen's has a known grave – Pte L/10669 Edward Jones lies in Y Farm Military Cemetery. It is evident that those men buried during the ceasefire were lost or destroyed at a later date.
10. National Archives, WO374/59326, service record of Charles Gardner Rought. The text is from his own notes, explaining the circumstances of his capture. A completely inexperienced soldier, Rought was well-known before the war as a rower of international standard, and was one of the coxed four that won a gold medal for Great Britain at the 1912 Olympic Games. He enlisted into the Artist's Rifles on 4 August 1914 (the day that war was declared), and was sent to France on 28 October 1914. The 2nd Queen's war diary describes him as one of four probationary second lieutenants who joined on 13 November. Rought remained in enemy hands until returning to England on 20 November 1918. Second-Lt Edward Atherstone Walmisley was even less experienced, for he only landed in France on 10 December and joined the battalion three days later. Twenty-one-year-old Lt Duncan Gavin Ramsay was killed in the attack and, according to Commonwealth War Graves Commission records, was originally buried in the churchyard at Fleurbaix, implying his body was brought in from no man's land. Ramsay was an officer of the Royal Sussex Regiment, attached to the 2nd Queen's from 12 November 1914.
11. Twenty-year-old Sandhurst educated Henry Raymond Syndercombe Bower has no known grave. He is commemorated at the Ploegsteert Memorial.

12. Heyworth had been appointed to command the brigade on 13 November 1914. He was killed in action on 9 May 1916 at the age of fifty-three, while in command of the 3rd Guards Brigade. He lies in Brandhoek Military Cemetery.

13. Both men were experienced and reliable officers – Askew was a veteran of the Second Boer War.

14. Imperial War Museum, 73-141-1, private papers of Harold Douglas Bryan. Bryan survived the war after being wounded three times. He had just returned to service after recovering from his first wound, which occurred on 26 October 1914. He was one of six brothers who served. His recollection that the Scots Guards held the enemy trench for three days is flawed.

15. Rather unusually, the 2nd Scots Guards named its four companies as F, G, RF (Right Flank) and LF (Left Flank).

16. Ottley was mortally wounded by a bullet to the neck. He died three days later at the Australian Voluntary Hospital at Wimereux. The son of RADM Sir Charles Ottley, he is one of the few men whose body was repatriated home before this practice was officially halted. He is buried in St Andrew's churchyard in Fort William. His promotion to Captain, which he applied for before the attack, came through shortly afterwards.

17. The records of the CWGC list forty-four men who died, although three including Henry Askew are shown to have died on 19 and 20 December. This is possibly at odds with the war diary, which reports that Askew was killed 'on top of the enemy's trenches'. Only three of these men have a known grave, and all are buried in distant locations that imply their remains were found after the war. The number of deaths is a little higher, if we count those who died of wounds after 20 December. They include Capt. Cameron Lamb, who was wounded in the first wave of the attack. He died of his wounds on 29 December and is buried in Wimereux. L/Cpl Brewer and Pte Clarke both received the Distinguished Conduct Medal for bringing Lamb back to British lines under heavy enemy fire.

18. Abraham Acton was killed in action at the age of twenty-one, on 16 May 1915. He has no known grave and is commemorated at the Le Touret Memorial. James Smith survived the war and passed away in 1968.

19. Sir Edward Hamilton Westrow Hulse, *Letters Written from the English Front in France Between September 1914 and March 1915*.

20. *Infanterie-Regiment Herwath von Bittenfeld* (1. Westfälisches) *Nr. 13*, raised in the area of Münster. This unit also faced the 23rd Infantry Brigade at Neuve Chapelle.

21. Sgt 2355 William Goff and Pte 5254 Ernest Newman are both buried in Fauquissart Military Cemetery. Goff had elected to extend his service with the regiment to twelve years in March 1914, having originally enlisted in 1907. He already had some service before that, with the Volunteers and briefly with the regular army, but had been discharged on medical grounds. In recent years, he had served in Egypt and India. The army could ill afford to lose such experienced NCOs in 'demonstrations', specifically designed to draw the enemy's fire.

22. G. B. Laurie, *Letters of Lt-Col George Brenton Laurie*, privately produced 1921.

23. Goodwyn recovered from his wound and, in late 1915, was posted to the Middle East to take command of the 16th West Yorkshires – the 'Bradford Pals'. He later moved to France and commanded the 2nd Manchester Regiment from August 1916.

24. Joy was killed in action in Mesopotamia on 11 December 1915, having been posted for an attachment to the 2nd Dorsetshire Regiment.

25. Lafone, still commanding D Company, was killed in the same vicinity during the Battle of Neuve Chapelle on 12 March 1915. He is buried in the Royal Irish Rifles Graveyard near Laventie.
26. Max Arthur, *Forgotten Voices of the Great War*
27. National Archives WO95/706, War Diary of IV Corps General Staff.

Chapter 6

1. Not to be confused with his namesake Henry Hughes Wilson, who was on the staff of GHQ. Henry Fuller Maitland Wilson (born 1859) was a veteran of the Second Afghan and Second Boer Wars. He had gone to war in command of 12th Infantry Brigade, but took over 4th Division from 9 September 1914. Later in the war, he commanded a corps in Salonika. Wilson was related by marriage to Hubert and John Gough, both famous generals of the Great War.
2. Keir was a gunner, having entered the army through the Royal Military Academy at Woolwich. A trained staff officer, he was also a veteran of the Second Boer War. He went on to command a corps in France, but was sent home in 1916 after serious disagreement with his commanding officer Sir Edmund Allenby. He retired from the army in 1918.
3. The period is remarkable in that for the most part many civilians were carrying on their lives within the range of shell fire. Houplines was considered too close to the trenches and the people were compulsorily evacuated from the town after 24 hours' notice during December 1914.
4. The terms St Yves and St Yvon both appear in contemporary maps and documents describing the hamlet at the north-east corner of Ploegsteert Wood. For clarity, St Yves is used throughout this narrative.
5. At 9.30 a.m, II Corps received a message from II Corps saying that it could give them just ten rounds of 6-inch howitzer shell. Late on 18 December, I Corps offered III Corps the use of a howitzer battery, but it was refused as there was insufficient ammunition for it to be useful in the forthcoming operation. A section of three light guns from a mountain battery were allotted to 11th Infantry Brigade at 6.20 p.m. on 17 December.
6. Lyon, aged fifty-seven, had seen service in the Malakand Field Force, Second Boer War and West African Field Force, and had some time as British Military Attaché in Bucharest, Sofia,
7. The London Rifle Brigade was also known as the 1/5th (City of London) Battalion of the London Regiment.
8. The divisional artillery brigades (14, 29, 32 and 37) were supplemented by numbers 4 and 6 Siege Batteries of the Royal Garrison Artillery, and half of 37 Battery RFA for the attack on the 'Birdcage'. It is of interest that the diary of 14 Brigade RFA, which was the most southerly of the division's guns being located around Le Bizet, and was under orders to 'demonstrate freely', said that it halted its bombardment at 10 a.m., 'as the ground was found to be too wet and marshy for an infantry attack'.
9. This may not be correct, for the 1st Hampshires were some way south, on the far side of the Somersets and the Rifle Brigade. Whether their trench could be seen from St Yvon is doubtful. It depends on the direction in which the officers were looking, but it may have been the trenches of the 1st Royal Warwickshires of 10th Infantry Brigade that they could see. The Warwicks complained of short firing at times through the morning.
10. Richard Morgan-Grenville, the grandson of the late Duke of Buckingham, was known by his hereditary title as the Master of Kinloss. Born in 1887, he was

Eton and Sandhurst educated and had been commissioned in 1906. He had already been wounded twice since the beginning of the war. Morgan-Grenville lies beside many of his men in Rifle House Cemetery.

11. A thirty-four-year-old son of a baron, Prittie had been commissioned in 1900 and had spent much of the time before the war on various duties in Africa and Egypt. He had already been awarded the French Legion d'Honneur for being 'the last man to leave a trench under very hot fire; and it was his action that saved the lives of many French soldiers'. He is buried next to Richard Morgan-Grenville.

12. According to *The Indian Corps in France*, although the 129th Baluchis play an important part in the fighting of December 1914, 'the name is a misnomer, as the genuine Baluchi is not now enlisted. The 129th consists of 2 companies of Punjabi Muslims, 3 of Mahsuds, 3 of other Pathans.'

13. The field artillery was all British except for mountain guns. This was a legacy from the Indian Mutiny, and subsequent decisions not to allow such weaponry to be in Indian hands.

14. The German unit facing the attack was the *Infanterie-Regiment Vogel von Falckenstein (7. Westfälisches) Nr. 56*, which was raised in Wesel and Kleve along the Rhine, not far from the Dutch border. A prisoner captured by the Baluchis confirmed the fact.

15. Mastan Singh was a native of Chhoti Hiron, Patiala, Punjab. He has no known grave and is commemorated alongside many of his comrades at the Neuve Chapelle Indian Memorial. CWGC incorrectly gives the date of his death as 10 December.

16. John George Smyth was later awarded the Victoria Cross for his exceptional work on 18 May 1915. He continued on to see service in the Second World War, reaching the rank of Acting Maj.-Gen.

17. *Kurhessisches Jäger-Bataillon Nr. 11*, raised in Marburg.

18. Brigade HQ was in Cense du Raux Farm, which is situated behind and to the right of the Le Touret Memorial and Military Cemetery.

19. Burke and Rundall have no known graves today, and are commemorated at the Neuve Chapelle Indian Memorial. Rundall was the author of a book, *The Ibex of Sha-Ping and other Himalayan Studies*. Published after his death and now freely available on the internet, it includes some excellent drawings. Spr 2162 Raj Muhammad is buried at the Gorre British and Indian Cemetery. Aged twenty-one, he was a native of Murarian, Korla, Kharian, Gujrat, Punjab.

20. *Kgl. Preussiches Infanterie-Regiment 'Herzog Ferdinand von Braunschweig' (8. Westfälisches) Nr 57*, raised in Wesel.

21. It is also possible that they had been killed by 'concussion' from the air pressure wave of a nearby explosion. The phenomenon of finding such men, apparently unhurt but dead, is often commented upon by men who served in the trenches.

22. Haking's name became almost synonymous with the ground between Givenchy and Armentières, for he was in command during some of the more disastrous of British operations of the First World War in this area, including the British-Australian attack near Fromelles on 19–20 July 1916. He also commanded the British XI Corps, which fought well here in the Battle of the Lys on 9 April 1918, holding on even though one of its formations, the 2nd Portuguese Division, was destroyed in a matter of hours by overwhelming German attack. On the Portuguese right, the 55th (West Lancashire) Division fought a brilliant defence – at Givenchy.

Part 2
Chapter 8

1. *Birmingham Gazette*, 16 November 1914.
2. Philip Wittkop (ed.), *German Students' War Letters*, p. 32. Aldag was killed on 15 January 1915, and is buried in the German military cemetery at Fourbes-en-Weppes. His letters included a report on a short truce on New Year's Eve, apparently requested by the British for burial of the dead but with fraternisation and exchanging of gifts. Unlike the Christmas truces, this New Year's ceasefire does not appear to have been widespread. Aldag explained the British motives for the truce, as 'they are only mercenaries, they are going on strike'.

Chapter 9

1. Farrar, aged twenty-seven, was a graduate of Queen's College, Cambridge.
2. Wenzel's unit was the *Kgl. Bayerisches Reserve-Infanterie-Regiment Nr 16*, which was under command of the 12th Reserve Infantry Brigade of the 6th Bavarian Reserve Division. This was the unit with which one Adolf Hitler served in France. It is also sometimes known as 'Regiment List', after the surname of its first commander.
3. Bruce Bairnsfather, *Bullets and Billets*.
4. Imperial War Museum, 87-56-1 (1694), private papers of C. A. F. Drummond. His reference to the Royal Dublin Fusiliers is at odds with the fact that the 'Dubs' were not in the trenches at the time.
5. This may have been Capt. William Alexander Henderson of the 2nd Argyll & Sutherland Highlanders, who has no known grave and is commemorated at the Ploegsteert Memorial. The recollections of George Allman Bridge are in the Liddle Collection.
6. In 1915, Welton was commissioned as an officer of the Royal Garrison Artillery, reaching the rank of major during the First World War.
7. Imperial War Museum, MISC 70 Item 1080 (10083), private papers of Arthur Sydney Bates.
8. Imperial War Museum, 84 9 1 (3881), private papers of J. Selby Grigg.
9. Private papers of J. Selby Grigg.
10. Rue du Bois is, in this instance, the hamlet alongside the Armentières–Lille railway line near Wez Macquart, rather than the better known road of the same name that passes down towards Neuve Chapelle.
11. The war the infantry knew.
12. Richardson, by then a captain with the regiment's 1st Battalion, was killed in action on 19 March 1916, aged just twenty-one.
13. John Terraine [ed.], *General Jack's Diary*.
14. Captain 'Billy' Coates was killed in action on 30 April 1915, and is buried at La Chapelle d' Armentières Communal Cemetery. His 'wart' (subaltern), Sudney Bunker, went on to become a lieutenant-colonel of the Royal Engineers, with a Distinguished Service Order and Military Cross to his name.
15. The records of the Commonwealth War Graves Commission show that the two men killed have no known grave. They were L/Cpl 7620 George Sutton and Pte 11419 James Farrell. Pte 9634 Joseph Richards was killed next day – he is buried at Ration Farm Cemetery. Pte 9713 George White died of wounds on Christmas Day at a clearing hospital in Bailleul, but it is not certain that he was the man wounded on the day.

16. Liddle Collection, private papers of Harold Startin.
17. The man killed was Rfn 2316 Leonard Tait. He has no known grave and is commemorated at the Ploegsteert Memorial.
18. The Imperial War Museum holds a letter written after the publication of Brown and Seaton's book on the truce (item MISC 208 item 3015, 8085). It came from Mrs Marian Richmond, the daughter of Rfn 2288 Arthur Lancelot Pearce. She explained that he had been one of the three men who went missing, and that he had become a prisoner of war. Pearce had been educated in Germany, spoke German fluently, and had been suspected as a spy because of it. Tragically, Pearce's mother committed suicide, and Mrs Richmond had always wondered whether she suspected that her son had defected to the Germans rather than been captured. The other men taken prisoner were 2133 Noel Byng and 1401 Herbert Goude.
19. Liddle Collection, private papers of Walter Mockett.
20. Imperial War Museum IWM93-25-1(2450), private papers of Ernest Gordon Morley.
21. Privates 9841 Alexander Butters (who served under the name of Kennedy) and 8327 Henry Teasdale are both commemorated at the Ploegsteert Memorial.
22. Private papers of Harold Douglas Bryan. His papers also mentioned a boxing match and football, the Scots Guards 'winning easily by 4-1', but the reliability of these notes is doubtful. They are all written in the past tense, evidently at a later date, and are very mixed up in terms of chronological sequence.
23. 7th Baronet Hulse, son of Sir Edward Henry and the Hon. Lady Edith Maud Hulse of Breamore House in Salisbury, was killed in action on 12 March 1915. He is buried in Rue-David Military Cemetery, not far from the site of the battalion's participation in the truce. This is not, however, his original place of burial. His remains were exhumed after the war from a burial plot at Wangerie Post, on the road between Fauquissart and La Flinque.
24. Sidney Bunker had been promoted to Lt-Col., and was in command of the battalion when he was killed on the Somme in July 1916. He is buried in Dernancourt Communal Cemetery.
25. Pte 1204 James Macintosh has no known grave; Pte 1101 Archibald Reid lies in Rue-du-Bacquerot (13th London) Graveyard, Laventie.
26. Liddle Collection, private papers of Spence Sanders.
27. The officer was Harold de Buriatte. He had been commissioned into the Bedfords from the Artists Rifles on 14 November 1914.
28. Thirty-two-year-old Capt. Charles Watts was a native of New Zealand. He has no known grave.
29. The man who lost his life was Pte 4902 Edmund Griffiths. He has no known grave.
30. Twenty-six-year-old Maclean Dilworth now lies in Cabaret-Rouge Cemetery near Souchez, many miles from Neuve Chapelle, and outside the area occupied by the BEF in 1914. He was exhumed from his original place of burial in 'Edward Road Cemetery Number 2', near Rue-des-Berceaux, in the post-war clearance of many similar small plots. L/Cpl 8749 Jarvis Walters and Pte John Clarke have no known graves.
31. Imperial War Museum, 74-154-1 (7753), private papers of Arthur Self MM. Self added that he visited Ypres in 1971 and, from the officers of the Commonwealth War Graves Commission, found that the man he had buried. L/Sgt 8569 Henry Lomax, now has no known grave and is commemorated at the Le Touret Memorial. Lomax had been killed on 19 December 1914.

32. Letter reprinted in the *Tacoma Times* on 11 February 1915, referring to previous anonymous publication in Britain.

33. Great War Archive, University of Oxford. Albert Raynes' letter was submitted to the archive by his nephew Peter Raynes. Twenty-year-old Albert was killed on 10 March 1915, and is commemorated at the Le Touret Memorial.

34. Imperial War Museum, MISC 26 Item 469 (5016), A German officer's recollections. This officer appears to have been in company of 6 Company. In later passages, he described the burial of Capt. Arthur Forbes Kilby VC of the 2nd South Staffordshire Regiment, who was killed near Cuinchy at the start of the Battle of Loos on 25 September 1915.

35. Thirty-four-year-old Capt. Archibald Robertson-Glasgow, of the 2/39th Gharwalis, is buried in Le Touret Military Cemetery. He was a veteran of the 1901 campaign in Somaliland.

36. Limerick native Fitzgerald died of wounds while serving with his regiment's 6th (service) battalion in 1916.

37. The records of the Commonwealth War Graves Commission list two men killed on Christmas Eve, two the next day, and one on Boxing Day. Rees may have been misinformed, or it is possible that the officially recorded date of death is wrong for two of the men.

38. Thirty-eight-year-old Baronet Sir Montague Cholmeley was reported to have been shot in the head as he led a charge down a trench towards the area that had been blown up. He has no known grave, but is commemorated at the Le Touret Memorial. John Nevill is buried in the adjacent cemetery. Of the men who lost their lives, only five have known graves.

39. Jeffreys' diary was published in an edited form, and is entitled *Fifteen Rounds a Minute: The Grenadiers at War*.

40. Both men are buried in Le Touret Military Cemetery.

41. He was buried in 'the garden of a house near Pont Fixe'. He now lies in Brown's Road Military Cemetery. It is not clear whether the two are the same location.

42. Goodwin had originally enlisted in 1901. A veteran of the Second Boer War, he was recalled from reserve in August 1914. He joined the 1st Battalion in France on 9 November.

43. A battalion comrade, Ernest Williams, gave an interview many decades later, in which he also mentioned football.

44. Tapp also noted that 'the Scotch [by which he presumably meant the 2nd Seaforth Highlanders on his battalion's left] won't have anything to do with them', which tallies with the brief account in that battalion's diary.

Maps

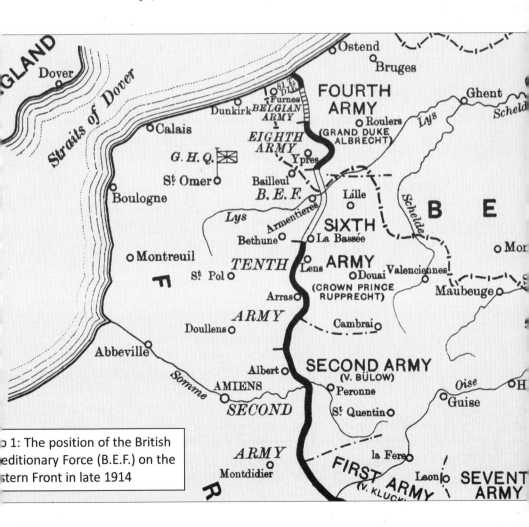

1: The position of the British
editionary Force (B.E.F.) on the
stern Front in late 1914

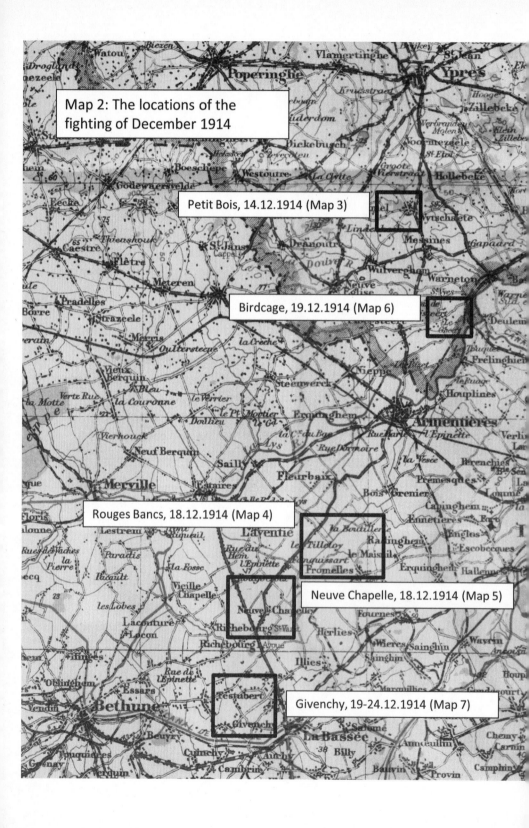

Map 2: The locations of the fighting of December 1914

Petit Bois, 14.12.1914 (Map 3)

Birdcage, 19.12.1914 (Map 6)

Rouges Bancs, 18.12.1914 (Map 4)

Neuve Chapelle, 18.12.1914 (Map 5)

Givenchy, 19-24.12.1914 (Map 7)

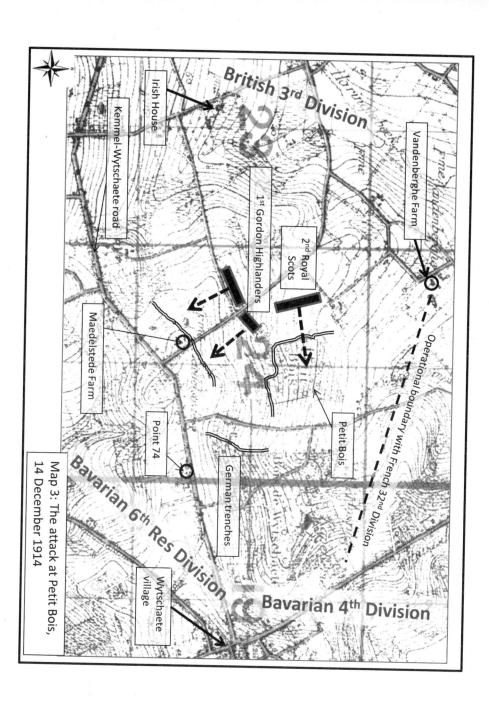

Map 3: The attack at Petit Bois,
14 December 1914

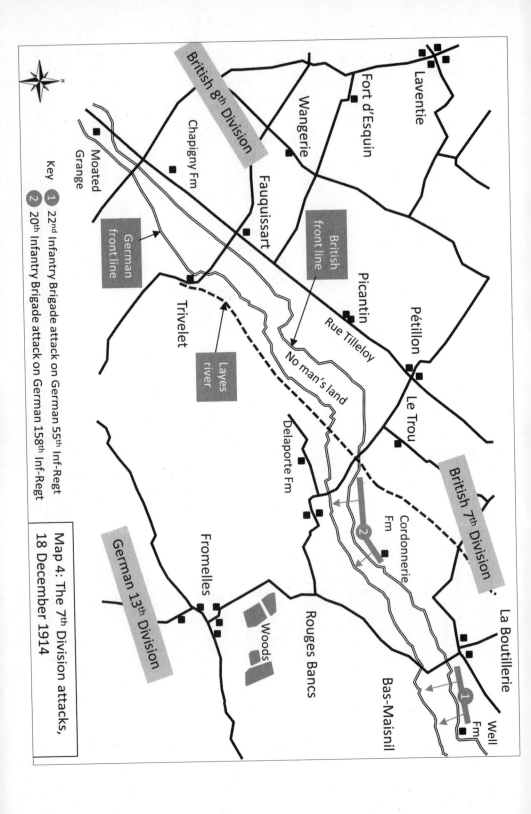

Map 4: The 7th Division attacks, 18 December 1914

Key

① 22nd Infantry Brigade attack on German 55th Inf-Regt
② 20th Infantry Brigade attack on German 158th Inf-Regt

British 8th Division

British 7th Division

German 13th Division

German front line

British front line

No man's land

Layes river

Moated Grange

Chapigny Fm

Wangerie

Fort d'Esquin

Laventie

Fauquissart

Picantin

Pétillon

Rue Tilleloy

Trivelet

Delaporte Fm

Le Trou

Fromelles

Rouges Bancs

Woods

Cordonnerie Fm

Bas-Maisnil

La Boutillerie

Well Fm

N

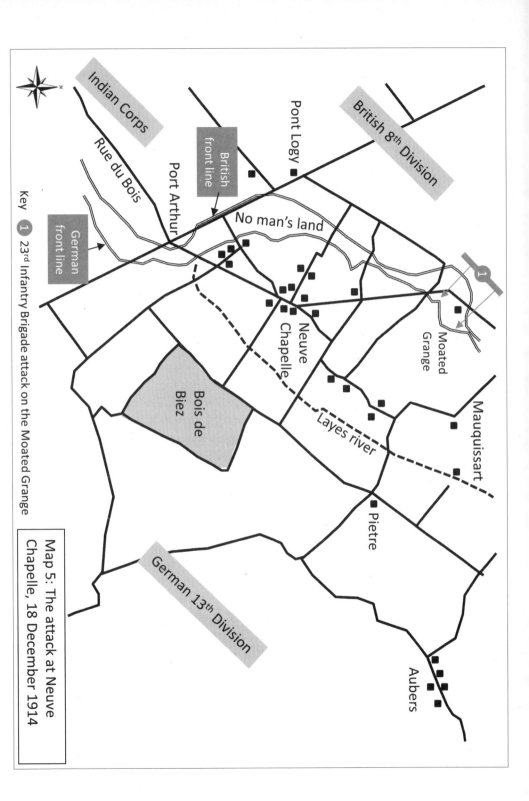

Key

1 23rd Infantry Brigade attack on the Moated Grange

Indian Corps

Rue du Bois

Port Arthur

British front line

German front line

Pont Logy

No man's land

British 8th Division

Neuve Chapelle

Moated Grange

Bois de Biez

Layes river

Mauquissart

Pietre

German 13th Division

Aubers

Map 5: The attack at Neuve Chapelle, 18 December 1914

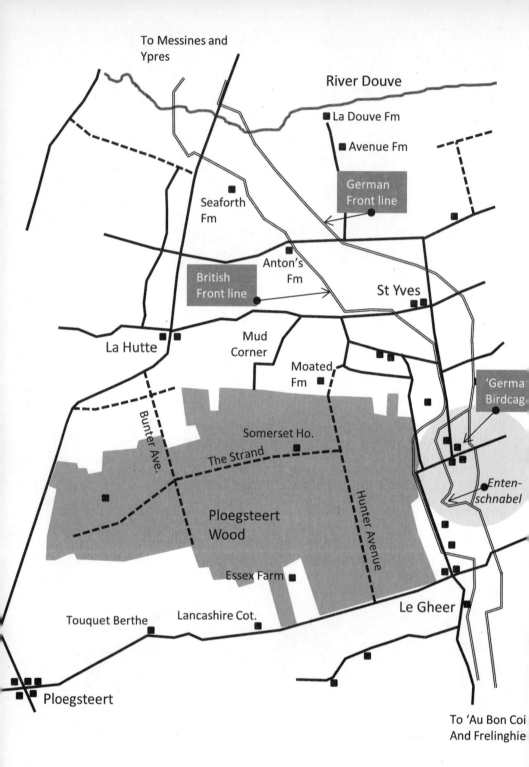

To Messines and Ypres

River Douve

La Douve Fm

Avenue Fm

German Front line

Seaforth Fm

Anton's Fm

British Front line

St Yves

La Hutte

Mud Corner

Moated Fm

'Germa Birdcag

Somerset Ho.

Bunter Ave.

The Strand

Hunter Avenue

Enten-schnabel

Ploegsteert Wood

Essex Farm

Touquet Berthe

Lancashire Cot.

Le Gheer

Ploegsteert

To 'Au Bon Coi And Frelinghie

Map 6: the Ploegsteert sector and the 'German Birdcage', 19 December 1914

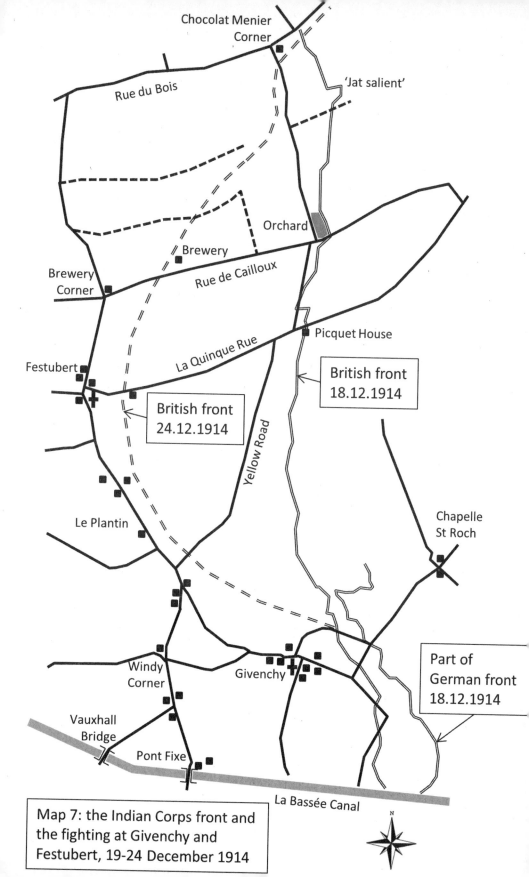

Chocolat Menier
Corner

Rue du Bois

'Jat salient'

Orchard

Brewery

Brewery
Corner

Rue de Cailloux

Picquet House

La Quinque Rue

British front
18.12.1914

Festubert

British front
24.12.1914

Yellow Road

Chapelle
St Roch

Le Plantin

Windy
Corner

Givenchy

Part of
German front
18.12.1914

Vauxhall
Bridge

Pont Fixe

La Bassée Canal

Map 7: the Indian Corps front and
the fighting at Givenchy and
Festubert, 19-24 December 1914

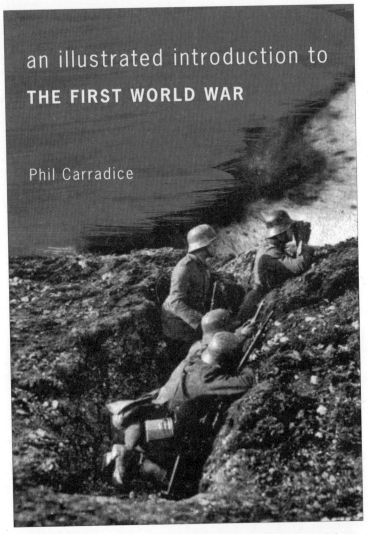

THE FIRST WORLD WAR IN PHOTOGRAPHS

1914

OVER BY CHRISTMAS

JOHN CHRISTOPHER & CAMPBELL McCUTCHEON

1914: The First World War in Photographs:
John Christopher and Campbell McCutcheon

1914: the first year of the 'war to end all wars', documented through
old photographs.

978 1 4456 2181 4
96 pages, full colour

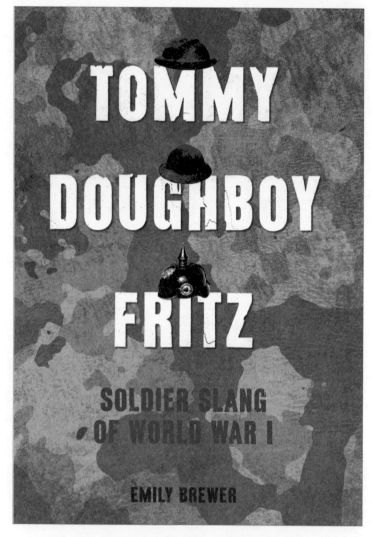